Congratulations
You Made It...
AGAIN!

To Joe–

Phil 1:6

Agape

Geof

Congratulations You Made It... AGAIN!

by
Michael F. Jaress

COMMUNICATION CONSULTANTS INTERNATIONAL
P.O. Box 1212
San Diego, California 92112

Library of Congress Cataloging in Publication Data

Jaress, Michael F.   1940-
        Congratulations, you made it...again!

        1.   Success.   I.   Title.
BJ1611.2.J37   158'.1   80-25559
ISBN 0-938320-04-1

Acknowledgements

I owe mention to more thousands of people...than there are words within this book. My life has been blessed with associates and friends that number in the tens of thousands. I THANK YOU ALL.

To the special people that helped me put together the book itself, I thank each of you personally:

My wife, Mary Ellen, deserves more credit than any other person on this earth for the completion of this book. She has been my "best friend", helpmate, and inspiration...at the times when I needed her the most. And when I needed her the most, she was always there to lend exactly what I needed...at that time and place.

My children, for their understanding when Dad would spend 14 and 16 hours in a row at the typewriter...because "he had to capture an idea." My special thanks to my son, Jon Cary, for his help in the illustrations throughout the book. He is a talented young man, and I am very proud that he would take time to work on a project with me.

My parents, Robert and Helen, (affectionately known as Mom and Dad) for all the beautiful examples they have provided throughout the years...and, the pathway they set me upon.

My secretary-editor, Colleen Carnevale, for her efforts in collecting my ideas and thoughts from hundreds of different lectures and seminars into meaningful sentences, paragraphs, chapters, and finally, a complete book.

If one should give me a dish of sand,
and tell me there were particles of
iron in it, I might look for them with
my eyes, and search for them with my
clumsy fingers, and be unable to detect
them; but let me take a magnet and sweep
through it, and how it would draw to
itself the almost invisible particles
by the mere power of attraction! The
unthankful heart, like my finger in
the sand, discovers no mercies; but
let the thankful heart sweep through
the day, and as the magnet finds the
iron, so it will find, in every hour,
some heavenly blessings.

—Henry Ward Beecher

PIVOTAL POINT: A point in time, place and circumstances when the decision that is made affects the quality of life from that point forward.

—Michael F. Jaress

Table of Contents

List of
Charts/Diagrams

Chart "A" Your Major Labels of Identification.........52

Chart "B" Feelings, Emotions,
and Attitude Labels..........................61

Charts "C" Primary Goal Charts .... 144 - 146

Charts "D" Labels and Actions
That Support Goals .... 184 - 189

Chart "E" Understanding Thought Cycles 196

Chart "F" Labels Identified as Essential For You.... 211

Chart "G" Writing Your "Major Purpose" 217

Chart "H" Habits - Stress - Procrastination
As They Appear in Diagram Form.... 224

Introduction

As a reader of this book, I would like you to sit back, for just a moment, and contemplate. Wouldn't it be wonderful if there was a way through a basic philosophy of life to improve every aspect of your life? If a basic philosophy of life would immediately remove the problems of the past, and the worries of the future, you'd want to hear about it, wouldn't you? Wouldn't it be a blessing if a very simple way of thinking would cause every day to turn out better? Wouldn't it be exciting if a single change in your thought patterns would cause you to learn more...to expect more...and to receive more? You could look forward to success, success cycles and to bettering yourself every day of your life.

Such a simple philosophy exists, it has existed from the very beginnings of recorded history. It has been adopted by some, but rejected always by the majority. It is a philosophy that I have incorporated into hundreds of speeches given over the last few years. To date, over 300,000 people have attended my lectures, speeches, workshops and seminars...and been offered this philosophy. Some have adopted the ideas, others have rejected the concept. But, all have benefited through the exposure. Some individuals automatically reject everything offered to them. You have probably known people like that...haven't you? They run headlong into brick walls in everything they undertake. You have probably stopped offering them help because inside, you already know that they do not want to learn how to make things work out "right". It is not in their "game plan" to succeed, to be prosperous, to be happy, to win. Their "game plan" is to collect as many bloody noses as is humanly possible...and to gripe all along the way.

You might ask, "How did you, the author, come to the point of learning this philosophy...and finally include it in all those speeches?" To answer that question, I must tell you, "I have been fortunate in my life." The philosophy was part of my upbringing as a child. At the early age of four (my earliest recollection of the systematic input of this philosophy), my parents offered a daily menu of the philosophy. Bits and pieces were talked about constantly. Meals were saturated with philosophy of life and living. I would estimate that well over 90% of all our activities and inter-family conversations contained some form of learning lesson built around the philosophy. The advice was gentle. The manner of presentation was always with love, and the results of following the philosophy were guaranteed; success at your endeavors. Over the years, I saw the workings of the philosophy in my own life, and in the lives of the people that filled my environment. I saw this way of viewing the world help my father and mother. In those early years, my dad drove a truck delivering coal from house to house; a dirty, hard, back-breaking job. The simple philosophy allowed him to approach each day and control that day...and *improve* that day. Until one day, he owned a fleet of trucks and equipment. Now, the thought that may be going through your mind is "Nice story, but lots of people raise themselves up." However, I have only told you the beginning of the story. At the point of the goal being accomplished (financial success), I watched as the whole world collapsed in the family business; an unfortunate accident, tremendous lawsuits, poor legal advice combined to bankrupt everything. The simple philosophy worked again. "Shaking the dust from his feet, and not looking back", the simple philosophy stabilized everything. It took a couple of years, but I saw my father consistently turn every adversity into a climbing step until he was vice-president of a multi-million dollar conglomerate of businesses.

Now, how does that fit into this book and philosophy? Well, day after day, month after month they offered the philosophy to me...the same advice...never varying...always the same...consistently the same. We (our entire family) lived the philosophy on a daily basis, and I consider myself very fortunate. You see, less than 1% of the population of the United States grows up with this type of philosophy in their home on a consistent basis. With consistent effort, everyone that hears the philosophy can eventually adopt it. And, if you adopt it, the world will reward you for your changed viewpoint. If you will use the philosophy for 30 days, remarkable changes will take place around you. Money and abundance seem easier to come by...people will be more likely to help you and provide you service...conflicts will soften and soon disappear...problems of the past and worries of the future will dissipate like fog does when the morning sun shines through.

I will explain the **outward demonstration** of the philosophy in the first chapter of the book. Then, we will work through the rest of the chapters to insure that the philosophy can become a way of life. As we work through the chapters, we (you and I) will understand and remove all the *stumbling blocks* that other people may put in your path. As we work through the chapters, we'll cover in depth the *six laws* of this universe that always work...why they work...and how to use them in your life. In addition, we'll work through the **"success cycles"** and **failure cycles"** that develop into patterns in life. We'll also talk about ways to acomplish up to *five* times as much (productive activity) in your 168 hours each week. It will be exciting...very exciting.

By the way, if you are reading this book, you are probably in one of three possible situations:

1. SUCCESSFUL, INFLUENTIAL, DEFINITELY DOING MANY THINGS RIGHT...AND ENJOYING THE FRUITS OF LIFE.
   (You are probably reading this book just to cover all the bases...to *enhance* your position)

2. STRIVING, BUILDING, LEARNING, AND

INTERESTED IN LEARNING TOOLS THAT WILL INCREASE YOUR HARVEST. (You are probably reading this book to *improve* your techniques and your position in life)

3. HAVING A HARD TIME OF IT IN A VARIETY OF AREAS OF LIFE...PERHAPS STRUGGLING WITH FINANCES, OR RELATIONSHIPS, OR YOURSELF. YOU ARE ALSO NOT SO SURE HOW ALL THE ROTTEN FRUIT ENDED UP IN YOUR BARREL.
(Of the three possible positions, you have the *most to gain*...but also, the *most to learn*)

Whichever situation fits you, "wear it"; it does no good to try to whitewash your past or to try to put down your accomplishments. **You are what your are!** This book is a book of hope and expectation for the individual that wants to live up to their true potential. We will not wallow in the past or berate ourselves for "what could have happened if...". We will make full use of techniques, concepts and the philosophy of "life" to insure that each day will be successful. Let's start with a full explanation of the philosophy.

I
Discovery

1
Philosophy
of
Life

What I need you to do at this point is to ask yourself a question, and to answer it truthfully. My question to you is this. IS LIFE WORTH LIVING? **IS LIFE WORTH LIVING?** DO *YOU* THINK LIFE IS WORTH LIVING? Surprisingly, many people, who ask that question of themselves... deep down, **cannot answer it.**

I have asked that question hundreds of times to large groups... hundreds of thousands of people, and normally I see 100% of the hands go up when I follow up with the question "How many of you feel YES, LIFE IS WORTH LIVING?" I suspect that a good proportion of those hands have been raised because no one wants to sit with their hand down ...while everyone else puts theirs up.

If your honest answer is YES, LIFE IS WORTH LIVING, then the basics of the philosophy and tools of this book are open and waiting for you. If you answered **NO,** or some other "fence-sitting" maybe, you need to come to grips with the fact that you have become your own worst enemy. Wrestle this question through and take a stand for life...or no philosophy will serve you, no abundance will seek you, no successes will please you or grace your tables.

I'm going to assume that your answer is in some way, of a

positive nature. You said "YES, LIFE IS WORTH LIVING!"

With that single statement, you have laid the basics for a *life-view philosophy.* What is a "life-view" philosophy? A life-view philosophy is how you look out from inside yourself and view this world in which you live. Some people have a warm, happy, loving, successful, prosperous way of viewing and evaluating this world. But, most people have a cold, sad, lonely, stingy, poor way of viewing the world in which they live. How can I say what life-view philosophy is adopted by most people? I'm sure you've read or heard the statement "THE WORLD IS A MIRROR...IT REFLECTS BACK THE INNER FEELINGS OF EACH INDIVIDUAL." The world is a *happy* world for *happy* people... The world is an *angry* place for *angry* people... The world is a *prosperous* place for *prosperous* people. I'm sure if you reflect a moment, you too will agree that most people must have a life-view philosophy that is *less* than wonderful.

When you can truthfully say "YES, LIFE IS WORTH LIVING", you have adopted a basic life-view philosophy that can be expanded to create a world that will award you with tremendous treasures, gifts and riches*. Let's put this philosophy to work. Here's how I view my waking up each day...every day.

When I woke this morning, at around 6:30 am, (even when we are on vacation or traveling, our hotel wake-up call is early...the earlier, the better) THE FIRST THING I REALIZE IS...**I AM STILL BREATHING.** That's the first thought that races through my mind, **"I AM STILL BREATHING."** At that point, I know that I am already *more successful* than all the people who died in their sleep that night...*because* I have already decided that "Life is worth living" for me. Your first reaction to that might be the thought, "What a *morbid* thought!" "More successful than all the people who *died* in their sleep, **how awful!"**

That's not a morbid thought. The truly adult person, who

---

* riches are much more than material wealth or money...the riches include harmonious living conditions, spiritual wealth, good health, and abundant happiness.

accepts and knows reality, realizes that "life" and "death" exist...they are facts. There's no question about "if" you're going to die. It's a matter of "when". Occasionally when I speak for a Life Underwriters Conference or Life Insurance Convention, I'll joke with the group about how they are always basing their insurance figures on mortality rates (3.5 per 1000 or 4.1 per 1000), but I have the **"straight, honest figures"** about the mortality rate. At this point, they sit up and think "HOW DARE HE TELL US WE'RE NOT USING THE RIGHT FIGURES." And then I unload my punch-line, "IN CASE YOU HAVEN'T FIGURED IT OUT...THE MOR-TALITY RATE IS *ONE* PER PERSON!"

I believe that the Lord allows us time on this earth to fulfill a major purpose. We are here to accomplish His purpose. There are reasons for us to be here. If the Lord allowed you to wake up this morning, then you have a reason for being here. Your purpose is not fulfilled. He still has work for you to do. With a philosophy that rewards you instantly with success, every day starts with success...on a positive note. With this philosophy, you can go out into the world and accomplish seeming miracles.

Now, this is not some sort of *"cheer-leaders"* "rah-rah sis-boom-bah" philosophy. This is a matter of the choice between life and death...and I am deadly serious, as you should be. If you will come to grips with the question of "Is life worth living?"...and, come to grips with your answer, yes or no...and congratulate yourself for the success you had this morning and every morning...as it is given to you, here's what can happen for you. You will realize that every day is a gift. You will stumble or make mistakes occasionally as you try new techniques, enterprises or methods of living. If some-thing doesn't work, it isn't a failure, it's an opportunity to learn. If you stumble, that's not a tragedy, it's an opportunity to learn. If you make a mistake, as a successful person, you'll understand the opportunity to learn. The people who learn the least about "life's lessons" are the people who go into every endeavor with a negative, unsuccessful attitude...and then become enraged inside when everything doesn't go 100% according to how they had it figured it could have worked out **"IF"**.

Life is showing us, through our mistakes, that there are better ways to accomplish our objectives. If you learn from a mistake, you'll have learned a valuable, helpful lesson. A mistake made today, if you learn from it, may put a million dollars in your pocket five years down the line. Sure, today when you made the mistake, you couldn't see the opportunity that was going to be presented five, seven or ten years from now. Perhaps all you could see and feel were the hurts, the disappointments, the frustrations in the supposed failure of today's plan. What you could not see was the opportunity awaiting you in your future. Can you see the benefits in changing your approach to mistakes? Can you see the benefits in approaching the gift given you today...namely, another day...another chance for fulfillment?

I can think back to times when I have shared this message with crowds of people. Each time, I have had the inner feeling that *at least one person* in each audience needed to hear the philosophy. I can remember one young man, in particular. It was a pivotal point in my life to hear what he had to say. Probably the single most important endorsement of my decision to include this philosophy in every meeting, every convention, every workshop or seminar. After we had our conversation, I knew that I would never again approach an audience and fail to present this philosophy of life.

A young man approached me, about three months after I had given a major address for a large sales group. The group had contained about 700 people, and the young man said, "You don't know me. But, I heard you speak at the **Board of Realtors meeting**...and I know your message was directed right at me. On the day that I heard you speak, everything was black. I had just finished a messy divorce and lost my children in the custody action. My "ex" got the house, and we only had one car...and she got the car. Here I was, a real estate sales- man with no property, no car, and no money. I didn't have

transportation for my clients...I had no listings...nothing in escrow to collect commissions on...in fact, the only reason I had a place to live is because one of my fellow Realtors had an extra apartment in one of the properties he manages...and he let me live there until I could get straightened around." This guy was so excited in the way he was telling the story...I knew something was happening positively in his life, so I listened some more as he continued, "Everything was going downhill, and on that morning, I went to the Board meeting, but my heart wasn't in it...I was feeling really bad inside and contemplating *suicide.* As I sat there amongst those 700 people, listening to your message, I heard what you said about 'Congratulations, you made it again.' So I went home to that crummy little apartment*, and I went into the bedroom, and on the sliding closet doors, I took a bucket of black paint and a brush, and I painted in foot-high letters, **'CONGRATULA-TIONS ROY, YOU MADE IT AGAIN'** I did that three months ago and some great things have happened."

I must admit, my first thought was, "I wonder what the apartment manager thought about those huge black letters on his white doors?" But for Roy, the message was working positively in his life.

He said, "Strange things have happened in the last 90 days. I've been waking up to that message every morning, and it's kind of changed me in a way. A real estate company with hundreds of offices offered me a position as manager of one of their offices...in fact, one of their best offices in the state. The company has a car program and I ended up with a new Cadillac. And, as the manager, I get paid an over-ride commission on all the salespeople in the office...so I started collecting commissions on all the transactions that were already in escrow. I'm making about $3,000 a month and just getting rolling. And I'll tell you something else that's really unusual, I met a young woman recently, and I think I've fallen in love."

I'll give you a little follow-up on the romance angle of this

---

* he still was in a learning phase...a free apartment provided by a friend when you're down-and-out is quite a blessing...it's rare to find friends when the going gets rough

story. Roy married the young woman that came into his life. She had children that she brought into their marriage, but I remember the excitement in Roy's eyes when I saw him about a year and a half later. He and his wife had just had a baby.

Now you know why *I can not* miss an opportunity...to tell this philosophy of life and hope. I've given speeches for marketing meetings, communication seminars, meetings, with corporate presidents, management staffs, and sales people, but since that day almost a decade ago, I've never failed to weave the story in some how. Sometimes it is very tricky to introduce a life-view philosophy into a serious discussion of profits and third quarter down trends...but, I always manage somehow. I feel that at least one person in *every* audience **needs** and **wants** to hear this message. Sometimes it is the top man in the organization. Maybe, the president of the corporation just that morning noticed that his family has dissolved, his holdings in another company are in serious jeopardy, and his financial worth to his present company is in question...if so, then with all his wealth, position, and status, he is still vulnerable...and needs a message of life and hope.

Let's take a look at Roy's remarkable turn-around in life. Let's not skip over the reason for his *recovery* to a life of happiness and prosperity. What had really changed about Roy? What had really changed about Roy's circumstances? What had really changed about the world and all that it holds in abundance? Why did the world reward Roy? What laws for success were responsible for his happiness and prosperity? Why did the laws start to work for him? How can he guarantee that the laws for success will continue to cycle favorably for him? What techniques can he use to instantly stop "failure cycles" other people might bring into his new job and marriage? How can Roy increase the number of "success cycles" in his world? What can Roy and his new bride do to counteract future problems? What can he do to make sure that future decisions don't upset his plans?

In fact...WHAT TOOLS AND TECHNIQUES AND METHODS CAN BE ADDED TO THIS PHILOSOPHY OF

LIFE? WHAT WILL WORK? AND, WHAT WON'T WORK?
The rest of this book contains the answers to the questions
above...plus the answers to hundreds of other questions...
NOT ONLY FOR ROY, BUT FOR YOU...AND MYSELF...
FOR YOUR LOVED ONES...AND FOR MINE.

2
A Special Message For You

This chapter contains a special message for you. A message of importance woven into the fabric of every success story, but unfortunately, ignored by all except the most astute seeker. As you read this chapter, the message will become more and more clear. As each example unfolds on these pages, the message will become stronger and stronger...until, you finally have what is sometimes called an "Ah-hah" experience. An ah-hah experience occurs when you suddenly know, fully and truly know, "why" something works the way it works. We all know individuals that have crammed their brains full of technical data and facts, but have not one bit of understanding or enlightenment...about anything. One "Ah-hah, now I truly understand" experience is sometimes worth a year of searching. I hope you have many ah-hah experiences as you mull-over the ingredients of this book. This chapter contains at least one such experience for each reader.

In the chapter just finished, you read of a young man, Roy and his return to life via a philosophy of life. If I were to assign a partial page of this book to *each* person that has used the philosophy, "Congratulations, you made it again"...perhaps, let's say, 1/10 of a page for each story...this book would need at least 500 pages just to cover the stories. And you, would become bored and say, "Ho-hum, how uninteresting." One example is all we needed, because now, the game is in your court. Now we bring it home to you.

You may be saying to yourself, with that little voice that discusses everything you read or hear, "I'm already a positive, uplifted person. It's a nice story, nice philosophy, but I've already adopted it." You may even have talked to yourself this way, "Big deal, some guy finally gets himself together and stops wallowing in his beer. Is that all he could put together, $3,000 a month, chicken-feed...etc., etc." As you read each word, and fully assimilated the whole story, you self-vocalized the entire scenario to yourself. You added to and identified with this true story...you judged and applauded Roy's performance...and, you may have negated the laws of success **working positively** in your life.

Now this book holds a complete bag of tools waiting to be used. But, it'll do us no good to move on to those tools until we can be fully honest with each other. I know that you have probably read at least one or two (or perhaps one or two dozen) positive-living books. And, in your mind's eye, you view yourself as a pretty positive individual compared to all those other people out there in the world. I believe you...you are probably very positive compared with *most* of the world out there. But, I'm looking deep within you...*with you,* and both you and I know it's not always totally wonderful. We both know of the days when you wake up...not so sure *anything* will go right. That's the day I worry about you. You grumble as you arouse yourself from that warm bed. You cut yourself shaving or put a run in your last pair of stockings...and grumble a little bit more. It's that kind of morning when you can look at a full closet of clothes, and say, "Look, nothing to wear!" On that morning, your toast will not be the "proper" shade of brown, and the eggs will be too runny or overdone. The weather will probably be in agreement with you, and just as you are about to put your key in the car door...you'll drop those crummy keys in the only "dumb" mud puddle. I'm sure the drop of muddy water (the one that dripped off the keys onto your light colored suit won't show too badly. And then, you'll drive to work talking to yourself all along the way. Perhaps one of your comments may even go like this, "God, why have you dealt me such a lousy hand in life?" Of course you and I know how the rest of that day turned out. Important appointments that you rushed to (usually risking your life by traveling too fast with one foot on the brake and one on the gas plus, your hand constantly on the horn) will be in vain; your client had complications and canceled out without giving a courtesy call. Your lunch was not "up to par"... and almost "came up" for good when you found an important message buried at the bottom of the wrong file... an important message to call by 10:00 am SHARP!... and you found it after lunch. The day progresses from bad to worse to *total despair*. And, to clench it all off, four dumb idiots almost run into you on the freeway going home. Maybe your spouse and kids will be lucky... maybe they won't be home when you get home. Maybe the dog will get lucky also... perhaps the gate got left open and old "Fido" can spend a safe night at the local pound.

Now, you tell me, how the positive laws of success work in your life... on a day like that. And I'll say "baloney". That entire rotten day has been a downer because in the first few moments... **You missed your chance** to have a day of praise, and a day of success. You can tell me that you "feel", or you "think" that the events that followed your first few minutes had nothing to do with each other. You'll not find me believing you. I know, for a fact, that based on the **laws of this universe,** those first few minutes put a damper on the rest of the day for you. And, as the laws continued to work, events followed events. A **"failure cycle"** was set in motion as surely as gravity exists. Everyone else got in tune with that attitude, they all played their parts perfectly, and helped you create a day that overflowed with negativity. You may respond with, "**NO, NO, NO, you don't understand.** Most of the time I am a super "up", "positive person". Yes, I do understand... I understand. I'm on your side... I do understand, that's why this book was written just for you. It is my contribution to you as a fellow

human...someone I care about. There are ways (tools) that you can keep in reserve for those infrequent days when problems arise...special tools for special people. There are ways (tools) to make everything all right.

These tools didn't just "pop-up" out of nowhere like bread out of a toaster. The formation of this book, took approximately ten years. In that time, I have had a living, breathing research lab in which to work and study. During the ten years, over 47,000 sales and marketing people have participated in our specialized training workshops and seminars (over the years, I've stopped trying to impress myself with the numbers ...all I see now are about 600 new friends each month.) I only wish that, somehow hundreds of thousands could have participated. But, I know that everyone that was supposed to be there...**was there!** In the workshops and seminars, the methods and concepts of this book were "fine-honed" for workability. Ther is **absolutely nothing** in this book that will not work. There is **absolutely nothing** in this book that violates truth. You will find truthfull, powerful statements and tools throughout the book, that *may parallel,* or be in *alignment* with many hundreds of books, perhaps thousands, of other books. You will find that all the tools, techniques, and statements will be in alignment with scripture.

We need to come to an understanding again. I want to ask you as the reader, "Do not turn-off or prejudge these writings on the basis of what you *think will come*...or what *you think* I'm going to write next. Since this book will contain some parallel truths that you have read or perhaps listened to before, there may be a slight tendency for you to let your mind wander off...or skip ahead. **PLEASE DON'T.** Also, since there are parallel truths offered in this book, that may have been offered elsewhere...with a different explanation, your mind may have a tendency to skip over or partially negate the *positive* aspects of those truths. I'll ask again, "**PLEASE DON'T!**"

Let me express it this way: A truth **is.** A **truth** is. What I mean by that is this: I cannot, and would not, try to make a *truth* appear to be untrue. The reverse also applies. I cannot, and would not, try to make an *untruth* appear true. To do so is impossible. The truth always floats to the surface, and remains a truth. An untruth is always exposed. It may take time, but it is always exposed.

Let me put that in a different light, and state it this way: A truth is in alignment with **universal laws.** An untruth will be exposed by **universal laws.** So as you read this book, DON'T SKIP. Don't skip a sentence, a paragraph, or a page, because you assume that you've already read it before. You *have not* read it before. You may have read or heard similar explantions, but never before have you been in this place, with this set of circumstances, and experienced this word as it is written right here. Don't skip for any reason.

Let me illustrate with an experience that should fully explain why I want you to read this as a fresh new experience. Remember back when you were a youngster, maybe 10 or 12 or 13 years old, and you wanted to carve your initials or a message into something? You looked at trees, poles, a porch railing, or maybe your desk at school. You probably used a knife, or a sharp edge on a ruler, or possibly a nail, because you wanted to put your mark on that piece of wood. You tried your mightiest to make that line you carved straight. One of two possibilities occurred. You either made the line straight, or you didn't. Those are the only two possibilities. And, you pulled that point down again and again...scoring the wood deeper and deeper. If that first scratch was crooked, all the lines on top of it fell into that first groove...and they too were crooked. Even if you corrected the line the second time you pulled the point down, you occasionally ran into that crooked groove again and again. So it is with the truth. If you internalize a truth in a way that is just the *slightest* bit crooked, it will remain crooked as it goes deeper and deeper into your thought patterns. **Don't get reactive**...I'm not saying you have *crooked* thoughts. What I am saying is, "The way a truth was presented, or laid in, (perhaps as little as one word was interpreted incorrectly, or negatively accepted) can affect your understanding and, your ability to use the truth for your own benefit." So if you skip over a truth presented in this book or if you skip one of the tools this book offers, **within that message** may be your greatest "Ah-hah" experience. Take the few seconds necessary to read each sentence. Don't automatically accept or reject. Talk it over with yourself and interpret how the message could benefit you **if you were to accept it** fully into your thinking. I do know this: Speed reading this book will do you very little good, and may be disappointing. Reading a truth without accepting it may even reinforce the negative aspect, the opposite of the truth, in your mind.

Here's an example. There are some passages from scripture that go like this:

"GIVE, AND IT SHALL BE GIVEN UNTO YOU."
"AS YOU SOW, SO SHALL YE REAP."
"JUDGE NOT, LEST YE BE JUDGED."

As you read those lines, automatically your mind began to identify with all the times you have ever heard the statements. There are millions upon millions of **"Positive Mental Attitude"** people, (**PMA** people) who will go right over those sentences as if they are reading them in a PMA book. They think, "Yea, yea, yea, I know." or "Right, right, sure...garbage in, garbage out." "Get on with something that is *new* or *interesting.*" When you hear a truth, and react to it in one of those ways, you **negate** the ability of that law to help you in this physical world. A derogatory remark, a passing-off as old news, a skip by with merely a glance and **you've negated** that law working *positively* in your life. If you've ever gone to a PMA meeting or company conference, you've probably heard the comments from others (usually loud enough so everyone can hear)..."A nice speech, but it's the same old thing." Or perhaps, "Boy, I sure wish those speakers management brought in would learn something *new* to say...I get tired listening to all that 'Help your neighbor jazz.'" Now, be honest with yourself, when you read the three scriptural statements, what were your deep down, automatic reactions, (called

"ANOTHER CRUMMY DAY OF EXCITEMENT"

semantic reactions) to those words? Did you *praise* the truth making comments like, "What a wonderful *truth!*" 'What *clarity* of thought...how fortunate that I have a chance to learn from those statements. It's so good to see the truth without all the whitewash or frills or fancy words." Or, did you automatically think comments that negated those laws working in your life?

As you read and learn to use the tools in this book, you will automatically prosper more in all areas of your life...one of the reasons for this will be:

A DECISION ON YOUR PART TO NO LONGER
NEGATE THE LAWS OF SUCCESS, TO NO LONGER
NEGATE THE LAWS OF THIS UNIVERSE
TO STOP BEING YOUR OWN WORST ENEMY.

It always amazes me to see how *enthusiastically negative* people can get about the "Horror stores" on the front page of the daily newspaper. But, what is their reaction to seeing the truth in print? Or their reaction to a co-worker reading something worthwhile..."Old Jim is getting soft in his head with all that *goodness* nonsense."

As you've probably noticed, the message, the *"Ah-hah"* may have hit you by now...or maybe it's just working into you little by little and getting ready like a volcano to let go any moment.

Another time over those three statements from <u>scripture</u> and a point will certainly be made. Did you know that I used "scripture" (the word) again...and I even underlined it so you couldn't miss my usage of the word. I used the word for **definite reasons.** Don't automatically accept or reject my reasons until you fully understand and can see the truth behind my words. When you see or hear the word "scripture", if the word is a part of your vocabulary, you have an automatic reaction...either positive or negative...an automatic reaction. And, **I know it.** And, I did it *on purpose.* To help you with an *"Ah-hah"* experience. Now, I'll give you the other reason: My wife, Mary Ellen, and I are Christians, as are tens of millions of people who might some day touch this book. You are or are not...as you have chosen...*thus far.* Speaking for myself, I would be suspect of any success philosophy, sales methods, daily living guide, training program, or psychological approach to life that was being offered...if the author was unsure of himself and **didn't know** if his works would stand inspection by both believers and non-believers. If you, as I do, take a stand for Christ, you will thoroughly enjoy and learn from every line in this book. If you are a non-believer, this book will fulfill all that you want from it...with one additional plus you may not have known would be involved. You will discover two more people of this world that truly care *for you,* and *your successes,* and *your well-being*...namely; Michael and Mary Ellen Jaress. We *care* and we'll *share!*

So, now we can talk, you and I. I would like you to read my work *differently* than you've read a whole lot of books in the past. Read it with self-interest. Mull-over the concepts. Don't automatically reject or accept. Seek out the truth, and then make your decisions. Read every page, paragraph and sentence, as though it were written only for you...with your self-interest in mind. In point of fact, it was written just for you. No one else was supposed to get *this copy*...it ended-up exactly where it was supposed to be...*in your hands.*

I am almost certain this will not be the last book you will ever read. I am equally certain this will be one book you will want to re-read. Time and time again. I never mean to offend when I implore you...DO NOT SKIP. My meaning behind the meaning, "There is so much I want to share with you, and I want you to have it all." In the next chapter, we'll cover exactly what you can expect for your efforts in reading, understanding, and applying the tools of this book.

Here's the message that was hidden behind the words...
"YOUR THOUGHT PATTERNS EXPRESSING *NEGA-TIVITY* HAVE *SEVERELY LIMITED* THE POSSIBILI-TIES FOR TRUTH TO WORK *POSITIVELY* IN YOUR LIFE."

You may say, "Wait a minute Buster, I am *already* successful in many ways...I've made out just fine without your telling me how *limited* I am. You must be talking about some of those failure types that I see all around the country." No, I am talking about you... and me... and every other person in this world! We are all fulfilling only a *fraction* of our potential. Every great thinker, by every measure of potential, has demonstrated that we as individuals (and as a world population) are existing at a small fraction of our true potential. As you and I (and everyone else) learn to accept some basic truths in the operation within this universe, we will operate at a much higher level... a much greater percentage of our potential. There is much to be learned in the seven words... *"and the truth shall set you free."*

I'll try to uncover as many truths as possible in one small book. You will find that most of the chapters are complete stories in themselves; that each could be the subject of a complete book... independent of all the other chapters. However, that does not mean that the chapters can be read in a haphazard order. I have placed the chapters in an order that will make sense once you have read the entire book.

I am not a novelist. I prefer to think of myself as a reporter... reporting the facts as I have observed them working in the lives of thousands upon thousands of people.

One interesting thing you will learn about me... as you read... I have an easy time explaining gigantic "concepts", but tend to want to "move on" once the major "concept" is covered. I know why this happens, and I'll share it with you: "I feel that once you know... truly know... the essence of why something works, it is only a rhetorical exercise to try to explain every little usage of the law." To be frank with you, I am often quite "blunt" in my approach to sharing knowledge. Mary Ellen is always at my side saying "Slow down, Honey ... add more details... just because you think it's clear, doesn't automatically make it clear. Maybe someone has a question." Bear with me... OKAY?

3
Expectations
and
Assumptions

It feels good to be honest...totally honest. I'm sure you've had that feeling many times in your life, in a variety of situations. That good, solid feeling that comes once a heavy burden has been lifted from your shoulders. That's why I didn't want to "soft-pedal" the first two messages of this book. You're still reading...we're still together. So I guess, my being honest has not turned you off or diminished your desire to gather the tools you want.

This book is a bag full of tools. Just as a workman has a bag of tools, *you* are in the process of acquiring a bag of tools. Each type of workman has a different type, or collection, of tools. And, each tool has a distinct function... *successful ways* to be used, and *inappropriate ways* that may cause damage rather than good results. So it is also, with your tools. You will need an individual collection of these tools. You will use the tools efficiently...they'll become customized to your hands...you'll add your personality to the tools and eventually be as proud of your tools as is any skilled craftsman.

Here is what you can expect in your life as you practice with your tools:

YOU'LL HAVE MORE HAPPINESS
YOU'LL HAVE MORE PROSPERITY
YOU'LL HAVE MORE RICHES

YOU'LL HAVE MORE PEACE
YOU'LL HAVE MORE RESPECT
YOU'LL HAVE MORE CONFIDENCE
YOU'LL HAVE MORE FUN
YOU'LL HAVE MORE FREE TIME
YOU'LL HAVE MORE FAMILY HARMONY
YOU'LL HAVE MORE LOVE
YOU'LL HAVE MORE HONESTY IN YOUR LIFE
...AND,
YOU WILL HAVE A REDUCTION IN THE FACTORS
THAT DESTROY BUSINESS PEOPLE; REJECTION, CRIT-
ICISM, AND FRUSTRATION

Now that you know what *you can,* and *will* have, will you actively seek out the tools? Will you pursue the tools agres-sively and make them yours? Only you will be the final judge of how successfully you make the tools yours. Only you will view the changes in your life. Let me repeat that statement, "Only **you** will view the *changes!*" The **rest of the people** that make up your world, they will view the *"results"* of the changes. Amazing "results" because of your changes.

"Changes?" you ask. Yes, changes. Let's discuss changes in depth. I repeat, "Let's (meaning let us; you and I) discuss changes, and why changes will be necessary. If everything is not exactly the way you want it to be...in your world...then, you will have to make changes! Many people in workshops respond with, "But I don't want to change!". Or, "Why should I have to change in order for the rest of the world to shape-up?"

It is tied to a *law* of the universe called "The Law of Cause and Effect." Everything you have in life right now...is an *effect.* Your happiness, the amount of riches you enjoy, your health, your family life, all are *effects*. And every effect has a cause. If you want to change the effects, you must change the causes. If you want more out of life, **YOU HAVE TO CHANGE SOMETHING, AND THE SOMETHING THAT MUST CHANGE IS YOU.** You caused all those things (effects) to come into your life. If you want more of the good effects, it will take some changes in your thoughts (causes). Sometimes I hear people say, "But, **look at all the success I've had** being the way I am. You're not going to get **me** to change!" And inside, I say to myself, "You're probably right, but I like you enough to help you change…and I also like you enough to let you be anything you want to be." Understand that it is "right" to change, and it's also "right" **not** to change …depending on the *effects* you want in life. If you want your life to remain **EXACTLY THE SAME,** all you have to do is just keep on doing and thinking **EXACTLY THE SAME.** The same causes will go right on producing the same effects. That's easy to figure out, isn't it?

But, I'll wager that if you walked up to your five best friends, and asked them, "If there was a way for you to get more out of life, what would be the three things you would want more of?" Instantly, each of your friends could rattle off his or her desires…"effects" they would like to come into their lives. And, so it is with you. In order to have that change come about, to have that *little bit extra,* something has to be done in a different manner, or order.

What follows is the easiest way to make changes. A proper thought pattern can help you view "change" in a way that won't scare you…or create resistance within your environment. Let me show you how to approach change by making major assumptions…three gigantic assumptions. I can make the three assumptions based on fact. The fact is, **you are** reading or studying this book. Therefore, you can help make the three assumptions. It will be easier if we make them together. The **first assumption** is that you could, if you wanted to, and applied yourself, you could be *totally honest* with yourself. This is your copy of this book. *You could,* if you wanted to, be completely honest when it comes to filling out some of the charts. You could, if you wanted to, be honest with yourself when you measured your successes and failures of the past. And, you certainly could be honest, if you wanted to, when it came to listing how you'd like life to treat you in the future. Knowing that you have that choice, I'm going to make the assumption that *you could* be *totally honest* with yourself.

My **second assumption** is that if you were totally honest with yourself, you would admit to having experienced *"down"* times and feelings in the past. In fact, if you were totally honest with yourself, you could even admit to yourself that at times you've felt rotten. You really have the choice to be totally honest, and *exercising* that option allows you the right to discuss your "down", depressed feelings without the fear that you've just thrown away all those dollars you spent for PMA books and tapes. For some people who are thoroughly indoctrinated with PMA, (PMA, PMA, RAH, RAH, RAH, SIS BOOM BAH...give a little cheer), this is a real test of their acceptance of **assumption number one.** By the way, I'm not against motivation conferences...I love them...they are very exciting and lots of fun. Just don't get so involved trying to maintain the facade that you lose the ability to admit truth as it applies to you. I have had the "down" times. You have had *not-so-hot* feelings also. We all have...to deny the existence of some negativity in life violates a law of success that will follow in a later chapter. I feel certain that you can join me in agreement on assumption number two. If it will help you finalize your acceptance of assumption two, I'll offer a little help from the chapter on the *laws of the universe.* Every person that has reached for potential...stretched to improve their position...and made it, has had more than their share of failures. And, some of those failures were bitter to the point of penetrating and hurting. To try to hide the mistakes of the past, to try to deny failures in life, to fail to accept assumption number two has never been the path of greatness.

And finally, assumption number three. The **third assumption** is that you have not solidified like stone. We'll assume that you have not petrified like solid stone, but are instead a living, breathing human being. You're probably thinking, "Finally, we've come to an easy assumption...those other two **were brutal!".** As you and I make this assumption, we are agreeing that you are not stiff, cold, solid, unmanageable stone. You have not solidified like rock. You are alive, vibrant with life, and capable of change.

We're making three distinct assumptions. 1) **You'll be honest with yourself,** 2) at some time in your life, **you've experienced thoughts that were negative and depressing,** and 3) that **you are still capable of changing**...unlike a solidified, stone statue.

There are people who can't be honest with themselves, who refuse to acknowledge they ever could be down, and who have solidified like rock. You've heard the jokes made about people being dead at 30 and buried at 65. Those people solidified at age 30, they became totally fixed in their ways; unemotional, unexcited, unenthusiastic, not open for change, not open for life, not open for anything.

Well dear reader, I'm glad you are mature enough to have worked yourself to this point in the book. The time has come for us to take a stroll into adventure. You have my assurance once again...while there is nothing radical within the pages to follow, *you will* be offered a new way of thinking about yourself and what you've come to be in this world of ours. I'll talk our way through the book just as though I were chatting with my closest friend, or a member of my family. There's nothing in here that you couldn't share with your best friend, or a fellow church member. You and I can make this journey together as often as you desire rereading these chapters. Everytime you come back to these pages, you will be a new person...in a different time, a different place, and with a different set of circumstances. You may learn as much on your seventh journey as you did the second time you came back through...and that may have been as much as you learned the first time through. How exciting to make an interesting experience of life come to life again and again. I guess there could be someone out there who says, "If you can't tell a story good enough for me to learn *everything* there is to know...right now, then I'm not going to read **any more!**" I don't know if that type person exists, but if they did, they'd *also* want to play a piano like Liberace with their first lesson, and hit a golf ball like Jack Nicklaus their first time on the tee!

Each person starts this book in a different place, a different time, and with a totally unique set of circumstances. With your unique set of circumstances, you...**and only you**...can determine what you want and need from these writings. You...**and only you**...determine your capacity for growth.

The foundation for the tools will be fully developed. Now, shall we take a look at your world as it exists today. Let us get into a complete understanding of how you, or anyone else, can start out in this world (day number one in your life), and finally come to a point in time, place and circumstances where you are reading this book. We'll start from day one and quickly work ourselves forward to the point of your living and breathing and experiencing this day...today's day.

4
What's
Your
Label?

You will find within this chapter one major concept plus some very easy tools that go with the concept. The major concept can be learned by an adult in less than 15 minutes. Once yours, no one, I repeat, **no one** can ever take the knowledge away from you. Once you learn the major concept, many useful tools can be added.

The major concept I call **"THE CLOSET OF YOUR MIND"** so you will have a title for it. It is an abstraction; an abstract idea or abstract visionary idea. I shall fully develop the concept in a moment, but first let me outline why you might want to read and reread the concept intently. Once you fully understand the concept, you'll know **why** you are **who** you are. You'll know **why** you are **what** you are; you'll know **why** you act the **way** you do; you'll know **why** some people can manipulate you and **why** others can't. You'll know **why** some things never seem to work out for you; you'll know **why** some people love and respect you and **why** others will have nothing to do with you. In fact, you'll know **why** you have limited successes and **why** your goals don't always come true. In addition, this concept will explain why everyone else does what they do. In fact, you'll be amazed as you have the "Ah-hah" experience with this concept; you'll know why about 95% of all the problems between people occur. If your goals in this world are dependent on the help and performance of other people, this concept, **"THE CLOSET OF YOUR MIND"** could be the key to gaining cooperation from those people.

The concept has to do with how you relate to others, and how others relate to you. The concept applies to every human being. So once you've learned it, *not only* will you know about yourself... you'll know *why* everyone else is doing *what* they are doing.

Here's a quickie quiz for you regarding the people in figure number 6. In each example, one or more of the laws of the universe is being exercised. In each example, it's quite apparent a building is being designed or about to be erected. In each example, blueprints have been drawn that will outline the expenditure of thousands, or perhaps *millions* of dollars, to create something that will have worth. I am **not** going to ask you which laws are being used. And, I'm **not** going to ask you what step of the construction phase they are in... it looks like they're moving into the physical reality of construction. **Here are my questions**...IF YOU WERE GOING TO SPEND HUNDREDS OF THOUSANDS OF DOLLARS TO BUILD A HOME, WOULD YOU WANT THE CONTRACTOR TO BUILD ACCORDING TO BLUEPRINTS? WOULD YOU WANT A "SAY" AS TO WHAT WAS IN THE BLUE-PRINTS? IF YOUR BLUEPRINTS CALLED FOR A SPLIT-LEVEL, FOUR BEDROOM, DEN, FAMILY ROOM, THREE BATH, ETC., ETC. HOME...WHAT WOULD YOU EXPECT YOUR HOME WOULD CONTAIN WHEN THE BUILDERS FINISHED? Correct, you'd expect a split-level, four bedroom, den, family room, three bath, etc., etc. home. See how easy the quizzes are going to be?

No one would build any type of structure without a set of plans. No one would expect a million, or ten million dollar piece of property be built without plans. So, now we come to you. You are at least a million dollar piece of property... perhaps even a ten or twenty million dollar piece of property. You may be saying, "But I'm not worth a million dollars!" or "At my current earnings, you've got to be kidding. I doubt that I'll even come close to making ends meet... let alone end up with

anything when I retire." You might as well stop all that
negativity "trip" in your mind. You're racing off on a *tangent*...and are going to miss the point I'm trying to make. The
point is this:

**YOU HAVE BECOME ALL THAT YOU ARE TODAY
WITH EITHER NO FORMALIZED BLUEPRINT
OR AN ALMOST TOTALLY INADEQUATE
SET OF PLANS.**

It's as though a couple thousand *construction workers* came
into or through your life over however many years you've
been alive. And as each *construction worker* entered your life,
he or she just added to, or rearranged the building any way
that worker wanted. They didn't want the finished product for
themselves. They didn't have to live in what *they* constructed.
Isn't that a great "Ah-hah" to experience? You and I are
multi-million dollar pieces of property (I use that term
because we have worth in the market place). We were put
together in haphazard fashions, by a multitude of amateur
builders, who didn't know what the *finished product* was
supposed to be.

It is no wonder so many people have trouble enjoying
their work, their style of living, and themselves. It is no
wonder so many people are "searching" for something different in their lives.

You might be thinking, "Wow, that's some concept!"
because of what you have just read. WAIT! **That's not the
concept**...I just wanted to show you the problem. The concept, "THE CLOSET OF YOUR MIND", is how we take
control of the problem and undo some of the bungling that
has been done. At this point, you might say (and rightly so),
"But, I like a lot about myself." Good, then you won't have
much to change...you'll always have the choice to keep what
you want.

Here we go with the concept, **"THE CLOSET OF YOUR
MIND".** Please remember to fully evaluate the material...
chew it over...talk about it with yourself. Evaluate how
effective the concept could be in your daily living. As you

evaluate the concept, comparing it against how you have been handling a variety of life situations, there will be moments when you'll think, "How simple." or "They wouldn't do that to me...would they?". Try to control your thinking and keep it on the central theme...**the concept.** Nothing constructive will be gained by your mind running off on a tangent "condemning" others, or "judging" yourself. It would also help, if you could read through the concept without trying to find "something wrong" with the concept. Make sure you have a pen or pencil handy...you'll want to jot yourself some notes in the appropriate diagrams and charts. We'll start in the proper place; in the beginning...

Take a look at Chart A. You see a large circle with a small circle in the center of it. That small circle represents you as a newly born baby. Inside the small circle, print these words "This is me, in the beginning." Realize that you were *whole* and *complete* when you were first born. When you were first born, you had no "labels". By the way, a label is a means of identification...or a means for identifying things of this world. As a little baby, you were *complete even without labels.* That center core was at one with God; *complete*...though without labels. Do you realize that without knowing any labels...**the words for things**...you automatically felt good about this world? Without knowing words like mother, father, milk, warmth, love, caring, sharing; without knowing any words at all, a baby can be happy, and whole. The world on the other hand, *does* need labels. It needs labels in order to identify that child. And so, the world assigns labels to every child as soon as is possible. A name is one of the first labels assigned...right after the father yells, **"IT'S A GIRL!"** or **IT'S A BOY!".** The name is given to establish the difference between that child and all the other children and adults who are in this world. The important point to remember is that the label is for the *convenience of the world, not* the child. When you were born, you were given all kinds of labels. I'm going to give you a list of my labels...to demonstrate how very extensive the list can be. One label is my formal name, Michael Frederick Jaress. Other

LIST THE MAJOR LABELS OF IDENTIFICATION
IN YOUR LIFE. LABELS THAT IDENTIFY
YOUR RELATIONSHIPS WITH OTHER PEOPLE
AND ACTIVITIES.

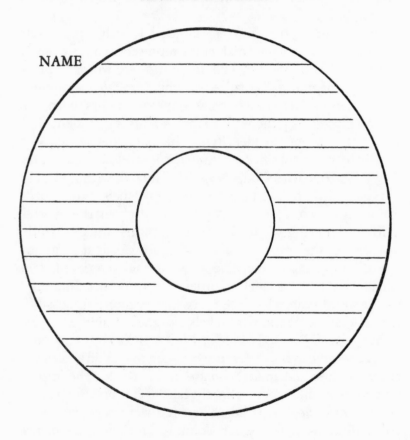

NAME

CHART "A"

labels include my "son" label, and a "boy" label. Here are a few more of the labels: brother, kid, student, ball player, school buddy, bowler, teenager, boy scout, explorer, fisherman, grandma's boy, nephew, class mate, friend, young adult, college student, Army ROTC Major, small bore rifle marksman, adult, Christian, husband, father, worker, salesman, manager, teacher, consultant, business owner, trainer, lecturer, author, president, vice-president, Board Chairman, Optimist, and on...and on...and on. Now lets look at your labels. There are perhaps 50 or 60 labels that identify you. Let's see what some of your major labels would be. I want you to use the lines in the outer circle for the exercise. Write the **major identification labels** you wear that allow other people in the world to know you...or to have some relationship with you. Start off with your name and gender, and go on from there. It should only take you about six or seven minutes to do that...AND **IT IS VERY IMPORTANT THAT YOU DO IT BEFORE GOING ON WITH THE READING.**

These labels that you have listed, are just like the clothes you have hanging in your clothes closet at home. The clothes are as much a form of label as are...the words (the labels) you just wrote down to describe yourself. The words or labels hang in **"The Closet of Your Mind",** and you select one to wear in the same way that you select the clothes you put on. Think about your closet and the clothes that are on all those hangers. Some of the clothes are *favorites of yours*. Some of the outfits are *out of date*. Some of the clothes *don't fit anymore*. Some of the clothes in your closet *never get worn,* and others are *worn quite frequently.* Some of the clothes you've *never really liked,* but they keep on hanging in there. At any rate, each day you walk into the closet and select at least one thing to wear. Even though there are many outfits that are not *"right"* for the day; being too old, too loose, too tight, too dressed-up, too casual, too...whatever, you always seem to find something to wear. When you go out into the world, you've got some *clothes-label* hanging on your body, you've selected something for the day.

What happens if all the people you see begin telling you

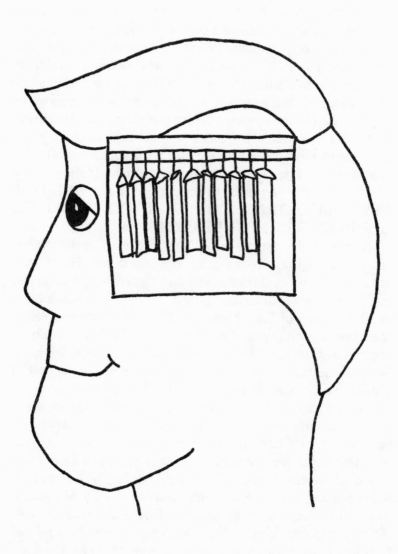

things like "Gee! That's a great looking outfit." "Hey, I really like that suit." "Your clothes look nice on you today." "That's a terrific color on you." No doubt, you would feel really good. Now what if someone comes along and says, "Gee, that's a good-looking suit, but the color's *not quite right* for your skin...and it does fit a little *too* tight." Guess what your reaction to that would probably be? You'd catch yourself looking at yourself in mirrors or window reflections at least 10 or 15 times that day. Each time you looked, you'd suck in your stomach and talk to yourself a little, "Well, it's not really *that* tight...I've always liked this outfit, maybe I'll just wait until the weight's gone to wear it again." A stray comment regarding your outfit might make you feel self-conscious about your appearance. Self-conscious enough, that you might decide to change the outfit. You would at least feel some *small degree* of discomfort with your label...the outfit. Criticisms of your labels can be enough of an irritant to literally ruin your day. Some people become very disturbed by chance comments regarding their clothes. They have outfits that fit perfectly, but they'll never wear them again.

Another problem you might encounter is that midway through the day, at lunch, someone accidently flicks a drop of gravy on your sleeve, and it leaves a spot. You have *choices* when that happens. You can wipe off what you can, and know that the next day you'll have to drop the garment off at the cleaners...and then forget about it. Or you can let it *ruin* your whole day, complaining about the incident to everyone in sight and make it known to the world that this has really gotten you upset. Your label was spotted so the day was a total loss.

A third example of what could happen to your label on this day would go like this...you're walking down the street on what has been a perfect day, and you pass a construction site. As you stop to watch, a runaway truck loaded with concrete tips over and smashes three cars next to you. Miraculously, you are unharmed. Your clothes are a torn, filthy mess, but you've escaped without injury. Do you say, "Thank goodness, I'm alive, nothing's happened to me." "Thank the heavens I've been spared from being maimed or killed!" Or do you say, "**My suit! My beautiful suit! It's been ruined!**" "**What an unjust world! What stupid idiot forgot to put up signs warning people about runaway concrete trucks!**"

Now here's the important message. Do you realize that your clothes are *not you*...NOT THE **REAL YOU**? They are labels, extensions of you. You can replace clothes if something happens to them. You can change your clothes when you want to change outfits. You can select the appropriate clothes for different occasions. You can decide which clothes no longer fit you. You can even discard some of the clothes from your closet if you choose to do so. The very same situation exists with your identification labels. Your labels are *extensions* of you. They are not the "real you"...that *complete you* that existed in the very beginning. Your labels are all added-on to the "real you". The labels exist in "**THE CLOSET OF YOUR MIND**", and you can do as you please with them. **You** decide which labels you will wear throughout the day and the evening. **You** decide which labels fit "right" for each situation during the day. **You** have the choice...if **You** elect to choose. **You** also choose your reactions to the labels...**don't you?**

Here's an example. Today when I came home from a business appointment, I walked into the house and saw my wife, Mary Ellen, standing in the living room. She was intent on looking out the window overlooking our flowers and gardens. So I reached inside "**THE CLOSET OF MY MIND**" and put on my "husband" label. With my wife I am: A husband, best friend, companion and lover. I am romantic and warm and many other things. I selected the labels that fit the situation, and in the wink of an eye...I was wearing the labels appropriate for it. I crept up behind her, gave her a big hug, and a squeeze, and a kiss...and got one in return. Suddenly, tearing through the hallway, came our two girls. They're excited and happy because they're going swimming. They sure are moving fast, but I manage to swoop up one of them in my arms, give her a kiss and a hug, I tickle her and she

giggles. What have I done? I've put on my "father" labels
...*appropriate* for the situation.

...BY THE WAY, DON'T YOU START SKIPPING AHEAD,
NOT READING A SENTENCE HERE, A WORD THERE,
OR, YOU'LL MISS THE "AH-HAH" COMING.

Next, I walk into the office area of our home, and see my
secretary talking with an associate who is also a good friend. I
wear the label employer with the secretary, and I wear the
friend/associate label with the person she's talking with. Do
you realize you've done that exact same thing every day of your
life? Through each hour of your day, you go through the
label-changing process, usually without even thinking about
it. You keep it all straight...*usually*...and it's amazing how
quickly you can perform the changes. The only problem in the
whole process is...**when you forget** and begin to think that
you are the labels. The problem occurs when you begin to
think that the labels you wear are the "**real you**". Let's go back
to the inside circle, to the inner core that is *really you.* That
perfectly *whole person* you were in the beginning, without
labels, is the person **you still are.** The labels hang on the
outside of you, like your clothes do. They are not an internal
part of the *"real you".* Your labels hang in "**THE CLOSET OF
YOUR MIND**" on hundreds of hangers...and you, **AND
ONLY YOU,** should have access to that closet. You, **AND
ONLY YOU,** can decide when, and how, and where, and why
a label should be worn...or changed. You see, you are in
control of the labels. You *own* the labels. The labels *don't own*
you. If you forget that the labels are *under your control,* you
could make this world a very harsh place to be. **Ah-hah!**

For example, let's say you wear the label "salesperson".
Now, we could use any *occupational* label...so, just because
you **don't** wear the "salesperson" label...**don't get to thinking this doesn't apply.** It will apply no matter your occupation...or major work function. Let's say you are wearing your
label, "salesperson", and everyone says you are a very good
salesperson. Then someone comes along who says, "Oh you're
a terrific salesperson. I really *admire* a salesperson that can

help people make up their minds. I could never do what you do, because I wouldn't be able to *push* people into making decisions like *you do*. But, frankly I guess I just couldn't *use* other people to get what I want." For many "salespeople", the comments would be so disturbing, so unsettling, that after some thought, they would decide to put that label back in the closet and never wear it again. But, what happens if that person is still in the occupational field that *requires* selling? A very serious problem...that's what happens. Just like the outfit that was retired to the physical closet, never to be worn again...the label "salesperson" is retired. Now, we have an individual...in the sales field...trying to earn a living... ashamed to put on the *proper* label...and probably failing. Sometimes, they try to give themselves labels marketing analyst, counselor, financial advisor, residential specialist, etc., etc., almost anything will do better than having to take the responsibility for controlling the label that would be *correct* for the task at hand...selling. As you've been reading, you naturally have substituted your major occupation label into the story and can see how chance comments about your label may have influenced many of your days.

A second example could occur if part way through the day, someone *accidently* spills some gravy on that "salesperson" label. You can say "Oh that's no problem, it'll clean right off." Or, do you get outraged and tell the person off...or worse yet, rehash the story of how rotten and inconsiderate the person was who accidently "soiled" your label? Who would you rehash the story with? Other "salespeople", your spouse, the guys at the club, your best friend, other customers, etc...that's who. There are *choices,* and *you* are the one who is making them. Do you control the labels or *do they* control you?

Maybe your label gets totally destroyed in an accident, so what? You haven't been harmed, because the "real you" is always untouched. Use the "salesperson" label again. Maybe you're in charge of a certain type of product or division for your company. Suddenly your company decides to cease production of your specialty...or your company sells-out...or the market disappears...whatever the case, you're out of a job. The inner core of you has not been touched, but your label has been ripped and torn apart. What do you do? Do you condemn the world for being so unjust, and wail over bad luck? Do you make pledges to get even with whoever was so inconsiderate to cause your label to be set aside? Or do you recognize that *you own* the labels, it's "**THE CLOSET OF YOUR MIND**", and you can choose *to own* the labels or have them *own you?* Your ability to see the difference between the "real you" and your labels is going to become more important as we continue with this concept...and use the concept in daily living.

When you were making out your list of major labels, I'll bet you didn't put down a whole variety of labels that were in your "closet". You probably left out labels like: **dumb, poor, clumsey, stupid, enemy, accident-prone, klutz, brat, little devil, inconsiderate messy kid,** etc. You probably left out about 100 descriptive labels of identification that people have applied to you in the past. You may *deny* having those labels in your closet, but if you understand the word (the label) you *have* the label...let me repeat that, "**If you understand the word, you have the label.**" It doesn't mean you have to wear it. There are plenty of clothes in the closet you never wear...and there are plenty of labels in the closet you never put on. The labels are there, but you don't have to wear them. Just be aware that the labels are there; hanging on hangers in "**THE CLOSET OF YOUR MIND**".

Also among the labels in your closet, there are thousands of labels called "attitudes". As we discuss all these labels, please remember that ancient bit of wisdom we all heard as kids, "**STICKS AND STONES MAY BREAK MY BONES, BUT WORDS THEY JUST MIGHT KILL ME!**" You just read the saying as it should read...not as you heard it on the school playground. I think as you follow the concept, you'll recognize how appropriate the above saying can become.

We are going to look at some of the attitudes that can be coupled with, or connected to, major identification labels. As we look at the combinations, you'll notice that some combinations produce *a world of abundance, a world of plenty, a world of fulfillment.* Other combinations produce frustration, misery, a world *lacking* in all areas. Become aware that attitude labels are exactly the same as identification labels; they hang on hangers in **"THE CLOSET OF YOUR MIND"**, you wear them by choice; **you own them.** Remember, if you **don't** own them...then maybe, they will end up **owning you.**

Some of the attitudes that immediately come to mind are: happy, sad, prosperous, poor, successful, failing, jealous, mean, depressed, angry, frustrated, enthusiastic, and energetic. All are attitudes that a person can wear. Now let's take a look at an expanded list of labels. **TAKE YOUR PEN AND PUT A CHECK MARK NEXT TO THE WORDS YOU UNDER-STAND:** (by *understand,* I mean you have at least some understanding of how the word is used...or what the attitude is.)

____ affectionate	____ angry	____ annoyed	____ bad
____ betrayed	____ blissful	____ burdened	____ calm
____ charming	____ cheated	____ cheerful	____ condemned
____ contented	____ crushed	____ defeated	____ depressed
____ despairing	____ distraught	____ disturbed	____ doubtful
____ dominated	____ eager	____ emphatic	____ energetic
____ exasperated	____ failure	____ fearful	____ flustered
____ foolish	____ frantic	____ frustrated	____ good
____ guilty	____ inferior	____ happy	____ helpful
____ horrible	____ hurt	____ hysterical	____ ignored
____ imposed upon	____ infuriated	____ intimidated	____ isolated
____ jealous	____ kind	____ left out	____ loser
____ loving	____ melancholy	____ miserable	____ nervous
____ OK (okay)	____ outraged	____ peaceful	____ persecuted
____ pressured	____ put-upon	____ rejected	____ relaxed
____ relieved	____ right	____ sad	____ satisfied
____ scared	____ shocked	____ spiteful	____ stunned
____ stupid	____ successful	____ superior	____ sympathetic
____ tense	____ terrible	____ thwarted	____ tired
____ trapped	____ troubled	____ vulnerable	____ winner
____ wonderful	____ worried	____ wrong	____ wrung-out

CHART B

Now that you've gone through the list, think about this for a moment. YOU CHECKED ALL...OR **MOST OF THE WORDS**...and I would be willing to admit that I learned these words without even once going to the dictionary for a definition...**will you** admit it also? You know those words because the world gave them to you in much the same way the world gave you your sets of identification labels. As a little child, you were *complete*...but the world needed a way to identify you...so they labeled you. Then, the world needed some way to identify your behavior...or the behaviors they thought **you might someday exhibit**. So, they (all those construction workers that tromped through your life) gave you all their interpretations of what these labels meant. Why did they do it? So they could identify your behaviors. For instance, if your business fails, and you start behaving like *a failure, a loser, a quitter,* the world can look at you and say, "He's got a *failure's* attitude, a *loser's* attitude, a *quitter's* way of looking at the world...look at his attitude."

Here's a very important point to remember when you look over those last few sentences. When the world gave you those labels, the attitudes that hang in "**THE CLOSET OF YOUR MIND**", most of the definitions for the labels were given to you incorrectly. And, on top of that, nowhere was it taught that you, **and you alone,** were to be in sole charge of which labels were to be used, which labels would apply, and which labels would never be put on. Think on that for a moment...you have hundreds, maybe even thousands of labels and attitudes in your closet. **And you only have to wear the ones you want.** If you wear the label, the world will identify you with the label. If because you were incorrectly informed, you wear the wrong label or a collection of inappropriate labels, THE WORLD WILL NOT MAKE ALLOWANCES FOR THE MISTAKES IN YOUR WEARING THE WRONG LABELS. The world will identify you and reward you based on the labels you wear...not the ones left hanging in "**THE CLOSET OF YOUR MIND**". Remember, the example about a business that fails? You do have a choice regarding the labels that you would wear after the business is lost; you could reach into the "CLOSET" and take out any assortment of labels you desired. You *could* put on labels that signify defeat, discouragement, and failure. If you put on the labels that are identified with "failure", the world will reward you with the proper "rewards" failures normally earn. You could reach into the "CLOSET" and select labels that signify any state of being...even labels that signify you have the ability to "rise above" temporary setbacks. In my career, I have seen the results of *both* reactions to business failures. Some people totally collapse when presented a problem that directly affects a label they "hold too dear"; they have forgotten that *they* own the label...they *are not* the label. I have also seen business people accept the challenge of temporary negative turns in their worlds. I have seen thousands of business owners "supposedly fail", wake up the next morning, put on successful labels, and start new, *successful* businesses; *they* own their labels...the labels *don't own them.*

The basic concept of "**THE CLOSET OF YOUR MIND**" is easy to read. It is an easy picture to visualize in your mind. "**THE CLOSET**" with all the labels hanging on coat hangers, is an easy abstraction to visualize, but it does take some in-depth understanding on your part. If you want to get the full benefit from the concept and the tools that can be implemented...you will take the time to fully "chew" on the concept...weigh its merits...and then fully implement the concept into your world. I'll help with the implementation. Some of the tools I'll share with you make it easy to use the "**CLOSET**" concept. Some of the tools make it easy to use the concept in dealing with the people that make up your family, social and business environments. We'll cover the tools as soon as we clear up the *misconceptions* regarding 10 of the labels that were given to you as a child. The important point to realize about the 10 labels; there is a *very high probability* that at least six or seven of the labels were given to you *incorrectly.* Approximately 95% of all the people that attend our workshops find that they were given the complete list of 10...*incorrectly.* Let's look at the 10 most misunderstood labels.

5
Labels
That
Compare

There are 10 words (labels) that seem to account for almost all the problems people have in this world. The words are not highly technical or difficult to spell, pronounce, or use in ordinary language. The problem is in the fact that the 10 words are used constantly in the wrong context; to describe situations *incorrectly*. It is no wonder that the 10 words are used incorrectly, fewer than one person out of every hundred has ever gone to the dictionary to look them up. It would not be so terrible if these were inconsequential words; words that didn't matter or were used infrequently...these are important words. These are words that affect the happiness and prosperity of every human being. These are words that hold marriages together...or destroy them. These are words that determine who will *"have"* and who will *"have not"* in the business world. These are words that affect the *quality* of life. A point to be made here: each of the ten words is nontangible, purely abstract, formless. The 10 words arrange themselves into **five sets** of two words each. We'll spend time on each set...how they were used in your past...and how you might want to see them used in the future. By the way, it will be useless to agonize over the past uses of the words. Once we cover the five sets of words, you will *own* the labels. At that point, you can make decisions about your future. You may learn some very important lessons about your past, but you *cannot* change it. Therefore, we won't spend much time in that time frame. Here are the 10 words arranged into the five sets. The sets form an example of one of the laws of the universe we'll study later:

SUCCESS & FAILURE
SUPERIOR & INFERIOR
WIN & LOSE
GOOD & BAD
RIGHT & WRONG

Ultimately, the 10 words revolve around the last pair; **RIGHT & WRONG.** The other four sets (eight words) are ways of expressing *right* and *wrong.* Let's take a look at each of the sets and see how problems are created when the words are used incorrectly in the label process.

SUCCESS & FAILURE

Everyone "knows" what it is to be a **SUCCESS,** and everyone "knows" what it is to be a **FAILURE.** They base that *knowing* on what others (the multitudes of construction workers that *didn't* know what they were building) have told them. Very few people are directed to the dictionary at six, seven or eight years of age, and carefully instructed in the proper method of determining how to measure **SUCCESS** and **FAILURE.** Very few people are lovingly instructed as to how failure can be eliminated from life...or brought to a full understanding of how everyone could become successful. I am going to make the assumption that you have not examined each of the 10 words, and that you might want *to fully examine* each of the words before we move into other important matters. This section of the book could become one of your favorites. I hope that you will reread it after you finish the rest of the book.

The dictionary definition of **SUCCESS** reads: *the progressive attainment of desired goals."* And, **FAILURE** is defined as: *"a lack of success."* Isn't that amazing! All we need to do is decide on the definition for success...work on success...and we have eliminated failure. **"THE PROGRESSIVE ATTAINMENT OF DESIRED GOALS"** tells me there are *two* essentials for being a success. *Both* must be present, or you would by definition be a failure. It seems so easy to eliminate that distasteful word, *failure*...let's pursue what is needed for success. The two elements need to be switched around; "DESIRED GOALS", and then "PROGRESSIVE ATTAINMENT" is the order for discussion. "DESIRED GOALS" has to mean something different for each person. If you know what you want to do, what you want to be, and what you want to have, you can formulate a workable set of "DESIRED GOALS." We'll spend time in a later chapter on charting what you want as your "DESIRED GOALS." And now, "PROGRESSIVE ATTAINMENT" It certainly seems plain enough, once you know your "DESIRED GOALS", you must make progress towards attainment. In other words, **ACTION DIRECTED TOWARDS FULFILLMENT.**

If you have both elements, you cannot be a failure...and the word failure ceases to exist...**for you.** Therefore, a successful person knows that their success **does not** rest on what other people feel is a so-called "success-oriented goal"...a successful person has *ceased* to judge their successes based on what other people want. A "SUCCESS" operates on a different plan of action than most people. Their goals may be to make a lot of money...or it may have nothing to do with money. If you progressively attain your own goals, you are successful. At this point you realize, I've gone full circle. You may also be saying, "Oh come on now...it sounds great, but that means everyone *could* be successful. And, that's just **not going to happen!**" I know it's not going to magically happen... but there is the possibility that everyone *could be* successful if they would understand what has happened in their lives, and could eliminate the negative labels they have accepted. That's primarily what this book is all about, people attaining **their personal goals** and **being successful.** You might ask yourself this question, "Why is it, as I look about the world, that most people are not playing the *success* game? Why are so many playing the *failure* game?" As you answer those questions, you'll see many of the differences between conventional thinking, and the truth **as the truth is.**

Again, I'll remind you...**A TRUTH IS.** I don't want anyone that reads this book to get the idea that I, Michael Jaress, thought up these truths by myself...the truth is...has always been...and always will be. It is only necessary for us (you & I) to discover it. I will take credit for some unique ways of exposing the truth...and I'll take credit for some concepts and some tools that you can use to implement the truth into your life. You can operate more efficiently, more prudently, more effectively...and with a lot less hassle if you operate your life in certain ways. I am showing applications of the truth (the laws) in the concepts, the philosophy, the assumptions, the tools...in *each* chapter, and in *each* method. We'll talk about the bare-root *laws* in a later chapter...after covering more applications.

WIN & LOSE

Think now of the words "**WIN**" and "**LOSE**" which are so often attached to thinking along the lines of "**WINNERS**" and "**LOSERS**". To "**WIN**", according to the dictionary is *"to gain the victory, to succeed in arriving at a place or state, to get possession of,* or *to gain as in a battle or contest."* The dictionary definition of "**LOSE**" is quite simple... *"to fail to win, to fail to attain."*

It certainly sounds to me as though *"winning"* is exactly the same as *"succeeding"*...first you must have something to be attained, and then, you must go after it. If you have a goal that you've set, and you gain that goal, then you are a *"winner".*

The only problem I see could be created is if an individual somehow set goals that were totally beyond human capacity for attainment. Therefore, an individual with their goals within reach (attainable) is "successful" and a "winner" if they will but strive forward and claim what is theirs.

What an "Ah-hah" experience as we delve into the true meanings behind the words that control so much of what goes on in our world. Our world (the world in which we operate) is sometimes hard to deal with. A big part of the problem is that most people don't know what rules are being used. So, they use the rules that are handed down to them from all those *construction workers* that float through and give their many views of what should be built. Do you realize that if a one mile race was to be run...and there were seven runners going to run in that race...there could be seven winners if everyone understood how "WIN" and "LOSE" really work. Instead, operating under the present system, many times the race has *seven "losers"*...**count them**...*seven "losers"*. You may say, **"WAIT A MINUTE! HOW COULD THERE POSSIBLY BE SEVEN LOSERS IF THERE WERE SEVEN RUNNERS?"** Follow this example and you will understand a little more about how it is that there are so many people in this world that operate as losers. The seven runners run the race...one of them crosses the finish line first...the time for the first runner is four minutes, five seconds...the time for the seventh runner crossing the finish line is four minutes, eleven seconds. Now, here is what exists in the minds of the runners...and in the minds of the spectators: 1) Six runners feel they lost the race, and the crowd is in agreement 2) One runner finished first, but that runner claims, "I just wasn't running smoothly. I am *really* disappointed...I should have been under the four minute mark. I'm thinking of retiring because I just don't seem to enjoy the race like I used to a few years back." And, the crowd is disappointed because no one broke the four minute mile. People in the crowd make comments like, "If I'd known the race was going to be run so badly, I'd have stayed home and watched a football game." or "It sure didn't look like they really tried in that last lap...there wasn't a one of them that could hold up." Usually those comments are made by "armchair athletes" who couldn't *walk a mile* in 15 minutes, and yet, they criticize all seven runners. When you use the labels "WIN" and "LOSE", I hope that you realize from this point on: Winning and losing is in relationship to the rules, and you should be able to control the rules...once you decide what it is you plan "to attain."

SUPERIOR & INFERIOR

Let's take a look at another set of labels, **"SUPERIOR"** and **"INFERIOR".** First we'll look to the dictionary for definitions. When we check on **"SUPERIOR",** we find *"of higher rank, quality, or importance."* And for **"INFERIOR",** we find *"of little or less importance, value or merit."* If we fully investigate the way these comparative words are used, it is easy to understand how negative the two words are...and what a negative influence they have become in our society. "SUPERIOR" and "INFERIOR" are measures of comparison. However, as measures of comparison, they are worthless; totally "SUPERIOR" would indicate a point of perfection, and the opposite "INFERIOR" would have to reference a point without any value. Unfortunately, most of the people in our world "act" as though they have fully researched the meanings of these two labels. They act and voice opinions based on the labels "SUPERIOR" and "INFERIOR"...and unfortunately, they limit themselves and destroy a great deal of self-worth in the process. Have you ever wondered "Why do so many people down-grade themselves in front of others?" or "Why is it so hard for most people to accept compliments?" or "Why is it that people are forever comparing their weakest points against other peoples' strongest points?" It's all wrapped-up in the discussions we are having right now about labels; the five sets of labels (10 words) that are commonly *misused, misunderstood,* and *misapplied.*

With some addititional understanding about the labels

"SUPERIOR" and "INFERIOR", you can remove most of the problems connected with the games people play using the words.

First, it helps to realize that the labels "SUPERIOR" and "INFERIOR" should not even come "into play" in most of the areas of your life. There are so very few occupations, skills, or attributes...in which you can ever hope to attain any serious level of competency. Therefore, there are very few areas where you are even "playing the game." This one fact should eliminate thousands of *unfair* comparisons that go on in your life. If you haven't set any goals in an area...if you have no interest in the area of endeavor...if you don't desire attaining "rank or quality or importance" in a particular field or skill, you cannot be inferior to anyone in that area. Occasionally someone will remark to Mary Ellen or myself, "You make public speaking look so easy...I could never stand in front of 600 people and cover information like you do." If the person means that statement as a compliment, we thank them...if they are expressing feelings of the "INFERIOR" label by putting their own talents and abilities *down* by comparison, we will usually talk a little with them about their goals in the field of public speaking. It takes only a moment or two to discover some facts about the individual...and to find out whether they are desiring entry into the field of public speaking. Most of the time, they have no goals or desires about the field...and we move the conversation into whatever is their area of competency; it improves the level of communications when you talk about fields where the other person has skills and achievements. But, in the rare occurrence where the individual has a desire to be involved in our field, we talk about their goals, their achievements, and their future. It makes them feel better...and stops an *unfair* comparison that might lead to the limitation of another person's life desires. As you learn more and more about the label "games", I hope that you will pay special attention to the methods you can use to improve the quality of life around you; the laws of the universe will make certain you receive an extra measure of success everytime you use the methods.

Second, it will help in the understanding of the "SUPER-IOR" and "INFERIOR" labels if you will realize that everyone views superior, inferior, and perfection in their own particular ...peculiar...and sometimes pathetic, manner. There is no established "norm." Certainly there are areas of your life where you do have goals. And in those areas, you are striving to attain *"rank"* or *"quality"* or some level of *"importance."* What hinders your rapid progression in those areas of your desires more than any other single factor? Your reactions to the labels we are discussing in this chapter...that's what!

You have a *certain way* of viewing "SUPERIOR", and a *certain way* that you accept yourself in relationship to where you feel you stand in the scheme of things.

You have a *certain way* of viewing "INFERIOR", and a *certain way* that you accept yourself in relationship to where you feel you stand in the scheme of things.

And, you have a *certain way* of viewing "PERFECTION", and many feelings, emotions and attitudes wrapped up in your comparisons; yourself compared *with* and *against* everyone else in your environment.

The labels are difficult to explain because they are as slippery as trying to catch minnows with your bare hands; everytime you reach for something to grasp...you come up empty-handed. Because "superior" and "inferior" are only in terms of comparison, everyone is trying to pick a beginning point on the scale that ranges from one end of the spectrum to the other. It is absolute nonsense to try to pick a point somewhere in the middle of the scale...and assign it as "superior." Therefore, we must pick our point for comparison from two extremes; total superiority (perfection) or total inferiority (whatever that means). If we use the field of sports as a testing ground, we can see the total absurdity in trying to pick either of those two points...someone always comes along who is a little less coordinated than what we had previously selected as the absolute worst (inferior) of all participants. I remember when I was captain of a rifle team in high school. Small bore rifle (target shooting) was a part of my upbringing...my entire family enjoyed the sport...my grandfather and my mother were national champions...and it was very easy for me to become a part of that sport. Every once in awhile someone would come along who could shoot worse than anyone I had ever seen before. I think the worst I had seen by the time I left high school, was a young man that could consistently miss the complete target...*in fact,* he would occasionally put a shot into the roof of the target range. Naturally, not many people wanted to practice with him! If we pick the field of sports again, we can try for the point of perfection. Shall we say that a four minute mile is **the absolute perfection point?** Shall we say that bowling a 300 game is **the absolute point of perfection?** Shall we say that batting .400 would be **the absolute point of perfection?** Shall we say that scoring 100 points in a basketball game is **the absolute point of perfection** for one person? Shall we say *(anything)* is **the absolute point of perfection?** As surely as we select our absolute point of perfection, someone will strive a little extra and break that record; hundreds have already broken the four minute mile...thousands have bowled 300 games (and some have bowled back-to-back 300 games)...professional players have exceeded the .400 mark...basketball has seen over 100 points from a single player in one game. BUT HERE'S THE IMPORTANT POINT TO REALIZE: It would be foolish to pick a point of near perfection, and then assign everyone that could not guarantee a 100% *perfect performance...every-time...*the title "inferior".

In fact, there is no perfection on this earth in any area of human endeavor we seek to understand. If you decide to play the comparison game, here is what you have to look forward to: 1) If you compare yourself *unfairly,* you will always feel **inferior.** 2) If you compare yourself with *perfection in your chosen field,* you will always feel **inferior.** 3) If you compare yourself with others that are not even in your field, you would be a self-seeking fool...trying to lift yourself at the expense of others. 4) If you compare yourself to others in your field that are in earlier stages of training, just so you can call yourself superior, you will never be thought of as a champion. The discussion of the labels "SUPERIOR" and "INFERIOR" is a never-ending pursuit that will prove fruitless. Later in the book, we'll set up a situation that will remove all the unfair comparisons from your point of view so you can get on with attaining your goals and your desires unhampered by these words that *mean nothing*...but cause so much damage.

GOOD & BAD

The next set of words I choose for discussion are "**GOOD**" and "**BAD**". Once we have finished this set, we can discuss "**RIGHT**" and "**WRONG**". At that time, everything will fall into place. "**GOOD**" and "**BAD**" are a strange set of words. We learn them as children along with all the other labels we've been discussing, but the strange aspect of "**GOOD**" and "**BAD**" is how both words were used to describe the same actions in our young lives. How totally confusing it must be for a little child to perform an action one day and be called a *"good boy"* and the next day do the same thing and be called a *"bad boy"*. By the way, a dictionary definition for "**GOOD**" would be...*"something that is good."* (that tells you little, or nothing) or...*"a good element or portion."* (tells us about the same) or...*"of a favorable character or tendency."* (favorable to whom?) Maybe there's some hope in looking for the definition of "**BAD**"...*something that is bad."* (crazy world isn't it?) or...*"an evil or unhappy state."* (compared to what?).

Perhaps by discussing individual occurrences in the life of a small child we will be able to see how the labels "**GOOD**" and "**BAD**" came to be applied. As an infant, and as a small child, you learned at a faster rate than at any other time in your development. Your learning curve peaked at age 3½. I believe it didn't peak until 3½ because before that age your environment correctly applied the laws of the universe to your development. People, without knowing how the laws work, can still apply the laws. The laws will work for you or against you...it doesn't matter who you are…it doesn't matter how old you are…it doesn't matter how much money you have or don't have. **It doesn't matter!** A *correct* application of the laws will always work to your benefit. An *incorrect* application of the laws will always work against you. As an infant, the laws were applied correctly…fortunately for you. As an infant and small child, up until the age of 2 or 3, you were bombarded with the application of "good" labels. Everyone told you how wonderful you were. You were given positive strokes with all the "good" labels…and according to the laws of the universe, you responded. You responded by learning at an extremely fast pace. You learned words and language at a rate 15 to 35 times faster than the average adult. You learned complicated motor reactions in a matter of days that would take an adult months or years to learn. You were a genius in the field of art. Picasso oft-times mentioned the fact that 90% of all children under the age of four were his equal…geniuses in the field of art.

Now watch and see how it all works out: In the beginning, any *attempt* was rewarded. An *attempt* at walking, an *attempt* at feeding yourself, an *attempt* at talking, an *attempt* at tying your shoes, an *attempt* at dressing yourself, an *attempt* at drawing, an *attempt* at writing…all were rewarded non-judgmentally with love.

Can you imagine a child of 10 months standing by a chair? Holding on so he or she won't fall…swaying back and forth-…balancing and judging that great expanse to the next chair. And suddenly, the child lets go and takes one faltering step. **PLOP**, down in a heap. Can you imagine the electric thrill that goes through the household? OR…could you imagine the child's mother coming over and kicking the child, and yelling, **"you dumb, stupid brat**…you are *such a disgrace* to our family…you failed to walk, and after watching us do it perfectly for 10 months…how will we ever face the neighbors?" As she drop-kicks the child once again in the direction of his bedroom she screams, "Get back in your bedroom **you failure, you loser, you inferior thing**…and don't come out until you can walk **perfectly!"** Can you imagine that? Of course, you

can't imagine the drop-kick. What would happen is this: The parents would be ecstatic...they would pick the baby up and hug it and kiss it saying, "You are such a wonderful baby!" and "That's mommy's wonderful little baby, come on let's do it again." Meanwhile father is on the phone bragging to the grandparents about how that first step was all part of *dad's masterplan* to develop a quarterback or a ballerina. Within a few short weeks the child becomes accomplished at walking. It won't be long though until the very action that received positive strokes will elicit negative strokes. Along about the age of two, the child may be taken to a shopping center with mom. What a magnificent experience...all those lights...all those beautiful things...all those huge hallways to run in, rather than the limited space in the bedroom. But watch out, it will probably irritate mom when you explore. Perhaps you were fortunate, as I was. My parents never seemed to be caught-up in the terrible "rush rush...rat race" of life. They were "marathon runners" in the daily living of life. As you know, a marathon runner is in the race for the long haul...not a mad dash...not a sprinter...but rather someone that has learned to pace themselves. I can remember when I was a child in Detroit. I can remember what great fun it was to go downtown to the J. L. Hudson store, and get lost in the racks of clothes. Can you remember what great fun that was? My brothers and I were not raised to be destructive of others' belongings; therefore, our mother did not have to worry about us destroying the store. Think to yourself what happens to most of the children you see in the stores you frequent now. Do you remember the feeling in the pit of your stomach the last time you saw a little 2½ year child being reprimanded in a grocery store or department store. The mother was probably following this line, "**Look,** I didn't bring you to this store so you could run around...**DO YOU HEAR ME?**" She may be yanking at the child's clothes or dragging him by one arm or even slapping or punching and all the while yelling..."You are *such a pest,* I can't trust you for one minute. You are such a disgrace, you'll never grow up to be *anything.* I WANT YOU TO

PUT YOUR HANDS IN YOUR POCKETS AND STAND THERE AND DON'T DO ANYTHING **BUT BREATHE! DO YOU HEAR ME!**" The very same activities; walking, exploring, wanting to try new things are now "BAD" whereas before (6 months or a year ago) they were wonderful.

When a parent does not understand themselves...when they do not like themselves...when they feel trapped in their own labels...when they do not own their own labels, they find it so easy to destroy even their most precious possessions. I don't want to sound negative about our society *in total,* but in a general manner, our society is destroying the self worth of the children at an earlier and earlier age. I have observed parents violating the laws when children are barely beyond the crawling age. And, we are right now graduating masses that cannot read, cannot write, and have no identities. They have been so bombarded with the 10 words we are discussing in this chapter...they no longer are willing to strive, to attain, *to be anything.* Our country is wallowing in the muck of millions of people...millions upon millions of people...that have had their self-images, their self-worth reduced and torn to shreds. Let's take a look at some additional examples of how "GOOD" and "BAD" enter into the life of the small child. As you'll notice in each situation, the parent does an overload in reacting to the act. A little child finally sits up in the high-chair, and the family decides it's time he learned to feed himself. Into his hand went a spoon, into the oatmeal went the spoon, up to his face went the oatmeal (notice I said "face"...not "mouth"), over the head and down the wall and on the chair and in his hair goes the oatmeal. His first attempt at eating has been a success, and his *"fan club"* goes wild. Mom gets a nice clean baby washtowel and runs lukewarm water and gently wipes baby off saying, "You are such a good baby, you did such a *good* job, here's your spoon Honey, let's do it again." What happened to all those good feelings when *you* were about 3 and they got you dressed for church...before feeding you breakfast (that's *their* mistake, but they don't recognize it) and disaster strikes. I would like to bring in one point here that is appropriate. During the morning (that morning when you were 3), Dad *accidently* spilled some of his coffee while trying to turn the page on the Sunday paper...and Mom got a spot on the front of her church dress while cooking breakfast (she forgot to put on an apron) but in an adult fashion, she went in another room and quietly sponged out the spot so it wouldn't show. Dad was trying to read the sport section of the paper while dipping his toast in the eggs and doesn't know about the egg drip on the front of his pants (he'll discover that after church and be infuriated driving home). But that morning, *you* made the mess...*you* accidently dribbled something on the front of you, and the barrage started, "**You dumb, messy kid.** Can't you do *anything* right? We give you the simple task of eating and you blow it. If I've told you once, **I've told you a thousand times** to pay attention to what you're doing. Maybe from now on *you can go hungry* until we get home from church!" Meanwhile, they've grabbed a dishrag to clean you off. The dirty dishrag that Mom used for last night's dishes. The one that when you squeeze it, the water comes out *gray,* and the aroma is enough to turn your stomach. It's amazing how many participants in our workshops react to this example. Some people react because they were the one that experienced the filthy dishrag...and some react because they did it two nights ago to their child. But even the dirty dishrag doesn't end the scenario. You were manhandled out of the chair...scolded...and scrubbed...and the labels were "scored-in" so very deep. It makes you wonder how little kids keep from getting broken legs. I'm sure you've seen parents in restaurants trying to yank their kids out of high-chairs. But, the child's legs are pinned between the tray top and the seat, and the whole chair goes up in the air along with the child. *How sad!*

How about one more example that will establish the routine destruction of self-worth in a child. Will you agree with me on a general observation (this is not a hard fact, but an observation)...the general observation: People who are outgoing, friendly, extroverted, people who can speak up in public, and ask for what they want, people who will go the extra mile to put people at ease around them...*those people* seem to enjoy the better things of life and are respected for their warm personalities. WILL YOU AGREE? Good!

Think about a small child just learning to talk...can you imagine the excitement in the family as the day approaches when that first word is spoken? The praise, the warm cuddles, the pride, and the fulfillment...I'm certain you can imagine that scene. "Good boy" or "Good girl" you talked, now Honey, do it again. Can you also remember the last time you were in a restaurant somewhere, and sitting in the booth next to yours was a little boy or a little girl...about 2 years old. Suddenly, the child pops up and looks at you and says, "Hi, my name's Jimmy...what's yours?" Before you can answer, the parent grabs the child and says, "**SIT DOWN...WE DIDN'T BRING YOU TO A RESTAURANT TO ACT LIKE AN ILL-MANNERED BRAT!** Don't bother people, you shouldn't get in the way and *make a pest* of yourself. Now, **sit down...shut up...**and stop crying or **we'll never let you come to dinner with us again.**" Praise one year for talking...and constant degrading for 17 years...will not produce a warm, outgoing, personable individual. Maybe this is why we have a nation of people that would like to be heard...but, just know "no one would **pay atent**ion to me." Maybe this is why public speaking is one of the greatest fears people have. Maybe this is why people live in a neighborhood for years and never meet their neighbors. Maybe this is why management talent (the ability to lead...*not* order people) is such a rare talent. Maybe this is why people spend thousands of dollars trying to get rid of "hang-ups" that shouldn't be there in the first place.

RIGHT & WRONG

And now, for the completion of the sets of words; the pivotal words upon which the four sets (we've just discussed) rest. The final set will be the two words "**RIGHT**" and

"WRONG". To the dictionary we go and find... *"being in accordance with what is good, just or proper."* as the definition for "RIGHT". We should be able to work with that definition with no problem. Let's take a look at "WRONG": *"not right"* or *"Not right or proper according to a code, standard, or convention."* These may be the *easiest* of the sets of words to come to a mutual agreement as regards definitions... and, the *most difficult* for everyone reading this book to fully understand. Knowing that, I would like you to take a little break right now... maybe get a cold glass of something to drink... or a fresh cup of coffee. When you come back, we'll go through the words "RIGHT" and "WRONG" thoroughly. Don't be trying to guess what's ahead. Don't start trying to prejudge or decide how you're going to react... and please don't skip any of this section because you think you "know" what is right and what is wrong. I was a Christian for years before I came to fully understand right and wrong. As the game is played now (by believers and non-believers) many people are needlessly hurt *spiritually, financially* and *and emotionally.* In addition, families are torn apart over misunderstandings about these two words.

Now, that you're back from your short break, read over the definitions once again. Isn't it amazing that right and wrong actions have to do with *what is acceptable*... what is the *normal* standard? What happens is this; people decide what is "RIGHT" and what is "WRONG" based on the reactions of people around them. What's really amazing is that the decision can be based on the feelings of a very small number of people... and the small number of people may not even know *what* they are judging, or *why* they are standing in judgment. If the majority casts its approval, then what you are doing is "RIGHT." If the majority condemns your actions, then it's "WRONG." Seems very easy doesn't it? The problem is this, no matter what you decide to do... I can collect together a group of people that will tell you, "It is wrong for you to do what you are doing!" And, no matter what you feel is "WRONG", there can always be collected together a group that feels it is "RIGHT." The biggest problem with the two labels is when an individual begins living their life based on what other people feel are "RIGHT" and "WRONG."

The difficult part to thinking rationally about the labels "RIGHT" and "WRONG" is that each individual reacts emotionally when the discussion turns to "Are you *certain* what you are doing is "RIGHT?" or "How are you sure *you* aren't "WRONG?" If as an adult reader you heeded my advice about not rejecting or accepting until you had fully thought through the discussion, then you are not angry with me or the concept we are discussing. If however, you are talking to yourself and saying, "How dare you tell me what I feel may be wrong...or that what I'm doing may not be right! I'll have you know I've lived a lot of years, and morally I know what is right and wrong. I read the Bible and don't need to be told what is right and what is wrong." That's exactly why I caution so many times in discussing a rather touchy subject. Reserve your judgments until you have fully considered each subject. Reserve your judgments until you have seen the implications "RIGHT" and "WRONG" have on the lives of anyone that does not fully understand how the words are used incorrectly. It is the *incorrect* use of the labels, and the *improper* application of the labels, that creates all the problems and limitations in the lives of people.

Let me start with some easy examples of using the labels "RIGHT" and "WRONG" and then work up to more difficult situations. The reason I am putting forth all these examples is: To demonstrate that "RIGHT" and "WRONG" are *merely agreement* on the labels you wear; that "RIGHT" and "WRONG" are *merely agreements* by the majority. And, if you can understand the labels and use them correctly, you can use the labels to cause the laws of the universe to work *positively* in your life and in the lives of those you love.

Let me start with some easy examples and work up to more difficult situations. When you eat, do you hold your fork with your right hand or your left hand? WHY??? See, you might not have thought about it before. You hold your fork in (let's say right hand) your right hand because that is what is *"acceptable, proper* and *according to convention"* in your family or social circle. If you violate the social norms, people will whisper behind your back…your family will scoff at you for acting incorrectly (wrong)…and people in general will think many of your actions are suspect. Of course, if you moved to Europe, you would want to change and hold your fork in your left hand and your knife in your right hand…so you would be doing it the "RIGHT" way. About 98% of all the things you do each day you do a certain way because you want to be accepted by the majority…you want to be "RIGHT" based on what the majority tells you is right. The clothes you wear, the way you eat, the way you walk, the way you talk, the way you act, the way you laugh, the way you look, how you maintain yourself, how you think, feel, act and react are all subject to this force-field of "DO IT RIGHT!" Let me give you some examples from another culture just to demonstrate how "RIGHT" and "WRONG" are used by each society to fit the individual into the mold. I AM NOT ADVOCATING AN OVERTHROW OF SOCIETY…I am suggesting that it may be in your best interest to become a follower of the laws of the universe rather than a follower of everyone else. We'll get into the laws soon; their source, their content, and their meaning in your life…and then I'm certain the full picture will be revealed to you.

Here's the example from another culture that differs from your usual everyday living situation. In your home, I would imagine the females are allowed to drive an automobile if they are old enough to secure a driver's license. I would also assume that the females are allowed to select their own clothes, and to go out to a restaurant or to the park by themselves if they want. It seems right wouldn't you say? WHY??? Because it is the *accepted norm;* the *accepted standard.* What would be the community reaction if you suddenly set up rules that forbid such actions for the females in your household? You'd be "wrong." You'd be petitioned against. People would shun you, and talk about you behind your back. Do you realize that there are many areas of the world where the societies have strict censures against females taking control over the simple function of what to wear, where they can eat, and driving cars is against the law? It doesn't matter that you have control over these functions in our society...when in Saudi Arabia, do as the Saudi do...or end up in jail. How about one more example to send a little shock through you. Is it right or wrong to force seven year old children to work in the streets begging for 14 hours a day? It all depends on the common customs; the *accepted norm*, the *accepted standard* of the majority.

Occasionally someone will try to bring up at least one really ugly example to prove that "right" and "wrong" are inherent in the action; to try to prove that something of this world can be classified as right or wrong by everyone's standards. Of course that is futile, even when we consider the issue of killing another human being. Is it *right* or *wrong* to kill? It depends on the situation and what is accepted as right or wrong for the situation. On the one hand, the Bible says, "Thou shalt not kill." And on the other hand, the Bible contains many accounts when the Lord commanded that "every living thing be destroyed; man, woman, child, slave, and every creature"...and used His most worthy servants as the instruments to accomplish His works. We can wrestle with the subject of "RIGHT" and "WRONG" on the large scale forever. We can argue the issue with all our philosophical might...but, can we come to one small bit of agreement: Right and wrong are, and always will be, just labels that are attached to acts. "RIGHT" and "WRONG" in our society are based on common agreement. If we can come to this agreement between the two of us, then can you see the implications of this realization as regards your labels? If you can get enough people to agree that you are successful, YOU ARE SUCCESSFUL. If you can get enough people to agree that you are a failure, YOU ARE A FAILURE. I hope that a voice just shouted in your mind, "HOLD IT, HOLD IT! You said that being a success or a failure had nothing to do with what other people wanted." I certainly am glad you're awake. Follow this:

1) If you set goals 2) and progressively attain them 3) you will be doing the actions successful people do 4) people will attribute the successful attitude to you 5) you will have common agreement...as people say, "You are successful. You are right. You are a doer. You have clout, or money, or position, or financial freedom. You wear the right labels so you deserve the "right" rewards. Each day as you roll out of bed, you'll reach inside "THE CLOSET OF YOUR MIND" take your successful labels off the hangers and put them on yourself.

What about the people who decide to wear the failure labels? Follow this: 1) They don't set goals 2) and therefore aim at nothing 3) because they aim at nothing, they get nothing 4) people will attribute the failure attitude to them 5) and they get common agreement in the way people treat them and reward them and talk about them. What is said about a person that decides to wear failure labels? People say, "You are unsuccessful. You do things wrong. You are not goal-oriented. You have no clout...you have no position...you have no financial freedom. You are wearing the right labels to receive exactly what we are giving you. You are receiving the right rewards; the rewards you deserve."

＊＊＊＊＊ DID YOU GET AN "AH-HAH? ＊＊＊＊＊

Both successful people and failures are wearing the *right labels* to get what they wanted and **what they deserved!** Here's another interesting tidbit, you are wearing exactly the "RIGHT" labels to get exactly what you have...RIGHT NOW. You have learned to reach into "THE CLOSET OF YOUR MIND" each day and select the perfect labels for everything that is going on in your world...as it is now.

I've had people come up to me at the break in a workshop or seminar and say, "**You're wrong!** I am not wearing all those negative labels you described. I don't reach into any closet in my head and pick out crummy labels to wear. My world is a mess because of what everyone else is doing to me...not because of any labels I wear." In a little while, I'll share some interesting techniques with you that take almost all the sting out of the situation where you are ripped at by someone that thinks you are wrong. Fortunately for me, I practice what I preach...so I don't get reactive and hostile. There's usually quite a story behind why the individual feels they don't deserve exactly what they have...I DO NOT BELIEVE OR DIS-BELIEVE THE STORY, I just like listening to them (they are really *quite imaginative* and very interesting.) It never takes much prying to get the story started. I usually try to get the person talking by phrasing back their last statement, "What do you mean your life is a mess?" Normally they say, "Well..." and they start..."I'm very unhappy with my job. I don't like the people I work with and the money is never enough. My family is on the rocks. We've been discussing separating on a trial basis. My health is shot. It seems I've been on edge lately, high-strung, and my diet isn't what it should be, I guess. I have been on a real downhill slide for about two years, but I don't think it has anything to do with my labels." *By now,* you can probably describe which labels this person takes off the hangers each morning...can't you?

Then at the next break, I'll have someone come up and in front of 10 or 15 people they'll say (just loud enough for everyone to hear), "I'm a self-made millionaire and I don't know if your label explanation really applies to my situation. I can see how failure type people might bring it on themselves with all their moaning and groaning, but my situation is different. Most people don't agree with me...in fact, if I had to wait around for the common agreement of everyone, I would not be where I am in life. I feel that I control my success by hard work and smart business sense...not some funny little "label closet" like you talked about." For those of you who know me (you've been to one of the workshops), you know that I have a humorous "me" inside that enjoys fun and jokes and good stories. Anyway, the "me" inside takes over and asks for the story that is to come (I've been called wrong so many times...I quit counting) and almost always it will be a good interesting story. I still don't like being called *wrong,* but I've learned to control *my labels*...rather than to let other people "punch my button" and make Michael reactive. So a rephrase… "I always like spending time with successful people. How did you make all that money? What do you do? "Well…" and they start… "I've always liked to call my own shots, and I've been very interested in computers and electronics. I had this idea about supplying a complete program and unit in an untapped field. No one else knew how to make the program financially feasible for the kind of dealers my company approaches. When people in the industry heard what our unit would do, some venture capitalists approached me with a couple of million to invest. Two years later, I sold off half my interest for six million. It was purely a good money deal, and had nothing to do with my labels. Anyone with *that* unit could have done it." **NOW, YOU TELL ME,** did the labels have anything to do with the *success* of our self-made millionaire? You can probably describe which labels that person takes off the hangers each morning. Can't you? Certainly you can. I can also guarantee that on the morning when our self-made millionaire reaches into his or her "CLOSET", selects ugly, miserable, failure labels…labels that say "I DON'T LIKE ME…I FEEL INFERIOR…I'M ALL WASHED UP"…on that day, he or she will be on their way out. The millions can disappear overnight. The world is abundant; it rewards in direct proportions based on a set of laws that always work. We are working towards a full understanding of the six laws. But first, we are removing all the stumbling blocks that would keep you from accepting and using the laws.

Some very important points to remember about this chapter are hidden within the stories about comparison words. Basically the points to remember are the same as the points to remember regarding "THE CLOSET OF YOUR MIND." If you will take the time to fully understand the concepts behind the words that were written, you will begin to use the tools long before we start the discussion of the laws.

Realize this: 1) It is *your* closet…of *your* mind. You, and you alone have access *now*. In the beginning, others gave you the labels for *their* convenience…but now, *you* own the closet. 2) You can decide which labels *you* want to wear…which are inappropriate...and which will give *you* the rewards *you* desire. 3) The labels you are wearing at this time are only one combination of thousands of combinations you could select. Most of the people in your environment have come to an agreement concerning the labels you are wearing at this time and place in your life...and, 4) You are wearing exactly the *right combination* to give you everything you have in your life...**right now.**

Have you found the five sets of words interesting? Can you visualize how actions and reactions to the five sets of opposites have created many problems in this world? Do you have a better understanding of how people are limited by the words (the labels) of comparisons? Doesn't it make you wonder how advanced we would be if only people knew what you know now about these 10 words? **WELL...THE BUCK STOPS HERE!** Once you fully understand the words and the concepts that are woven into the games people play using the words, I think you'll want to take *the limits* off yourself. There are some cautionary notes I'll share with you in the chapters that follow...plus a great number of tools that you can use to help implement change in whatever way you would like to change. In the chapters that follow, we'll investigate positive goal structuring as opposed to the negative goal structuring taught in schools. We'll fully cover success cycles; how to start them, how to maintain them, and how to move from one success cycle into the next larger success cycle. We'll cover all the laws of the universe in great detail. It gets more interesting as we use the tools.

Let's talk about change for awhile. We started to discuss change in a chapter at the front of the book, but let's talk about change again. Let's talk about the nitty-gritty of who will cause you the greatest problems when you decide to make some changes in your life. You are going to be the major benefactor in all the changes that will be made. You are going to take control over the effects in your world. You are going to make things happen for the better in every area of your life...and this will help everyone in your environment, but your family, friends, and associates won't see it that way.

6
Changing
Your
Labels

This entire chapter was written just to let you know what will probably happen the minute you decide to change any *major* labels you are presently wearing. There is a high probability that your friends, family members, and your associates will react in strange ways when you change any *major* label. What do I mean by a *major* label? Do I mean changing your label to being a "Tarzan" living in a tree in some far off jungle? No, I mean changing a label such as; being a happier person...being a more successful person...being a warmer, friendlier person...being more industrious...being more goal-oriented...being more concerned about your health...being more spiritually oriented...wanting to improve yourself...wanting to "smell the roses" instead of living your work 24 hours a day...wanting to spend time getting to know your children ...wanting to show love to your spouse...wanting to be concerned with the growth of your church...wanting to help others when it would be easier to turn away...wanting to give instead of take...wanting to lead instead of being led...etc., etc. Along the way, you may make some decisions that affect your world of your work, and you may make some decisions that affect your style of living. But, the changes will only be made *if you* want them to be made. And you will only want to make the changes if you feel they are needed to create the kind of *effects* you feel will positively enhance your world. Just remember, there are *reasons why* some people are successful and others are not. There are *reasons why* some people are happy and others live a life of misery (even though surrounded by friends and a family.) There are *reasons why* some people seem to live a life that is blessed, and others feel that death cannot come quickly enough. There are *reasons why* some people are in the right place at the right time...and others never know what time it is. There are *reasons why* everything works exactly the way it does. It is not a gigantic mystery hidden from all but a special few. The reasons have always been open for inspection. The problem is that most people do not want answers for their problems. The answers have been known for thousands of years, but most people cannot stand the thought of finally being without their *overwhelming problems.* Sometimes people will agree to give up one of two of their problems...but not until they have carefully selected a much larger problem to nurture along. If you can take my being that honest with you, then I can safely assume that you can handle the simple process which if followed will change the *effects* in your life. If you get upset because I say that most people don't want answers to their problems, then you won't be able to handle the simple laws that work in this world. Here's the answer for whatever needs to be changed to remove a problem; everything of this physical world is an *effect*. Every problem, every situation, every reward, every punishment, every thing is an *effect*. If there are many effects in your life that you like (I hope that you have much in your world that you like), you'll naturally want to keep them. With some of the people we see in our workshops, very few changes are wanted...while others have very little about their world that they want to have remain the same. Just remember this, if you want to change one effect or a thousand effects, the process is always the same; change the *cause* to change the *effect*. One of the immutable laws of the universe is the law of **Cause** and **Effect**. We'll cover the law in more depth in a later chapter, but for now, let's discuss "cause". The *cause* is always self-contained because *cause* is always *thought*. Everything of this physical world in an *effect*. There are no, I repeat, **no** physical causes. All cause is in an energy form which we call thought. To change an effect, we must eventually seek the source of the effect and change the thought (cause) so as to create a new or different effect. If a person desires to be happier; that is, to create an *effect* of greater happiness, he or she must seek the cause and change the cause. Most people of the world approach the problem incorrectly; they try to manipulate other effects into some new arrangement that will make them happier. Trying to change *effect* by manipulating *effect* is a blind alley leading nowhere. Let's look at an example that I have used in hundreds of workshops.

I'm going to use an example from my experiences in working with children to illustrate the changing of an effect. I've tried to find another experience in the business world that would replace this story... with the same "impact"... but, have been unable to find as good an example.

Once upon a time, I was working with a group of very smart young children; ages 5-7. It was at a time when I was introducing some of my value structure games into teaching groups. One of my associates at that time was a man that had at one time been a director of testing for the county in Dallas, Texas. Ben and I were seeking ways to show small children how they could control their reactions when people picked on them. Children at the genius level in our society experience tremendous frustration in being forced to live two lives; one life at an advanced, accelerated learning pace (beyond their peers and parents) and a second life as a normal healthy young girl or boy, who wants to play and be loved and giggle and have friends.

I was working with a group of about 20 children one day, so I took a variety of labels for feelings, emotions, and attitudes that most people experience in life and printed them on cards about 15″ x 15″. I picked one of the boys who was a great actor. Bobby always liked to play up to the group... at six years old, he was a natural for the stage. I said, "Bobby, I'd like you to go over to the table and pick out the 'happy' label, put it on, and demonstrate the feeling that is normally worn when a person wears the 'happy' label." Away he went, he rifled through the cards, found the 'happy' label, and pinned it on. And, went into his act; smiling, strutting, and playing up to his classmates. At this point, I said, "Now Bobby, I want you *to pretend* it is 4:30 in the afternoon...you've had a hard day at school ...and you're hungry...real hungry. And so, you walk into the kitchen and real nicely you ask, 'Mom, could I have a cookie please?' Your Mom turns around Bobby, and she really chews you out for coming into the kitchen an hour before dinner. She yells at you, and tells you to get out of her sight before she whips you. NOW, BOBBY, HOW DO YOU FEEL?" I'll tell you, if looks could kill...Well needless to say, Bobby got his chance to do some more acting (and he really started believing he had been maligned...and cheated out of his cookie) and did he get mad. He stomped over to the table with all the labels spread out on the top, picked out the "mad" label, tore off the "happy" label, and pinned on the "mad" label. I let him rage for about a minute about how it didn't even matter how nice you asked...people still picked on him, and yelled at him (not a bad observation...by the way). At that point I stopped him and asked, "Bobby, *who* has made you so mad?" He thought a minute, and tried to rationalize why he'd gotten so worked up just play acting. I then asked the crucial question, "Well *who* changed the label?" He thought, and you could see the "Ah-hah" spread throughout him...and the room. he said, "*I* changed the label. *I* made me mad." "Right Bobby. No one makes you mad. No other person can ever change your labels. You decide what you will be, and then you decide what labels you'll wear!" That's what I told him and his classmates that day. So it is with Bobby, so it is for me, Michael Jaress...and so it is for you, the reader. You pick *your* labels. No one makes you *anything*...unless you give them permission to control you. If you decide to wear the label because the world expects you to wear the label, then perhaps you, like Bobby, have been in the habit of continuing to accept whatever *effects* were the rewards for your thoughts. Perhaps you disliked the effects, but didn't know the *causes* behind some of the problems.

If you realize that you are in control of the causes...and *therefore,* you are in direct control of the effects, then you can choose any combination of labels (thoughts hanging in "THE CLOSET OF YOUR MIND") to wear. I want to prepare you for the ancillary effects that will occur in the lives of the people that occupy your environment with you. On the day that you make your first changes, some of the people in your environment may act a little disturbed. Any change will eventually make someone feel that everything is NOT PROCEEDING EXACTLY RIGHT. They may want you to go back into a comfortable "mold" they want you to stay in for the rest of your life. I'm sure you have realized by now (especially after my mentioning it a dozen times) your labels were given to you for the *convenience* of the world at large. The world needed a way to identify you, your abilities, and your actions...so they just fed you the labels that were necessary. Anything you do to change yourself *in any way,* is not going to be 100% comfortable for everyone else.

Let me give you an example that I think will shine light on the situation. Don't try to decide if this is really how it works, or try to decide if this is *right* or *wrong,* just read and see if this is how things *seem* to work. Everything that an individual becomes is because everyone in his or her environment *agrees* it is *"right"* for that person.

Let's take an individual that is a lawyer (or any other occupational label) in a large corporation. And, let's say that person says, "I am a lawyer because I wanted to be a lawyer ...not because a lot of other people agreed I was to be a lawyer. Other people have nothing to do with it...I became a lawyer of my own free will." This individual obviously *does not* understand the label game. He or she is a lawyer only because of the common *agreement* among many groups of people all along the way in their career. During college years, that individual was *counseled* as to his or her aptitude for the field of law; they were *accepted* into law school because recommendations were given by people that *know* what a law student should be. They had to take a complete curriculum *dictated* by the *agreement* of many people as "the *right* set of classes to learn the skills a lawyer should have." When a small but influential group of people felt that our person had the *"right"* amount of needed knowledge, a degree would be *granted*. Next our individual would apply to take the bar exam; a test set up by *agreement* among many people in the field of law as a *proper* and *fitting* test to determine the applicant's *acceptability* into the field. Upon *passing* the bar, our individual would (by *agreement* amongst a large group of people) be *granted* the right to practice law within certain confined areas that met with the *approval* of another group of people. And now, our "lawyer" is ready to begin earning a living. Out into the world they go to offer their services to the highest bidder. After interviewing with many law firms and corporations, a *majority* of key individuals in one of the companies put their *"stamp of approval"* on the application and a decision is reached; based on their *agreement*, our lawyer is hired and formally given the title lawyer. As each week goes by, our individual performs various functions that the employing company's staff feel are the *appropriate* (right) things a lawyer should perform. Because there is a paycheck every month, our individual knows that he or she is doing what the group *agrees* is the necessary minimum requirement to be considered "a lawyer" with the firm. Should something go wrong along the way (the group *stops agreeing* that our individual should be retained as a lawyer), our individual will be stripped of their credentials as a corporate lawyer with the XYZ firm...and be out on the street again. But, let's say that nothing goes wrong and sooner or later the individual becomes a fixture on the legal staff of XYZ company. Now by common *agreement*, they can continue to do their function for the next 30 or 40 years. They are a lawyer, they wear that label by common *agreement* of hundreds, or perhaps thousands of people all along the way. The people that were instrumental in the

counseling are happy, the people that were involved in the training are happy, the people that eventually hired the lawyer are happy...they are all in *agreement*...you may by their permission, wear "THE LAWYER" label.

DOES THIS MEAN YOU ARE HAPPY BEING A LAWYER?

DOES THIS MEAN YOU ARE A SUCCESSFUL LAWYER?

DOES THIS MEAN YOU ARE A GOOD LAWYER?

DOES THIS MEAN YOU ARE RIGHT AS A LAWYER?

DOES THIS MEAN YOU ARE A SUPERIOR LAWYER?

DOES THIS MEAN YOU FEEL LIKE A WINNER AS A LAWYER?

No, it only means that a group of people decided to grant you a title. This is true of virtually every occupational label you can acquire...so you can probably substitute your occupational title in the place of lawyer throughout the example. Do you realize that this type of label agreement can be found in every area of your life. Are you married? If so, it means that many groups of people (involving many regulations) by common *agreement,* give you *permission* to wear the label "wife" or "husband". Because you followed the procedures properly, a group of people have *agreed* that you can rightfully wear the label. If you have the piece of paper that shows the *agreement* of the people, you are acknowledging the label. If you then live together, raise a family, are seen together, etc., the common *agreement* is that you are living as husband and wife. If one of the partners skips town, never to come back again, although the formal piece of paper still exists, the common *agreement* amongst the majority of people would be "They don't live together as husband and wife. They don't have a relationship." That's the way all the labels work, they are always by common *agreement* of other people. If we wipe out the need for common agreement of some outside group of people, you would not need or have been given labels in your formative years.

You may be saying, "Wait a minute, I'm a _____ because I want to be one.", and with that statement you are agreeing with what everybody else says your label is. By the way, that's a fill in the blank...you fill in whatever title you carry. Our lawyer friend would be shocked if suddenly **NO ONE** was in agreement that he was a lawyer. He wouldn't have a job. His college would say, "I'm sorry but you don't meet our standards. We don't recognize you as a lawyer." His family would plead with him "Please give up this nonsense talk about being a lawyer. No one will hire you...the colleges don't accept you as being a lawyer. The neighbors think you've gone off the 'deep end' with all this foolish nonsense talk. You are wrong to keep on with this stupid idea of yours!"

Just as an aside here, this is exactly what happens to many career people when they retire after 30 or 40 years service with the same corporation or the military. Their label has been stripped away; No one recognizes their label any more. In the confusion that follows, it's no wonder that the average longevity after retirement is sometimes as low as 17 months (an actual figure for one of the Fortune 500 Corp.)

Now, can you change your labels? That's the big question, can *you* change your labels? At this point, you might gulp and think, "Well...I didn't think it would be hard, but now I don't know." The truth of the matter is this...**YOU CAN CHANGE...AND IT WILL BE EASIER THAN YOU MIGHT HAVE THOUGHT...ONCE YOU FULLY DECIDE WHAT YOU WANT TO CHANGE.**

All I'm doing is preparing you for the "flak" when you try to change some of the emotion, feeling or attitude labels...so later in the book, there is a tool that you can learn that makes certain you're not hurt by the "flak" when it's thrown your direction. The name of the tool is **"THE LABEL RIP OFF GAME"** so you'll recognize it when we come to it. I think it will help you in dealing with your friends and family if you can just remember, they by common agreement feel that you are wearing *exactly the right labels; right* by their standards. Do you realize that if you decide to change, then they must have been "wrong" in coming to that agreement. People will throw a lot of "flak" rather than to be proven wrong.

You may be wondering, "What is this *flak* you are talking about?" Let's take a look at our friend the lawyer (or any other occupational label)...and discuss the "flak" that will be flying when he or she makes a decision and announces plans for a change. If our lawyer has grown tired of doing the same thing day after day, for 20 years, wouldn't you think they would want a change? Certainly, they *could* want to change; studies done on the entire spectrum of occupations in the United States, show that over 80% of all the labor force is in some way unhappy with their present work situation. Our laywer has his or her *own personal reasons* for desiring a change. Maybe money has been lean in their particular company...perhaps the challenge has gone out of the picture...it could be that they have been passed over for a promotion or an area of responsibility they wanted. They are no longer a *starry eyed* college graduate...out to set the world "straight." They are no longer simply looking to provide services in exchange for a salary that is "secure" (whatever that means.) Our lawyer understands that 89% of the people in the United States, who are in the upper income brackets, own their own businesses. Our lawyer also knows that while forming a small legal firm (setting up a small practice) would be a safe avenue, it might be an exchange of "one desk for another". Therefore, our lawyer announces the desire to entertain business ventures outside the area of legal services.

Here comes the "flak"...the statements of people that can't stand the thought that they might have been *wrong* in assigning the lawyer label to their friend and associate, "the lawyer." The spouse says, "You can't just throw away your career. All those years at XYZ company would be down the drain. Honey, you are a lawyer...that's where you belong!" Our lawyer's friends will say, "I just can't imagine you giving up everything you've worked for all these years. You are a lawyer, you went to school to be a lawyer, you're respected in the community as the head of one of the divisions at XYZ company. You'd be dumb to give it all up and start over...only 15 more years and *you'd have it made* (whatever that means) in retirement." Of course, people in the local bar association have a vested interest, and will rise to the occasion with statements such as, "You're a professional and we can't understand your wanting to give it all up for some whim." "It's always risky starting a new business, and running a little business seems so much beneath you." "We wouldn't want you to fail you know...but, I think you should consider the personality necessary to be an entrepreneur. As a friend and colleague, I want to be honest with you...you've never been on your own, and I don't think you have what it takes to run your own ship!" Nothing like some good, positive feedback to help you in making decisions...right?

Can you see how very negative and destructive those comments were intended to be. People with their words, and their tones of voice, and their insinuations, severely limit the desires and goals of everyone else in the environment. In our workshops, we call comments that are destructive...**"LABEL RIP OFFS."** Later in the book, this chapter will become even more meaningful as you learn simple techniques that will 1) Take the sting out of their comments, or 2) Shut them up, *or* 3) Get them to join your side.

Let's look at a few more examples of an individual deciding to make changes...and the typical "flak" that will fly when the new changes are announced. I will pick from all segments of society for a very special reason. I want you, as the reader, to realize that you are *not alone* in your desires to change...and, you are *not alone* in being hassled by your environment everytime you want to make a simple little change.

A housewife for 20 years has been happy being the center of attention in the house, but now everyone has grown up and become very self-sufficient. Our housewife makes a decision to change. It doesn't matter whether the change would be to:

1) Seek employment; 2) Go back to school for an advanced degree; 3) Become a professional painter and exhibit art; 4) Go into social work; 5) Become involved in community volunteer work; 6) Become a karate expert; 7) Take up a sport seriously; 8) Become an undercover agent for the CIA. The point is, IT DOESN'T MATTER WHAT SHE CHOOSES TO BECOME AS A *"NEW LABEL"*...she will receive some "flak" depending on who would have to admit that they have labeled her incorrectly. The discussions will vary in their intensity, but mainly they'll go like this, **"You can't, it's wrong,** you have a family that needs you right where you are...**in the home.** How could you be so *inconsiderate* of your loved ones. You *can't* just decide you want to do something and do it. What *right* have you got to be doing things just because *you desire to do them.* There are responsibilities you know!" If this housewife is not careful, all those great positive friends will have her back where she was...bored, becoming a less and less useful member of a family that is moving on...building their lives.

Let's take an example of a student, about 15 or 16 years old. He or she has never been a "good" student. This student's teachers expect him or her to be a *poor* student, and so do all the classmates. Everyone is always harping about the "poor" performance of the student; teachers, coaches, parents, counselors, minister, friends, etc. No one expects the student to do well. The labels have been applied beautifully, and everyone knows exactly what to expect. Suddenly, the student experiences a desire to change. Perhaps it's the result of a chance comment made by someone they respect, or a realization that they will not graduate with their class if they miss one more essential subject. Perhaps it comes from a sudden "Ah-hah, so this is what it is all about." With this sudden understanding, insight, and renewed ambition, the student begins doing the tasks that will earn better marks. Everyone in the environment will rise up, take notice, and throw "flak." "What's *wrong* with you? I just can't understand why you couldn't have gotten better marks all along...what are you doing, *cheating?*

What's got into you lately? Are you *sick* or something? What's the deal...do you need the car for a date? I don't know what's *wrong* with you, but we'll see how long you can keep it up." You do realize that after a few days of this...our student may escape back into the former role as a means of being "right". If you are "wrong" for being a good student (when you weren't supposed to be), then you must be "right" when you are a bad student (everyone is comfortable...and that's what counts ...isn't it?)

How about an example of someone just starting out in the world of business. Let's say that our young business builder joins a firm, works for six months, and decides to make a lateral move to another company. Here comes the "flak" from friends, associates and family, "**Son** (or **daughter**), this is just not the way you should run *your career.* I realize that you were not given the area of responsibility promised, but that's no excuse for you being a *quitter.* You'll never get *anywhere* in life jumping around." Associates might say, "I thought you were made of *tougher stuff*...just because the assistant manager *hated the ground you walked on,* you didn't have to move to our major competitor." Friends might say, "You really blew it. You had a super job...making much more than *I do* after four years with my company. I just can't understand your making a move so soon. You'll get a *bad name* in your field." It's surprising how much "flak" there is...isn't it?

What if a young couple decide to get married because everyone in their environment feels that is what they should do? The wedding date is announced...six months in the future. The young couple have known each other for three years, but during the six month period that approaches the wedding date, they *constantly* fight about every detail concerning the wedding. In their discussions about what life will be like after the wedding, they *both* come to the realization that they will be unhappy living together for the rest of their lives. **What should they do?** Should they call off the wedding? Should they follow through and then get divorced a year later? Should they get married, and live a life of *unhappiness* so no one can say *they* were wrong? Let's say they decide to call the marriage off. Can you imagine the "flak" they will have to put up with from friends and family? You do realize that not a single one of the friends or family members will have to *actually live* in that marriage, but they are certain that it is the *"right"* thing to do.

How about the "flak" heaped on people that are about to retire? Imagine a man about to retire at the young age of 62. If he decides to go fishing 365 days a year, he will get "flak" for *wasting* his life over a fishing pole. If he decides to build a part time business to keep active, he will get "flak" about the fact that he should *slow down* and *take it easy*...that's what retirement is for. If he decides to travel the world and spend all the money he has accumulated, he will get "flak" about being a *wastrel* and perhaps be judged feeble-minded. If he decides to play the financial markets and pyramid his savings into a fortune, he will get "flak" about the fact that he does not spend his money on his younger generations...perhaps picking up names like *"tight-fisted old uncle* _____*"* If he makes any one of the choices above (or a thousand other combinations), he will be thought wrong. But, if he a few years later makes a decision to change, he will again receive "flak" because he's doing something different.

You may be thinking about all the changes you would like to make in your world. When we start the second section of this book, you will find an orderly way to make your world whatever it is that you would like it to be. And I can assure you this: If you will follow the methods and the processes, you can *change* your world so it will reward you with *any style of life* you desire. If you will use the six laws, the tools, the methods, and the processes, you will be able to make small changes or large changes...a few changes or many changes...material changes and emotional changes. And, you'll make those changes with the least amount of "flak" possible. In fact, as people in your environment begin to reap some of the *spin-off rewards,* you will get some eager supporters to help you with the changes. **Isn't that exciting?**

Here's a final example to demonstrate dramatically why I am so excited about sharing change with you. This example will also demonstrate why I feel that when an individual makes decisions that are *"right"* for them...eventually it turns our *"right"* for their environment. It is always "right" for an individual to be in control of their labels; you control your labels...I'll control mine...and as each person controls and decides what is right for themself, then through proper application (correct application) of the laws that work in this universe, everything will work out "right."

My wife, Mary Ellen, was a nurse before we met. She was a good nurse, because she enjoyed some of her work. She spent five years in higher education to receive her R.N. One day, she thought seriously about her future...where she would end up on a nurse's salary...how she would provide for her two little girls...what it would be like to always have the kids staying with day care centers until she got off work...always struggling to make ends meet. I didn't know her at that time, but I certainly admire her ability to evaluate...identify...and come to grips with her future. She decided she wanted to own a business that would give her financial freedom. That was her goal; financial freedom. She decided that she did not want to spend the next 40 years of her life dealing with hospital staffs and doctors, always just making ends meet, putting up with the local "pecking order" where excellence and professionalism were paid off with "maybe" a pat on the back. She decided to build *her own* business, and immediately the "flak" began to fly from all sides; doctors and nurses, friends, and church members...all had a vested interest in maintaining the status quo. "You're a professional person, how can you give all that up?" "Why you wouldn't throw away *all that training,* have you no *consideration* for your children?" "You want to start *a business!* I thought you were a *better person* than that, Mary Ellen." "Now that you're thinking of *abandoning* your children to build a business...are you going to abandon God also?" Doctor friends still sneer when we say hello. I always find it amusing when people decide that they will snub you because you had the audacity to change and be what you wanted to be. What's also amazing are the number of people that will hold a grudge for years because you changed a label and they didn't think you should have done it. Some people will even continue holding the grudge after they have seen that the change was *a really good improvement.* They just don't like the fact that they were incorrect in the labeling process.

Back to Mary Ellen...and why it is so very important to follow through on your dreams...your goals. Because she made that decision, and progressively attained her desired goal, she was successful from the beginning. On the day she implemented her decision and started to follow through, she was successful. We met through a mutual friend in her business world and my business world; a meeting that would not have come about (for a variety of personal reasons we know this to be true) in any other way. We were married 10 months after we met because I fulfilled her goals of the type of man she would want...and she was everything I could possibly imagine a woman could be. What happened to her goal of financial security...of financial freedom? She traded a $13,000-a-year life of struggle, for a thriving business she built with her own drive and ambition. A business that provides her a six figure income, time to spend with the kids in the morning and afternoons and the evenings, plus travel to all parts of the United States, Canada and Europe...weekend trips to any fun spots this world has to offer. Plus, something else that cannot be measured by any amount of money...friends and business associates that are fun, and up, and positive...and *non-judgmental* about her success. By the way, as the reader of this book, we may already know you from some of our travels and workshops...and we just want you to know, we really appreciate your sharing and caring and help along the way. As people share some of the ideas in this book, it seems as though we are all sharing in a larger success story...A PART OF THE WHOLE...WOULDN'T YOU SAY?

* * * NOW, YOU TELL ME...
WAS MARY ELLEN'S DECISION * * *

TO CHANGE HER LABELS...A "GOOD" DECISION, A "RIGHT" DECISION, THE DECISION OF A "WINNER", THE DECISION OF A "SUCCESSFUL" PERSON?

With proper planning and understanding, you will always make what turns out to be the *"right"* decision *for you,* the *"good"* decision *for you,* a *"winners"* decision *for you,* the *"successful"* decision *for you!* Everything in this physical world is available as rewards for the labels we wear. Automatically by wearing the appropriate labels, the laws of this universe align the physical effects and present them as rewards for the use of those people wearing the "right labels" for receiving.

I want you to remember that we will be working on some tools and techniques that will give you a *"flak suit"* to wear as you make some of the changes you decide are appropriate for you. Please notice I said the changes *you* decide are appropriate *for you.* I will offer you some thoughts to consider ...some concepts that provide direction...and some areas for consideration, but you will be the one that makes the final decisions based on what *you want* and on what *you need.* **OK**?

7
Goals . . .
and the
Flat Side of Life

Throughout each chapter, I have asked that you think ahead regarding the changes you would like to make. Basically, when you thought ahead, you were thinking of the different areas of your life, and the changes you wanted to make in each of the areas. This may have been easy for you...or it may have been difficult...for many readers, it has been an *almost* impossible task. Many readers of this book will find it very difficult to effectively change their life goals. "Why?", you might ask. "Surely everyone could imagine what areas need change!" No, in fact, many readers will be in a quandary. Wanting to change, but *not knowing* what needs to be changed to *create* their desired results. The reason is simple; if you had the blueprints for a two story home, containing four bedrooms and a den ...but you wanted instead, a split level home, containing three bedrooms and an expanded family room. WHAT WOULD YOU HAVE TO DO WITH YOUR BLUEPRINTS? Correct! You would have to change the plans...correct the blueprints! The problem that many readers will face is: THEY DO NOT HAVE **A WELL DEFINED SET OF PLANS** OR **BLUE-PRINTS** THAT CAN BE PULLED-OUT AND CHANGED.

When it comes to a discussion of goals, I have found that people fall into four generalized groups...and, I am sure that after you think about the four groups, you will probably agree with my findings. While we might want to gather statistical data on the groups if we were going to prepare a paper for publication, we (you and I) don't need to gather percentages...we only need to discuss the four groups, and see where *you* stand. The groups are:

1. A very small collection of people that have never heard the information, **"You should set goals."**

2. Those people that have a fully detailed, well defined set of goals covering all areas for the development of their potential...a statistically *very small* group.

3. A large group that says, "Yes, I believe that everyone should set goals, but it *frightens* me...so I have always put it off!"

4. A very large group that says, "Yes, I believe that everyone should set goals, but I just never seem to get around to it...*maybe* one of these days, I'll find the time."

Group number one people have become almost nonexistent in our society; everyone from the richest of rich, to the poorest of poor, has heard the message in language they can understand..."**SET GOALS!**"

Group number two people do exist...they *are* in our society. They represent a definite minority; less than 3% (I'll explain how I am able to approximate this figure later in the chapter.)

And now let's take a look at group number three. The group that understands the need for goals, but experiences some fear or apprehension when the subject of goals is discussed. They don't experience a *deep-rooted, heart-stopping* fear, but rather, an uneasy, unsettling *queasy* feeling; an apprehension regarding the future. Psychologically this is termed "free floating anxiety"...a label that we can discuss. You will probably recognize some of your friends or associates once we fully discuss this group, so don't start thinking that big label is something to be avoided like the plague. Of course, there is also the possibility, a *statistical* possibility, that upon further discussion...you might be a member of group number three. We'll discuss group number four in just a moment, but first, let's fully look at the situation in group three.

We'll tear apart the words as our first step. **Anxiety** can be described as..."*Generalized feelings of apprehension and fear.*" If a person had no formal plans for the future, for surviving in this rather complex world, the future could definitely be a rather foreboding place to think of in terms of spending the rest of your life. As for the term **free-floating,** it's a nondescript lable meaning..."*unable to locate or account for the source.*"

Now, we have some idea of what we're looking at; a feeling of fear or apprehension for which we cannot locate a source; whose presence can't be isolated. It will also help us to understand better, if we know that there are two general methods for handling fear and apprehension in this type of *stress* situation:

1. If the individual attempts to accurately assess the problem and to formulate a course of action for coping with the problem...*then,* the individual is said to use an **effective coping behavior.** (That means they're doing it "right")

2. If the individual resorts to denial and/or rationalization of the problem...*then,* the individual is said to use an **ineffective coping behavior.** (They're doing it "wrong") Coping with a problem by denying that it exists or trying to rationalize away the problem is said to be **ineffective,** because that type of coping does not actually deal with the *stress* situation but only alleviates the fear or apprehension temporarily.

Can you see how an individual would have to be following the second method (the *ineffective* coping behavior) if they resorted to avoiding setting goals as a means of not facing the actual problems caused by the future? It is my belief that each person desires to move forward into the future...because we are eager to spend the rest of our lives there. Our hopes, our expectations, all our growth as individuals has to be accomplished in the future. We are...*what we are...today.* Our future, even the next ten minutes, is where **we are going;** minute by minute and second by second. What great anxiety it must create for the individual that selects method number two in dealing with the problem of the future; wanting to look forward to the future...but, burdened with the fear and apprehension of what is going to happen there!

Can you also see what would happen if the individual found a **solid concrete method** for setting goals...a **no-nonsense... straight forward approach** that guided them through the goal setting process? You guessed it! He or she could 1) Properly assess the problems of the future, and 2) Formulate a plan of action that would alleviate the problems, rather than merely "gloss over" the anxiety. I am certain that some readers of this book are actually members of group number three because some of those thousands of construction workers decided *everyone* should wear labels of fear and apprehension. As they went merrily about their work, they did their philosophy of..."Fear the Future." IF YOU ARE A MEMBER OF GROUP NUMBER THREE: **AVOIDING** SETTING GOALS BECAUSE YOUR FAMILY NEVER SET GOALS, **AVOIDING** THE SETTING OF GOALS BECAUSE PLANNING FOR THE FUTURE HAS ALWAYS MADE YOU FEEL A LITTLE UNEASY...FOLLOW THROUGH IN THIS BOOK. YOU HAVE EVERYTHING TO GAIN...AND ONLY YOUR FEARS AND APPREHENSIONS TO LOSE.

And now, for the final group...group number four; perhaps the largest group of the four. Group number four people are not afraid to think about the future, and they are not afraid to think about goal planning. "Most" of the people in group number four know how to set rudimentary goals; the very basic of basic goals. "Most of the people in group number four have read a good collection of the "Positive Mental Attitude" books, and have even repeated the "key" words often enough that a listener would think they supported the teachings. But, somewhere along the way, an *error* was made...maybe one of those "scratch an initial in the old oak desk" errors. I choose to propose that there must be an *error* in labeling somewhere in the past. To think otherwise would mean we would have to assume that this large group of humanity knowing full well what happens to people that have no goals, purposely **choose to set NO GOALS!** So, we have a strange choice to make in looking at anyone that ends up in group number four; the group that admits to understanding the needs for goals...but never gets around to setting that which they know they need. The two choices we have are: 1) There is a basic flaw in the original process, and goals were not presented in a proper manner (therefore, the need for goals was not developed properly or, 2) There are people *that just don't care to better their situations.*

I'll more fully develop choice number one in a moment, but first, I'd like you to think through the full impact of someone being in that choice we just looked at; people that *just don't care* to better their situation. Do you realize what that would mean. It would mean that a person knowingly is *not interested* in bettering themself, is *not interested* in living up to their potential, is *not interested* in helping their children have a better way of life by setting a good example, is *not interested* in making themselves into a fully balanced individual...a *full expression* of all they could become. Presented in that manner, I doubt many people would like the information to be made public about their decision to "**just not care!**" An amazing thing is going to happen to you some day soon. You will finish this book and feel so good, you'll want to share an extra copy with someone that has been leading a life filled with problems. You'll feel so good, you will almost shove the extra book on them...all the while saying good encouraging words about what the book contains. Tell them you want to loan them a copy. Tell them it will help them in every area of their life. Tell them you need to pick it up in about a week because you promised it to someone else (creates a necessity for performance)...and, when you go back to pick up the book, **it will be unread!** You will know where that person wants to be. They do not want answers for their problems; they enjoy their problems and would feel *cheated,* or less than whole, without the weights around their neck.

Now we are down to the group (a very large group) of people that may have had some basic flaws or misunderstandings in the way goals were originally presented (the need for goals was not fully developed). Many people have a half developed idea of proper goal structuring...because, they have never taken "a course" in proper goal structuring. Many people have a half developed idea about proper goal balancing...because, they have never taken "a course" in proper goal balancing. Many people have a half developed idea about how to use the six laws of this universe to progressively attain their goals ...because, they can't remember "any course" that fully taught the laws. And, many people have never written a complete, well defined set of goals...because, no one ever took the time to help them do it.

How wonderful it would have been if the world at large could have included all that training in your formative years ...rather than turning the job over to all those "builders" that wandered through muddling as they went. By age six, you could have been given: 1) Proper goal setting methods. 2) Knowledge and wisdom concerning labels, communications, and life-view philosophies. 3) Some expertise in the development of career planning (blueprints). 4) Instruction in the six laws of the universe; *how* the laws relate to each other, *how* the laws relate to you, *how* the laws relate to the future, *why* the laws relate to each other, and to you, and to the future. With proper instruction in the laws, you would have known (not surface knowing...but, deep down *gut-level* knowing) what a truly wonderful miracle this world is, you would have known how everything works, you would have known why the laws were *made known* to us, and you would have had an insight into what's to come. Are you ready to have another "Ah-hah" experience? The laws have been here for thousands of years...*billions* upon *billions* of people have been given the chance to learn them...you can look them up any time you want to...and most people experience some *uncomfortable* feelings when you tell them of one *well-read* book that contains the six laws...in fact, you may twinge or have an emotional pang as I lead you into the six areas of goal planning, and relate the areas to the six laws. Have you had an "Ah-hah" as to where the laws can be found? I thought you would.

It is a shame that some people feel uncomfortable when the Bible is mentioned...or when this universe is suddenly discussed in the same paragraph with our Lord's Word. It is very sad in the business world to watch people run headlong into *the same brick walls*...time after time after time! The difficult part for me is when I see the laws being violated time after time...offer a solution...and see the look of scorn or shock. I'll haul out my beliefs for you to survey. In that way, you won't be shocked...you'll know where I stand. I believe in the Lord's Word. He has given us certain teachings that when followed, **work.** He gave us the laws so that *we* (his children) would not have to suffer on this earth. You and I are created in God's image, and *for us,* He created an abundant world. He provides us all that we need for our physical well being. He provides us all that we need for our mental well being. He provides us all that we need for our spiritual well being. He provides us with the tools for building a happy family. He provides us the means for finding friends and companions that are pleasant. He provides us *the talents* for creating financial well being. He provides us the *knowledge* and *talents* we need but, **WE MUST DO SOMETHING WITH THE KNOWLEDGE AND THE TALENTS!** A little later on in the book, I'll more fully develop some thoughts regarding "talents"...and a catch phrase that is used often in business **"Use it, or you lose it!"** But for now, back to goals, goal planning and tools.

Here's how important I feel it is to have a well defined set of goals. As a business consultant with a wide variety of clients in the past, I can pick and choose any new client companies that approach me. I won't even consider a client company if they do not have a formalized business plan covering at least *the next five years.* You can't act with wisdom if you don't know where you are going. I don't care how much money the company has, they can't possibly use my skills without formal plans and goals. The company needs a blueprint for development just as a skyscraper needs a blueprint before development...*before* the groundbreaking ceremony.

I have two questions that I usually ask before getting into the goal section of our workshop. I have asked these two questions, in the same way, to approximately 40,000 professional people; sales and marketing professionals, business owners, middle management and key executives from all across our country. Always the same two questions: 1) DO YOU BELIEVE IN SETTING GOALS? LET ME SEE THE HANDS OF EVERYONE THAT BELIEVES IN **SETTING GOALS!** *and* 2) OK...NOW, HOW MANY OF YOU HAVE A COMPLETE SET OF **WRITTEN GOALS FOR ALL AREAS OF YOUR LIFE** TO COVER AT LEAST **THE REMAINDER OF THIS YEAR?** Less than 3% of the people can answer yes to the second question! Many of the professionals shoot their hands up with that first question...but, they look so "sheepish" when I ask the second question, and they have to bring the hand back down. Imagine *less than 3%*...and these are highly educated groups, people that understand the doctrines of PMA, people that have read some or all of the "success" books, and **almost all** have not set formalized goals for the important areas of their own lives. If you've been running your life without a full plan of action, you may have had thousands of days of pleasure *siphoned off* and lost forever, you may have had millions of dollars of *unclaimed money* going down the drain, you may have put your future in "hock" *never to be regained.* Let's take a look at the six areas of a person's life. As you can see in the illustration, if you try to stack them one on top of another, you may start trying to list them in order of priority. Rather than trying to weigh them and decide on an order of importance...let's put them around a hub so they form a wheel. That way there is no number three (which would be better than number four, etc.). There is no top or bottom, nor beginning or end. They fit together in *a balanced relationship.*

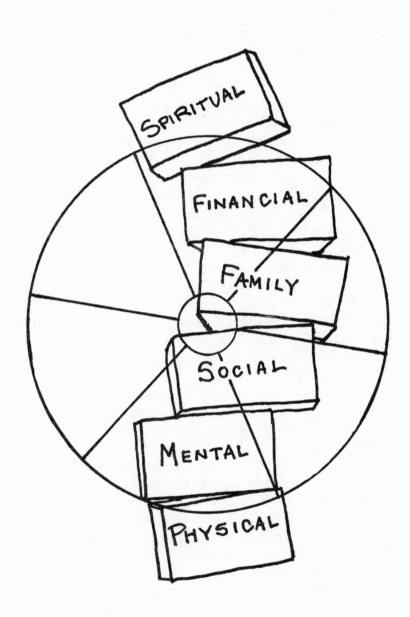

Now that you have the six areas in a circle or wheel, I have a few stories for you to digest. You have a little voice that talks to you all the while you are reading...talk it over with yourself as you slowly read the stories. See if this does make sense! No speed reading, just honest evaluation. Live the stories and see what is going on in each story. There's an *Ah-hah* in several of the stories.

Life works best when it is in balance, just like a tire or wheel runs and wears better if it has been properly balanced.

Remember when you wrote all your labels around an inner core? *You* are the hub, and *around you* are the labels that signify the six areas of your life...and the six areas run and wear better when they are **properly balanced.** People run into problems when things are out of balance. In fact, our country has various institutions for people that get *too far* out of balance. And now, **a story about balance...**

Let's say that you are driving on the freeway, on your way home from work, and you have a flat tire. You put on the spare, but it is a temporary tire (not much mileage in it) so, you limp into the nearest "Big G" tire store. When you get there you ask, "How much for a tire that will match my three good ones?" The attendant there tells you it's going to cost about $49.00. You sigh and tell him to go ahead and put it on. He pulls your flat tire out of the trunk, removes it from the rim, puts the new tire onto the rim, and asks "Would you like the tire *balanced?* We have a special today...only $2.75." And you say, "No, that's OK just the way it is. I don't want it balanced. In fact, you don't *even need to put air* in the tire." The tire man tells you "You can't run it unbalanced. You won't get many miles out of it. This tire is designed to give you 40,000 miles of life, but you'll be lucky to get 5,000 miles if you run it *out-of-balance!*" But you tell him off "Look *buddy,* it's *my* tire, and I'll do what *I* want with it, now put it on *my* car!" By now, the tire man is muttering under his breath "What a nut...I've seen everything now...this is stupid." You insist "Come on, lower it to the ground, I'm running late for dinner. I don't have time to *waste* with your *balancing act.*" So he lowers

the car to the ground and says, "Look at it, **it's flat!**" And you respond, "It's only flat on **ONE SIDE!**' He goes off shaking his head, with your $49 in the cash till, and a story to tell the missus tonight when he gets home. *You*...hop in your car and drive it home. It's a pretty rough ride, but you finally get home, and call your spouse out of the house and say, "Honey, I blew a tire on the freeway, but I stopped and bought a new one on the way home, come on out and see it!" You and your spouse walk around the car to the side with the new tire, and you stare in amazement. **The tire is 100% ruined.** Gashes and rips everywhere. Cords popping out. Whitewalls slashed and chewed, it's just barely hanging on the rim. Your short ride from the tire shop has completely destroyed your $49 tire...and you start boiling inside...really ticked off.

You could immediately make **two wrong assumptions:** 1) You could assume that this world, which has hard concrete freeways, is responsible for ruining your new $49 tire. Or 2) You could assume that the "Big G" company has sold you a real lemon...that they make a lousy tire.

If you make *the first assumption,* you blame it on the world because this hard, rough world destroyed your tire, tell me who decided to run the tire flat? *Ah-hah*...**you decided to run the tire with a flat side.** The world with all its laws of physical reality, gives you results for your actions. You were the one who decided to run the tire flat and unbalanced. You were given an adequate tire that would serve your needs, and **you set it up** so it would be ruined.

If you make *the second assumption,* you decide to call up the "Big G" company that produced such an *inadequate* tire. You're going to call them and tell them what a rotten tire they produce. You ring up their number at their regional office, and get as high a level manager as you can get. And you start in, "Look, I want some action fast. Your company puts out **a lousy tire.** I bought a tire today and it only lasted **15 miles**...you have really given me **a rotten deal!**" The official would probably talk very softly, and in the nicest way possible ask, "Oh, my goodness, what could have possibly gone wrong. We always make sure that every tire that leaves us is in perfect shape. Was there a problem with the way the tire was balanced or perhaps something went wrong elsewhere?" You tell him, the "Maker" of the tire, "I *knew* you'd claim there was nothing wrong with your tire... I *knew* you'd try to defend your work... I *knew* you would probably try to twist it around and make it *my* fault!" The official would very softly ask again, "Was the tire used in an incorrect method? Did you have it properly balanced? Was it placed correctly on the rim?" Along about the time you said, "Of course I didn't balance it! In fact, I ran it without air ... (click)" That click was the "maker" of the tire hanging up on you. Now, who's fault was it that the tire was ruined? Of course, **you!** In this little story, *you decided to run the tire unbalanced...* **flat!** You could not blame the problem of the destroyed tire on the world... nor on the maker. You must accept the blame yourself.

Now apply that example to your life, and this world, and the Maker. If you decide to run your life with a "flat side", that's OK. Everyone makes their own decision as to how they'll run their *own life.* You can run it balanced, out of balance, or with a "flat side"... **it's always your choice.** But, if you decide to run it out of balance or with a "flat side", you could make *two wrong assumptions* when things go wrong.

You might make *assumption number one* and blame the world for the problems, "This world is a crummy place. There's no one you can trust, friends are only out to get what they can from me. My family is made up of self-centered "stupid" idiots... but, they really don't matter to me. Work is a real pain. I can't stand those people, and the pay's lousy. I never get any recognition because they all conspire against me. I don't feel good anymore. My health is failing, and the "creep" I have for a doctor wants to take away my only pleasures... he'd probably like to have the money I spend on a few cigarettes and an occasional drink for himself. What hypocrites people are... always asking me if they can help. My kids really think they're cute... asking me to get myself "right" spiritually! The church has nothing but lying, hypocritical people in it...just trying to get their little bit." **Wrong assumption! The world is.** It just...*is.* It exists. And the "freeway of life" chews up people that run out of balance or with a "flat side"; just like the freeway chews up tires. You probably have heard many people complain and gripe about how the world has treated them *so poorly.* They are making *wrong assumption number one.*

What if a person gets to a point in their life and makes *assumption number two;* that everything in their life doesn't run smoothly because...**the Maker is at fault!** So, the individual looks to the Maker and says, "God, you didn't do "right" by me. Here I am _____ years old (that's a fill-in the blank), and my life is a mess. Every year seems to get worse and worse. It all seems like it's for nothing. I never seem to make any headway in the business world, *You* haven't opened any doors for me. My family is disjointed...spread apart...each in our own little world...no warmth, why haven't *You* filled our hearts with this warmth I've heard about? I have so few years left on this world, and if the *next* years are going to be like the *last,* **YOU DID A LOUSY JOB AS MAKER!"** The complaint to the tire maker if an individual ran a tire flat...when given the information about balancing, and air, and what would happen...would fall on deaf ears. On top of that, the tire is shot in just a few miles...a very brief span of time. *A life,* on the other hand, spans many years...and depending on *how much out of balance* or *how long* it is run with *a flat side,* sometimes there is much to be gained by reversing the problems. You cannot blame the Maker if you knowingly, or unknowingly, run your life with a flat side...that would be wrong assumption number two. You may yell, "Unfair, unfair-...*how can I be held accountable* for something I was not taught? No one taught me about the laws...and goals...and what would happen if I ran with a flat side!" You are accountable...and will receive according to the laws in every case. It sounds harsh, but follow through on this feeble attempt on my part to explain...before we continue with the stories. Do you understand *why* gravity works? Have you studied physics and memorized the formulas that dictate the impact that mass makes at *ever increasing speeds* dictated by the pull of gravity? Probably not. Would the fact that you didn't know *why* it works or *how* it works help you if you decided to step off a ten story rooftop? All the way down to the concrete below you could yell, "It's not fair. I didn't know. No one taught me. I heard something mentioned once about this, but I didn't think it applied in my case." SPLAT!

You, like the billions and billions of people that have gone before...and the billions and billions that will come to be...*each of us* is given a whole complete life. *We are given* the tools (talents) to discover methods that will help us develop into a balanced life. *We* are given choices, and we must live with our choices *until* we decide to make other choices that will give us different rewards. It is my hope that you will reflect on the story of the flat tire. It is a silly little story that demonstrates the responsibility each of us carry in exercising our method for living this life the Lord has given.

Each individual that reads this book is affected by *this story* in a different way. Just as each business person that hears it in one of our business workshops is affected in *a special way... special to them.* Don't be shocked that right in the middle of a business management seminar, we introduce a story that brings the Maker into the picture. Why should He ever be left out? You and I...and everyone else...in the beginning received a *whole, complete start.* Remember? In the beginning...a *whole complete being* without labels. Now that you are old enough to make choices, to live in this world, to decide how you're going to run your life...you have to make a choice regarding running your life with a "flat side". I've had people say, "Oh no I don't *have* to make any choice...not because *you say so!*" Have you ever heard the saying *NOT TO DECIDE IS TO DECIDE!* Think about it...and maybe see the "Ah-hah" experience as it applies to people that experience difficulties *but firmly believe it is not by their choice.*

We bring this story into business discussions of goals because it demonstrates the responsibility that each of us must exercise for our life that has been given to us. When you were given that life as *a complete unit*, you were entrusted with its care and development. You were given a full, *complete* life; a *perfect* life. This doesn't mean that you were given a perfect Adonis or Aphrodite covering, *but*, you were beautiful in the eyes of God. It doesn't mean that you were born with millions in the bank, *but*, you were wealthy in the eyes of God. It doesn't mean that your IQ was going to be 200, *but*, you were a genius in the eyes of God. It doesn't mean that you were meant to be a great church leader with a congregation in the thousands, *but*, you were a perfect vessel in the eyes of God. It doesn't mean that at birth you knew how to raise a family, *but*, you were the perfect family enhancer at birth. In the eyes of God, you were *exactly perfect* for the task of being His.

Just a reminder for the rare person that is a little shocked by this subject matter, I am not talking *religious doctrine* or *churchianity*. I am talking about your *personal relationship* with the Maker and what He has given you. Don't skip over the material because *you think* you know where the message is going. Unless you've read this book before, you would be *incorrect* in assuming you knew *exactly* what the point (to be made) was in the stories I just unfolded.

The point to be made in the story of the flat tire: You and *you alone* have the choice as to how your life will run. You will always be responsible for running your life *"in balance", "out of balance",* or with a *"flat side."* I am putting out a message that a mature individual can accept; You are responsible for yourself, your attainments and achievements in life, and ultimately your successes and failures in life.

All of the laws of the universe contain the essence of "balance", and therefore, the laws work for individuals that contain the essence of "balance". How can a life be run "in balance"? If you have six areas for living, what can be done to put these areas into "balance"? Well, one of the ways that will probably not work for you is to come up with some mathematical formula or equation that divides up the hours into a form of mathematical balance. All the areas should interact so the result will be a smooth, comfortable ride. Think of a child's toy...a child's musical top, as in the illustration that you see. Remember back when you were young, those musical tops that you pumped? The faster you pumped the more smoothly the top would run...with pretty music...it went so fast, that all the colors ran together into one smooth connected rainbow of colors. It hummed along, *in perfect balance*. A little attention every now and then, a little extra activity (an occasional pump on the handle), and the musical top provided you hours of entertainment. Your life deserves to run that smoothly. With a little attention, all six areas mesh together...around you as the hub...smooth, balanced, and full of rewards. **THE ATTENTION NEEDED...IS...SUCCESS PLANNING.**

Occasionally someone will say to me, "I think it's just great the way you talk about the six areas...but, the only area I am interested in is...(you guessed it) **THE FINANCIAL AREA OF LIFE.**" The person usually tells me that once they have made a lot of money, *then* they'll pay attention to the other five areas. What that person is failing to see (which could be a great "Ah-hah" for them...if they see it) is, their reluctance to exercise wisdom and understanding in terms of balance will always create a money problem for them. They will either have *too little money* or *a lot of money*...but, either way, they will have a money problem. "Wait a minute!", you say..."How can someone have a money problem if they have *a lot of money?*" You only need to look around in our society to answer your own question. Once you understand why people have problems, you will see many, many people that have *a lot of money,* live a life *out of balance,* and experience great frustrations and many problems. **NOT BECAUSE THEY HAVE A LOT OF MONEY...BUT BECAUSE THEY HAVE NOT BALANCED OFF THE OTHER AREAS OF LIFE!** Many religious leaders do a *great disservice* to their congregations by using harsh, insolent, and abrasive language when they speak of money, wealth, or financial matters. The Lord commanded us to "propser"...He also warned us to put everything in its *proper* place and priority, "Seek ye *first* His

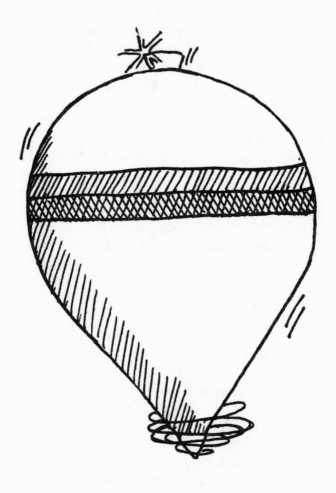

kingdom and His righteousness; and all things shall be added unto you." My assumptions are: 1) Understanding labels, I can see many people living in unhappy conditions needlessly, and 2) Many leaders have not discovered the laws contained within their own reference material; the Bible.

Let's talk some more about that person that wanted information on the financial area of life, but was not interested in the other five areas. They have a money problem...and want to concentrate only on the financial area. Remember the musical top? What happened when the musical top got *out of balance?* It wobbled and spun erratically...and finally crashed in the wall and stopped spinning. A little attention to the top and it would have continued spinning in perfect balance, but out of balance, it fell on its side. Something else you could have done with that top if...you had known the law of balance...you could have added weights around the outside rim. You could have counter-balanced small weights or large weights, and the top would still have spun in balance. A gigantic flywheel (weighing many tons) is nothing more than a perfectly balanced top...running smoothly around its hub or center. And so it is with the financial area of life, attention to the other five areas will allow you to reap rewards in *all six areas.* **BALANCE** is the key word. Planning for success in all six areas maintains the balance in life.

Have you noticed how the subject of *"balance"* keeps weaving its way into the discussions of life, and living, and goals, and success? Balance is a "key" word...I repeat "key" words often in public speeches and in these writings. I don't do it to bore the listener or the reader...but rather, to cause many impressions. With the person that we're talking about that wants to improve upon their financial area, I would take each area and demonstrate how planning goals in each area would affect the other five areas. If an individual is experiencing difficulty in one area, it is usually another area of life that needs the attention...and because there is a lack of attention, there is an *imbalance*...and subsequently, the difficulty. If the six areas are *out of balance,* planning goals in an area that gets *little*

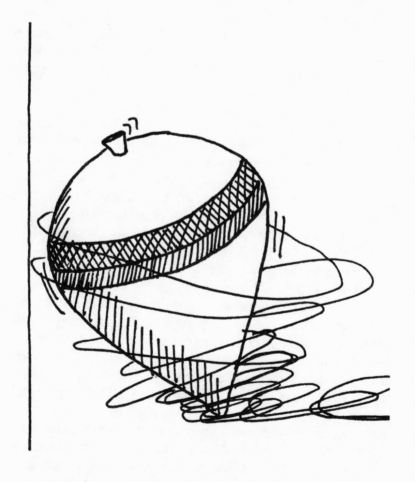

attention has the tendency to bring the entire wheel into better balance. Trying to plan goals in an area that already receives *too much attention* has the tendency to throw the wheel off even more.

Upon investigation it turns out that the individual is really well trained at their profession. In fact, the individual makes a very good living and enjoys the work they perform. They have money and are in word labels *"making it"* in the world. But, they want and need more financial success to fulfill whatever their thoughts are regarding that nebulous term; **"success"**. It also is discovered that the individual has *no* written goals in the six areas of life. However, they do have a semi-informal set of goals sprinkled throughout the six areas. "Semi-informal goals?" you might ask. Yes...semi-informal goals. You see, without some semblance of goals, they would not be experiencing the prosperity they now enjoy. The informal set of goals in the financial area turn out to be items such as: 1) Bills that must be paid on *a type of schedule* 2) work hours that must be met with *some regularity* 3) *well defined labels* that command prosperity and recognition in the market place. **What is success?** The progressive attainment of desired goals. They have *measurements*...and they are *progressively attaining;* therefore, they have a degree of success in the financial area. Now let's take a look at the informal goals in the other areas of life. The goals in the other areas of life are not so neatly arranged; they are less clearly defined...in fact some areas are almost totally neglected. AND NOW, comes the admission; that point at which the individual expresses what disturbs them. It goes something like this, "I know I could do much better in the business world. In fact, I could probably make twice what I'm making now, but...I seem to be torn in *a dozen directions* at once. Sure I make a good living right now, but my family *deserves* more attention. We never seem to have the time to spend with the kids...and they've grown up so fast. It seems like we're on a treadmill that never stops. We don't even have time for fun things with friends anymore. My Mom and Dad are getting on in years...and we really ought to at least keep in touch, but there just is not enough time in the week. Just last year, we talked about how we wished we could get a little more involved with our church. The fellowship we used to have was always uplifting, and I'm sure we would benefit...along with the fact that we have the means now to help others that haven't been as fortunate as we have. This constant racing has got me a little worried about my health. I used to keep in pretty good shape, but lately I never have time for any type of physical activity. **WOW!** Time sure slips by...it's been almost two years since I last played tennis. I sure used to enjoy the weekly matches. **ONE OF THESE DAYS I'M GOING TO SLOW DOWN AND START ENJOYING LIFE AGAIN!" Sound familiar?** What does this individual need to do to solve the situation? What is the situation? Or, shall we call it the problem? Or, shall it be called catastrophe? Or, shall we call it a shame? Whatever we call it...it is sad that life gets so far out of balance. In trying to remedy the situation, we must first understand what the individual wants and needs to accomplish...what outcome they desire *after the change.* I would state the situation in this manner; "To maintain or increase happiness in life, while increasing the financial rewards from the business world." This would be the start for **a statement of success.** As the goals are more thoroughly defined, they can be added to this statement of purpose, but for now, we have stated the "raw, bare bones" purpose to be accomplished. "Wait a minute!" you might remark, "Why did you add something to the goal of making money?" I'll explain more fully in later chapters...but for now, consider this: Would you want the situation stated thusly...*to decrease* happiness in life while *increasing* the financial rewards from the business world. **"OF COURSE NOT",** you would say. Well then, I have correctly stated the purpose or objective. Let's follow through on this example. If the individual tries to increase the financial rewards by intensifying their work goals ...and excludes the thoughts and goals related to the other five areas, he or she would throw their life more **OUT OF BALANCE.** If they do that, they just might make life miserable...and suffer great loss in five areas...and ultimately they might end up with less money. What the individual needs is "success" in the five neglected areas to bring their life into better balance. How can they bring success into the five areas? By **setting desired goals** that can be **systematically, progressively attained.** If this individual put some time into thoughts of what to accomplish in any of the five neglected areas, and progressively *did something* (action is necessary), the individual's wheel would be better balanced...and therefore, life would run more smoothly. Attention to a neglected area has a tendency to bring about better balance.

During this next year, you will hear many examples that demonstrate exactly what I have outlined on these few pages. You will hear of individuals that are told "slow down, take care of yourself, stop driving yourself so hard at work, you've had a heart attack, take it as a warning, remember to smell the roses!" Some people that you will hear about will restructure their lives, they will develop an interest in areas outside their work area, they will put their life in balance. They'll pay attention to the physical body, and to their family life, and to enjoying the time they have with friends. Mentally they'll clean up their thought processes while appreciating the positive aspects of being alive. Their attention to the spiritual area will be increased, and they will pace themselves better at work. Other people will experience the same *medical shock* (by the way I just used heart attack because it is such a prevalent problem...we could substitute any one of a hundred other serious problems and watch similar reactions) and react the opposite. They *refuse* to restructure their patterns, they *refuse* to think positively, they *purposely* avoid family and friends, they *refuse* to follow medical instruction, they seem to mentally decide that...Life is not worth living so I might as well just work until I drop...**AND THEY DO.** In the final days, weeks, months, or years, they seem *to intensify* the imbalance in their lives.

Enough talk about people that won't restructure and obtain balance when they have something as attention-getting as a heart attack. Why wait until that point in time...or that set of circumstances...to start getting into action concerning the restructuring? Why wait until you've about ruined the time on this earth? Why wait until "the top" is crashing into the wall and about to fall over? Read through the next chapter with one eye on the book and one eye *on your life.* It is worth it to ferret out potential problem areas. It will become important as you make changes...that you make compensating changes in all areas. In the next chapter, I will bring into view the different ways a person can run through life with a "flat tire" or "out of balance".

8
There are a lot of Ways to be Broke

See that little guy with the empty bag! You probably think that his look is because he has *an empty money bag*. What is amazing is that a person can end up "broke" in more ways than just financially in this world.

An individual could end up "broke" in the **family area of life.** Being "broke" in the family area doesn't necessarily mean coming from a broken home or being divorced. Many homes are places where strangers come together after a long hard day to share a TV and sleep for eight hours, so they can get up the next day and do it all over again. If the family core group lacks **warmth, understanding, caring, sharing,** plus fun and **living** and **loving, happy times**...then you are "broke" in the family area of life.

The **social area** provides an unusual area for self development. Your own personal workshop or laboratory. A laboratory where all types of experiments can be carried out...and the results investigated. A Reader's Digest article established that during your lifetime you would associate with approximately 400 friends and family members; people close to you. Of the friends, associates, or whatever you want to call them, how many of them can you truly call **FRIENDS** (with all the implications we apply to really close, good friends)? Another

area to look at in the social area of life is *the quality* of people you attract to you. "What do you mean by that remark?", you might say. I mean take a look at what you surround yourself with. Are there a lot of "label rippers?" Are there a lot of *backstabbers?* Are there a lot of unhappy people that always have something negative to say? Are there some very *unkind people* in the group that openly put down everyone and everything? It is possible, to be surrounded by people, and still be "broke" in the social area of life.

The **physical area** of life. The physical body is a once-in-a-lifetime opportunity to take care of a precious "irreplaceable" commodity. If you'll remember our original philosophy, you'll recall the mortality rate; **one per person!** Many people are "broke" in the physical area of life by the time they are 20, or 30, or 40, or even *the very young age* of 60. While other people that have respected this once-in-a-lifetime gift, are just hitting the prime of life at the exact same age. Your chronological age *has nothing* to do with your being "broke" in the physical area of life! Your life-view philosophy, your goals and your caring for and your respect for your physical being are the determining factors in your "wealth" in this area.

In the **mental area** of life, there are a variety of ways to be "broke", but each way, ultimately revolves around where your thoughts dwell "most" of the time. Do you have a positive or negative philosophy about life in general? In the law of cause and effect, where all cause is "thought", are your causes (thoughts) primarily destructive and self-defeating...or are they uplifting and self-enhancing? Are you "broke" in your thoughts or "wealthy" beyond all measure of money? In everyone's world, there are thousands of small insignificant situations that could be viewed negatively if an individual wanted to waste the time to focus on each situation or incident. When those small insignificant situations occur in your world, do you automatically react in a negative manner; allowing the incident to overwhelm you...and through your sour reaction to poison the air around you? Or, are you an easy person to be around? Have you developed a "That's no problem" attitude that goes along with your success philosophy? Do you look for "the positive" within each life adventure? Do you keep your mind open and consider other people non-judgmentally? Or do you keep yourself "broke" by running everyone into the ground, by attaching to the negatives and griping and complaining for weeks about situations that no longer even exist? Mentally, do you keep yourself open for constructive, uplifting new ideas? Or, do you keep yourself "broke" by knowing it all and never listening? Some people never do listen...but, of course, you already realize that!

Spiritually...what an area to explore! How do you feel deep inside spiritually? Have you set goals in the **spiritual area** of life? Have you come to grips with your worth here...and your eventual purpose for existing? When I speak of "broke" in the spiritual area of life, many people want to jump right out of their chairs and punch me for having the nerve to insinuate...that they might be "broke" in the spiritual side of their lives. Now you might think that I'm only talking about people that never give a thought to salvation ...but **I am not**...there are millions of Christians that have no plans for their next 10, 20 or 30 years on this earth. *By definition,* when they failed to formulate goals for living their spiritual life on a daily basis, they gave up the successes they could have had in that area of life. When *they failed to set goals* that *they could progressively attain, they* relegated their lives to a "no-growth" policy...and subsequently, threw the six areas of life out of balance. It is Scripture; You are to *abide* in the Word (which means to live continuously) and to grow in the Word. The individual that does not set goals for *living* and *growing* is running the spiritual area of their life in such a manner as to throw the wheel out of balance. Consider this: Think ahead for as many years as you plan to live, maybe 20 or 30 or 40 years. Think ahead to the end of your days on this earth. On that day in the future, perhaps many years from now, looking forward to physical death, and looking backwards over your entire life...what will you *have to see* in your past...what will you *have had to accomplish*...for you to feel that your life was a success? Do you have the confidence now...that on that day...you will be looking back at a successful life? If today was your last day, when you looked back over your life as you've lived it so far...are there areas that you have neglected? If you and I sat down over a cup of coffee tomorrow morning, could you describe the areas you neglected? Would there be any changes in the way you ran your life that *you wish* you could just reach back into the past and change? You might say, "Well sure...if we sat down tomorrow, I know of a couple of areas that I would like to change." **Good!** Then you have a chance right now...and in the years to come...to make the changes that you want! As we spend time in the six areas, you will be formulating the plans that will assure you success. And on that day 20, 30 or 40 years in the future, when you look back over your life, you will have done the best that you could to live "a balanced life". **A balanced life...a life of fulfillment-...filled full to the brim with happiness, joy, prosperity, and service.** A life that provides a *quality example* for your being on this earth.

What about the **financial area** of life? Are you "broke" in the **financial area** of life? Are you in control of your money and your possessions or are they in control of you? Do you have a definite plan of action for the handling of your finances? If you divide the number of years you have been working into your net worth, has it been worthwhile? Do you have financial freedom...or are you a slave to the system that now owns you? Is there too much month at the end of the money? Are you able to comfortably acquire material possessions...or do you apologize every time you spend a few dollars to buy something new? Some people have to apologize and explain to their family and friends why they change cars, redecorate the house, buy a new outfit, send the kids to camp, get their hair done, or spend a dollar on something frivolous. Have you and your family a **WELL DEFINED SET** of financial plans that will guide you this year...and the next...and on and on? Do you have the confidence that you will be able to take care of yourself financially...even beyond retirement? 54 of every

100 Americans that reach the age of 65 cannot write a check for $200. Why? Because they ran their lives with "flat sides"; they had no plans.

Once we look at the six areas of life, and individuals begin to see that goal planning is more than just picking a figure of "X" dollars per year... at that time, we can fully realize why so many people in the world experience so much frustration and lack of abundance. Here we are in a nation of abundance... and all around us are people experiencing extreme difficulties in meeting their needs. Here we are in a nation that allows you ownership of material possessions... and all around us are people that are not owners, but slaves to the things which they should own. Here we are in a nation that allows freedom of speech... but, around us we find millions that cannot express love and happiness to their family and friends. Here we are in a nation that spends hundreds of billions of dollars on health care... and our people are among *the least healthy of all nations in the world.* The list goes on, and on, and on.

The key to a smooth ride through life is "balance". Now you may know of people that don't fit your measure of "success" in any way; very little money or material possessions, not in really good physical shape, not particularily at the top of the class in brainpower, not interested in friends or family, spiritually drifting... and yet, they seem to just float through life without too many hassles (a fairly smooth ride). The point to remember is that they are *in balance at a very low level of attainment.* Though they have very few attainments, there is "balance" at that level... hence, life seems to run smoothly. If life runs smoothly, it is easy to be somewhat contented. If you are obtaining all that you want... without hassles... *in relative balance,* it's easy to be complacent.

The unhappy person is often one who should know better, but still insists on running their life with one or more "flat sides". Very high goals, desires and objectives in one or two areas... and neglect or flat sides in the remaining areas.

The law of **Cause and Effect** (one of those six laws that keeps popping up throughout the chapters) works equally for every person. It always works. The law exists independent of mankind; *equally, fairly without change.* When we discuss running life with a "flat side", we are discussing the Effect portion of the law. You may very well have had some instructions in the law of Cause and Effect...perhaps in a class somewhere in your school years. The problem is...the way the law is taught in the classroom; it is related to **an action-reaction principle**...rather than the application of the law in its true essence **energy-manifestation...or thought-physical.** Remember earlier in the book when we covered Cause (thought) eventually creates Effect (the physical situations)? The important point to realize right now is that everything in your life today is an Effect of thought; yours or someone elses. Are you comfortably sitting in a chair reading your book? Think about this, the chair is the effect of an effect of an effect, etc., etc. going back to the *thought* of the chair (which is the *cause* of that chair existing). The fact that the chair is in your possession is the effect of an effect of an effect, etc., etc. going back to your *thought* of needing or wanting a chair to sit in. The book you are holding is the effect (pages and print bound together) of an effect (printing proofs in a book publishing plant) of an effect (typed manuscripts, edited, and placed in sequence) of an effect (notes and messages that were collected over a 10 year period) of an effect (classes and many workshops) of an effect (physical experiences in business) etc., etc. going back to a *cause; thoughts that existed in my mind as observations. Thoughts* that when manifested (brought into physical view) worked. The clothes on your body, your dwelling, your vehicle for transportation, your job, the company in which you work, the food you eat, your spouse if you have one, your children if you have them...everything you acknowledge in your physical world is *an effect.* There are no physical causes, *only physical effects.* There is only one cause; thought-...and cause eventually ends up manifesting (bringing into view) the physical.

Now there will be some readers who will read this message and turn off (I sincerely hope that you are not one of those few) for a couple of reasons. **First,** if a person turned-off because they could not stand reading about a law that has given them every good thing they have ever had in their life...that would be a shame (if their thoughts turned negative and critical, you *now know* what they will manifest).

Second, what a shame it would be to come this far into this book, and then to fall back into the old label patterns of rejecting and criticizing without full examination. If you were one of those readers that immediately starts making negative remarks to yourself, please stop and reconsider! What kind of negative remarks am I talking about? Remarks that criticize, remarks that prejudge, remarks that are based on insufficient information. Remarks like, "Up to this point I was going along with most of the information in this book, but I don't like all this spiritual mumbo jumbo." Do you realize what I said concerning your ability to bring your thoughts into the physical realm of being? For instance, when you thought about breakfast this morning...you activated physical effects in your stomach. As you thought about what you wanted to eat, various types of food floated through your mind and you selected what it was you knew you could manifest (bring into being). Soon you were sitting down in your kitchen or out at a restaurant of your choice, and you were eating what you wanted for breakfast; you were eating the effects of your thoughts (causes) for breakfast. I am going to take you through a rather extreme example of ordering breakfast ...just to show you how thought (cause) can be turned into effect (physical)...if you are willing to commit the necessary resources for fulfillment. What if your thought for breakfast included the buffet selection in the Hanohano room that sits 30 stories above Waikiki Beach in Hawaii (Sheraton Waikiki hotel). Couldn't you bring that into the physical? Just by *realigning your resources*...using your thoughts to decide where the money would come from to pay for the airline ticket...you could hop on a plane anywhere in the United States before 8 am and touch down in Hawaii before noon (remember the time changes). You see...*thought* preceeds *effect.* Everything you would like to have come true in your life is "out there", somewhere, waiting for your thoughts to bring it into physical effect.

WHAT DO YOU THINK HAPPENS WHEN A PERSON VIOLATES ALL THE LAWS? Of course, they reap all the wrong effects. WHAT DO YOU THINK HAPPENS WHEN A PERSON THINKS *VILE, UGLY, NEGATIVE* THOUGHTS ABOUT THEIR WORLD? Of course, they reap (manifest in the physical) *vile, ugly, negative* effects. WHAT DO YOU THINK HAPPENS WHEN A PERSON HAS NEGLECTED TO SET ANY GOALS IN AN AREA OF LIFE? Of course, they have nothing to reap because they have not sown. WHAT DO YOU THINK HAPPENS WHEN A PERSON WORRIES ABOUT AN AREA OF LIFE BECAUSE NOTHING IS HAPPENING THERE? Of course, they reap the negative effects of their worries. WHAT DO YOU THINK HAPPENS WHEN A PERSON: 1) Violates laws that always reward justly 2) Fails to sow balancing goals in all areas of life 3) Worries and fumes and rants and raves about their lack in particular areas, and 4) Puts out negative, ugly, vile thoughts about how unjust the world is? **"Ah-hah!"** Can you see how most people have been running the six different areas of their lives? It is my contention that most people in our society do the following:

1. They violate the laws...because they never learned the laws in the beginning.
2. They fail to set balancing goals...because they never received the full story concerning goals.
3. They accentuate their lack...because our society does not understand the impact of the ten labels we studied.
4. They make one of the two wrong assumptions...because they inwardly know *someone or something* must be at fault.

You are obviously a fairly rational thinking human being (if you were not, you would have torn this book to shreds...or burned it...or thrown it away in anger by now), would you agree with the four statements I have just made? Is your agreement based on just a feeling...or would you say your agreement is based on your actual observation of the hundreds of people you have seen in the years of living you've had? Have you looked at some of the lives that have been literally thrown away, and wondered, "What a waste...Why did they end up the way they did? *One flat side usually wrecks everything.* The fewer goals an individual has in a particular area, the greater the chances that they will eventually run their life with a "flat side" in that area. It does not matter which area you choose to pick. If you pick any one of the six areas and designate it "the flat side", it can be shown how that flat side will eventually destroy the wheel. As the "flat side" throws the wheel more and more out of balance, the individual will career closer and closer to destruction...eventually destroying the other five areas in total.

In the same manner that planning a goal in a neglected area has a tendency to balance the wheel...creating a flat side by totally ignoring an area sends "the top" into a death spin. I could go on and on with hundreds of examples out of my recollections. I have seen some startling examples of people with flat sides; people that are, or have, followed the four steps I just listed above. One example sticks out in my mind as a classic of *personal destruction*...a man I met in the early 70's. He was not quite 40 years old at the time of our first meeting. His *flat side* was the mental area of life, and here's why. He was absolutely destroyed in a mental sense, at having filed a personal bankruptcy over problems in his construction firm. I will admit, filing a $14,000,000 bankruptcy would unnerve most people...but his reaction seemed excessive. He was trying to destroy himself physically with alcohol...and was succeeding. He had already abused and misused most of his friends and social contacts. But, rather than telling you what he was doing to destroy his world...why don't I tell you what he was left with after the bankruptcy. He still had a beautiful home overlooking the Pacific Ocean valued at approximately $200,000 (1980 value in excess of half a million). He had three brand new cars at the time (Pantera,

Jaguar, and Corvette). The only job he could find at the moment was a $75,000 a year temporary position with an unlimited expense account. And **he was miserable.** How's that for a poor position to be in? Given time to work out his life, I'm sure he could have risen to his former position of prominence in the construction industry. But in his state of mind, I doubt that he lasted very long. I met him twice, and each time he (and the group that had attached themselves to his expense account) *poisoned the environment.* Such is the story of someone in the last erratic spins of the top...totally consumed by the idea of failure, and his whole life was going down the drain as a result. I'm certain that people that charted the history of Howard Hughes saw what was ahead as he slowly threw his life out of balance. There was a time (early in his career) when he represented a fairly balanced life. How evenly balanced, I do not know; A man of the world, with extensive social contacts, physically vibrant, financially successful, mentally active...with drive and ambition and purpose behind the scenes propelling him into prominence. What went wrong? We may never know because of the cloak of secrecy surrounding his last decades. Was he *"happy"* secluded away from all personal contacts? Did he enjoy a *"balanced", fulfilling* life? What would he have wanted in the way of warmth and love in his final years? What did he have to look forward to...as he laid aside the five areas of life that could not bridge the gap of death? Who knows? The test for you is this; *what was the cause* of his life being so out of balance? If you said, "His thoughts", you're right.

Would you like to know what I feel to be terrible wastes? The terrible wastes I see are people, young and old, who live their lives in near despair; NO GOALS...NO DIRECTION ...WITHOUT PURPOSE...WITHOUT HOPE. I see thousands upon thousands of people drifting, sinking helplessly deeper and deeper into everyday problems that sap their energies. I see a nation full of people that have given up their enthusiasm for living. They live an existence where day follows day...and each day lacks the excitement of being alive.

An existence where everything blends together into a drab nothingness...and nothing seems to provide the happiness promised by all the TV commercials. I see people living their lives with two, three, four and five "flat sides"...and when they reach out to try and tell someone, that someone doesn't care (because they too are experiencing the same kind of life). I see tremendous "surface activity", but little "in-depth" happiness.

I am not retreating into negativity...just reporting problems as I see them. I am concerned...very concerned, and I want very much to be able to help in some way.

So I say, week after week...month after month...year after year:

"YES, LIFE IS WORTH LIVING."

Start with a simple life-view philosophy that offers hope, and let's take a look at some of the areas in which you might like to experience changes. BECOME LIKE SOLOMON AND SEEK WISDOM. With wisdom will come understanding which is more precious than gold or silver and *will bring you such* if you desire it. TAKE CONTROL OVER THE SITUATIONS rather than allow the situations of life to control you. **BALANCE, BALANCE, BALANCE** the key word in a life that runs smoothly.

It has taken one half of this book to complete a most difficult task; the task of properly identifying the problems. I learned a long time ago that properly identifying the problem almost guarantees your discovery of a workable solution. A problem properly identified is half solved. I think you will find the rest of this book easier reading because we have covered the groundwork thoroughly. The chapters are shorter...the subject matter more tightly defined...the pace quicker. Your task in the chapters that follow: To see yourself...your repeated patterns...your success and failure cycles...your areas of strength...and your neglected areas. Are you willing to follow the voice inside you that says, "Might as well follow through and give it a chance...I've got nothing to lose and everything to gain."

The next chapter contains the six laws of the universe and how the laws work for you or against you. Incidently, the laws are working *for or against everyone* ... depending on the individual's "proper" or "improper" application of the laws.

Let's make some decisions regarding what you would like to have in the six areas of your life. I'm not asking you to make all your major life decisions ... right now. What I'm asking is that you briefly state (in one or two short sentences) the result you would like to see in each area. Concentrate on sentences that describe positive results. Make each sentence a positive expression of the result you desire. Make each sentence a positive expression of the happiness the results would create within you. Remember ... you are expressing happiness! This is not a lesson in advanced composition ... your feelings concerning the results and accomplishments are more important than proper grammar.

It is important that you write ... that you express yourself in each area. We want to immediately start with the wheel "seeking balance". Go ahead and start the process. Use the charts on the following three pages.

PRIMARY RESULTS I DESIRE IN THE:

MENTAL AREA
MY GOAL IS

SPIRITUAL AREA
MY GOAL IS

CHART C

PRIMARY RESULTS I DESIRE IN THE:

SOCIAL AREA
MY GOAL IS

PHYSICAL AREA
MY GOAL IS

CHART C

PRIMARY RESULTS I DESIRE IN THE:

FINANCIAL AREA
MY GOAL IS

FAMILY AREA
MY GOAL IS

CHART C

9
Understanding the Six Laws

A quick recap of the ground we've covered is appropriate at this time. Many people will have reached this point and be ready for the adventure ahead. And, some will have reached this point only to find out they missed all the "Ah-hah's" along the way. One thing I have learned about lessons in this life; if you miss the lesson, it will be presented again and again and again.

We have been working backwards throughout this book; backing into lessons. Our ultimate lessons will be when we work on "success cycles" and "failure cycles" and the establishment of "ultimate purpose" in relationship to your major goals. Rather than approach subjects that are overwhelming when approached head-on...we have begun the approach in a zig-zag fashion. I mentioned in the last chapter that, we are approaching by first understanding the problems. The answers (solutions) are the ultimate lessons that we will take a look at in the second half of this book.

We have moved rather quickly through the material that, if written for technical journals, might have encompassed fourteen or more books. Some of my friends and business associates claim I sometimes make "light" conversation of the most difficult of subjects. It is my belief that we (as adults) do not need to be talked "down to" like 8th grade school children when it comes to the important matters of life, but I see nothing wrong with simplifying and understanding analogies and stories that represent *the essence*. Here's what we have covered thus far:

LIFE-VIEW PHILOSOPHIES

NEGATIVE INFLUENCES OF THOUGHT

BASIC ASSUMPTIONS REGARDING CHANGE

ACQUIRED LABEL STRUCTURING

LOSS OF IDENTITY & VALUES AS A
    SOCIAL NORM

NEGATIVE BEHAVIOR MODIFICATION:
    SEMANTIC REACTIONS

BREAKDOWNS IN POSITIVE GOAL ORIENTATION

BALANCE: A "KEY" FACTOR IN
    SOCIAL DEVELOPMENT

APPROPRIATE & INAPPROPRIATE BEHAVIOR RE:
    LIFE PLANNING

THE SPIRITUAL ASPECT OF WHOLENESS
    BEING INHERENT

We've covered some "heavy" subjects concerning life and death. Some of the material, the concepts, and the techniques may have duplicated prior life experiences or lessons. I would certainly hope that some of the concepts *parallel* your thinking; one of the processes that helps greatly in the learning of "something new" is the partial identification with what is already known. It is always good when you see in print the written expression of a deep "gut-level" feeling you've carried around without being able to fully understand. I do hope that some of the concepts in the first half of this book have triggered off some of those feelings down deep inside you. I also hope that you have experienced some "Ah-hah's" along the way; I like to feel that "I have been an instrument" in some manner. It satisfies some of my goals...and helps me set the foundation for more important concepts to come.

Now let's take a look at the six laws that always work in this universe. You may be surprised by some of them...they seem so simple; deceptively simple. However, only one person in a thousand (or ten thousand) can rattle off the six laws from memory. And I have only met three people in the instructional field that had a firm grasp of the laws; that includes my experience in teaching, training, success rallies, public speaking, and consulting…with hundreds of teachers, instructors, consultants, motivational trainers, ministers and counselors. I really have no definite percentage figure regarding how few people understand and use the six laws. You may need to read through the laws more than two or three times. Once you accept the fact that they always work, you will find the rereading of the first half of this book even more exciting. A quick run through of the six laws, and then a more in depth discussion.

The first law is the **LAW OF ORDER**. There is order to everything; you may not fully understand the order, but it always exists.

The second law is the **LAW OF VIBRATION**. Everything has a rate of vibration; no thing (nothing) of this universe is at rest. At the point of seeming rest, a new vibration rate is always set in motion.

The third law is the **LAW OF OPPOSITES**. Everything has its opposite; as far as you can go in one direction, on the other end of the scale you will find a balancing opposite as an "equal."

The fourth law is the **LAW OF CAUSE AND EFFECT**. Every physical (effect) has as its origin a thought form (cause). Energy manifests matter in perfect balance.

The fifth law is the **LAW OF ATTRACTION**. Like always attracts like; opposites complement, while likes attract.

The sixth law is the **LAW OF DUALITY**. Through the understanding of occurrences on a limited scale, we can understand occurrences of greater magnitude; similarly the reverse applies. As above, so below.

We'll go through the laws in greater depth soon. First, I wonder if you are having any difficulty grasping the importance of the laws? Does it create a problem for you to see the full explanation of everything in this universe reduced *to six short paragraphs?* Or are you sitting a little bit stunned by the simplicity of it all? What I just listed for you are the laws that govern everything! Does that make you happy...that the laws are so simple? Or does it frustrate you? I can't know what you're thinking right now; do you think it..."totally brilliant?"...or a "not-so-funny joke?"...or "to simple to be true?"

LET ME TELL YOU THE IMPORTANCE TO BE ASSOCIATED WITH YOUR FULLY UNDERSTANDING AND USING THE SIX LAWS CORRECTLY...If **you really understand and use the laws, you will:**
...never make a bad business decision.
...always have harmony in your family life.
...surround yourself with prosperity and success.
...have hundreds of like-minded friends surrounding you.
...live your life with a healthy body and a healthy mind.
...be a wonderful example for all people to emulate.
...glorify God in your every action.

This is not a scoffing point in this book...this is a point of serious consideration in the treatment of your life to come; day after day after day after day...**from this time forward.** This is the time of introspection I discussed back in the opening passages. This is the point where you might be tempted to say, "Yeah, yeah...I know. Can we get on to something else. Let's talk about the financial area again!" At this moment, you are looking at the six laws that govern the "why" behind everything that goes on in this universe. Scientists are trying so hard to understand...but, they are forever studying *effect.* Studying effects *is a never-ending process;* there are billions upon billions of effects interacting and becoming an effect of an effect of an effect, ad infinitum (forever and forever). Think back over the six laws and understand "why" things work. Every invention has to adapt to the positive application of the laws...or it is destined for failure. Every business application will work for you or against you; fail or succeed based on its relationship to the six laws.

The life within your body will change its vibration rate and move into a new cycle instantly if you violate the laws in certain ways...and you will instantly die. If you understand the laws, you can attract to you that which is pleasant, appealing, prosperous, healthy and positive. Our entire world civilization sits on the edge of destruction because mankind has learned to manipulate effects...but fails to understand the six laws. I HOPE THAT AT THIS POINT YOU WILL NOT FOLLOW THE REST OF MANKIND BY IGNORING THE LAWS...TOO MANY PEOPLE HAVE ALREADY MISSED THE POINT. Use the laws for yourself...and your family. Put them to work in your life and in the lives of those most important to you.

I must admit to you the reader that I have not always known, nor used, the laws. I ignored the laws for most of the years of my life; and paid the price for every transgression. In the start of the book, I mentioned the excellent philosophy that was presented to me as a young boy. The early training *was not* training in the six laws. It was training in a philosophy that pulled me through the repeated "bloody noses" I received as a young man...fighting against the six laws. Some lessons of life took quite a while to sink in; I had a habit of making the same mistake time after time after time...until I finally learned. Perhaps, you too have had similar experiences ...whole segments of your life devoted to learning one "Ah-hah". What a thrill it was a few years back when I finally learned "why"...and stopped madly dashing into "brick walls' making the same mistakes. Let me share with you the reason I started this book with the philosophy **CONGRATULA-TIONS...YOU MADE IT AGAIN!"**

I've made mistakes...you've made mistakes...we've all made mistakes. I wanted to share the philosophy because I knew there would be a lot of people reading this book that had experienced frustrations, failures, down times, and temporary setbacks in their lives. I knew that regardless of your success level now...there are times when you feel those "old feelings" crowding in on the beginning of your day. It takes so little to kick off a "failure cycle"...and I wanted to give you something that would lift your days...and give every day a fresh new start. I would like to share with you how I learned this life-view philosophy as a child of four. I think it is interesting and gratifying to know what a parent can mean in the life of a child. You might want to consider the philosophies you give to your children and grandchildren as you progress *through their lives*. Don't forget, you are one of those "construction workers" that wields a hand in the development we talked about earlier.

My lessons started earlier than four...but that's when I first remember the philosophy. A philosophy that I enjoy sharing with you. Let me tell you how I learned the philosophy as a child of four. A lesson that you can pass on to your children. A lesson that turned into a public speech 25 years after my learning it. A lesson that 300,000 people have heard. A lesson that saved the lives of some of those people, and enhanced the lives of most of the others.

When I was four, I made a decision that I would be a professional bowler. At four, I chose between golf and bowling ...and bowling won. It was a difficult decision. With all the sports that existed in my family, choosing one main sport was difficult. Everyone in the family had their specialty...plus a few extra sports they were merely good at. My mother and her father were championship class on the rifle range. My dad was a scratch golfer and a fair bowler and a superb shot with the bow and arrow. "Grandpa" Jaress (my dad's father) owned a bowling house and was a solid bowler. What a rock of Gibralter he was...he still bowled in three leagues a week when he was well past 90 years old. At four, I took up most of the sports semi-seriously, but bowling seemed my natural...so a bowler I became. It would not have mattered which sport I selected, because the lesson was always the same. The lesson in golf, small bore rifle shooting, baseball, archery, bowling, tennis was always the same; "Play the shot you have at hand...you can't replay the frame that's gone!" Day after day, for years ...learning to play the frame at hand...learning to squeeze the shot at hand...learning to hit the drive at hand. It didn't matter which sport we played, we always heard the same advice, "Don't worry about the shot that's gone. Don't try to replay the shot you missed...concentrate on *the new chance you have at hand!*" At the bowling lanes before special matches and tournaments, it was necessary to practice over 100 games a week...every frame independent of all the rest ...play the shot at hand, forget the shot that was missed ...concentrate on this next shot. On the rifle range where you often "hold" on the bull for 5, 10 or 15 minutes waiting for the wind to blow steady for just a few brief seconds...and then squeeze off the round. Round after round, hour after hour...so very patient waiting...squeezing off each shot independent of all the rest. Play the shot at hand...make it the best that you know how...squeeze. On the golf course, hit the best shot you can...forget about the shot that ended in the rough three holes earlier...play this new shot the best you know how ...concentrate...hit through the ball independent of all other shots...go for perfection on this one new chance.

I learned that once you've played the frame...ALL THE WORRY IN THE WORLD WOULD NOT CALL IT BACK. I learned that once you've played the shot...THINKING ABOUT THE CHANCE THAT'S GONE WILL SPOIL YOUR CHANCE FOR SUCCESS IN THE NEW FRAME AT HAND. I learned that even a rotten frame did not lose the game for you...IT WAS YOUR CONCENTRATION ON THAT ROTTEN FRAME THAT RUINED THE NEXT FRAME, AND THE NEXT, AND THE NEXT...that ultimately ruined the entire game for you. Over my bowling career that spanned 20 years, I bowled three 300 games, bowled in hundreds of tournaments, and with my father's backing and interest pioneered junior bowling for all kids. I never forgot the lessons...it's been over 15 years since I bowled my last professional tournament, but every year or so I take the kids bowling and amaze them (and myself) with a good game over 220...I still play one shot at a time.

The philosophy of shaking off the dust...and approaching

each frame or day as a new chance for success applies to every field of endeavor.

The business person who remembers that will turn defeat into success. The salesperson that remembers it will be the super star in the company. The sports figure that remembers it will go on into new fields when their playing days are over; and be successful. The minister that remembers it will not sour in his ministry because of short term defeats. The inventor that remembers it will discover the secrets he seeks to unlock. Husbands and wives that remember it will live each day as though it were a "honeymoon" day. Children that remember it will enjoy school and eagerly cram the day full of learning. Friends that remember it will grace their friends with happiness rather than reliving the problems of "past frames." And, when you remember it, you will accept each day as a wonderful gift...an opportunity to fulfill your purpose in life.

Shall we talk some more about the six laws? I think it would be very helpful if you saw how the six laws work on your behalf when you do something as simple as setting a goal. I am going to take you from step number one through the six steps; this is exactly how it works every time you set a goal.

#1　You look about and see the order of things in your environment. Everything that is there *is there* because it is in its proper place in the order of things past and present. Everything that is happening is happening in its proper order or sequence. Everything has a purpose for being exactly where it is...right now.

#2　You think about the changes you would like to make. Everything in the universe vibrates. Some things vibrate fast...others vibrate less fast (the molecules in the book you are holding vibrate at approximately 660,000,000 miles per hour). Some things vibrate so fast...you cannot see them. Some of those things you cannot see are thoughts, but even without seeing them physically, you have them...all things vibrate.

#3　You sift the thoughts into things you want and things you don't want. If you understand the aspects of positive mental attitude, you concentrate your thoughts on the more positive aspects; good, right, success, win... as they relate to your goal. Because the "law of opposites" will offer you both ends of the spectrum, you do have to make a choice as to where your thoughts will dwell.

#4 You bring the thought (cause) into the physical manifestation (effect) *either directly*... such as a realignment of resources... or symbolically. When you write your goal on paper, you physically manifest the symbol of the object desired.

#5 If you directly sought the desired results, you let "like attract like" (your thought attracted its "like" replica in the physical). If you are indirectly attracting the desired results by first writing down the goal, the vibrations of the thought coupled with the physical likeness of the symbol will tend to attract the desired results. The symbolic representation will be a constant stimulus. Eventually "like attracts like".

#6 Once you have received your desired results, you may decide that you want more of the same results... or you may decide you want a bigger result in a different area. What you have done on the small scale, you can repeat on the larger scale. Because patterns repeat, and the laws work equally... you can obtain similar results by following similar order... on a larger or smaller scale... as you wish.

Using this example, can you see how easily changes can be made? Can you see how someone that understands the laws could create almost any effect they desired? Can you see how the realignment of physical effects comes about? If you can learn to create desired effects on the small scale, what about on the larger scale... can you see that?

In just a moment, I will more fully detail the workings of the laws. They are not some metaphysical mumbo-jumbo that work because you recite a magical incantation. The laws are the hard facts of reality as it exists: **THE TRUTH IS... THE TRUTH IS.** Remember that phrase from the beginning of the book? People often don't want to see the answers for their problems. For this reason, the truth is often missed as people scurry about *seeking reasons* (effects) for their problems. Once you've read this book, you will see people in a new perspective; you will see people refusing to accept responsibility for what is happening in their worlds. In the business world all across the United States, Mary Ellen and I see many, many business people that would like to have you believe otherwise. They would like you to believe that their problems are because *something,* or *someone,* out there is making everything go wrong in the six areas of their lives. When we come back to the six laws, we'll find that they work equally and fairly and justly and independently and eternally in everyone's life.

I have seen literally millions of people that have had the laws working negatively in their lives; through their actions these people have assigned themselves a variety of "failure" labels. Why have they assigned the "failure" labels to themselves? They unknowingly did it when they refused to accept the responsibility of understanding **the laws and the positive applications of the laws.** Unfortunately, they compound the problems when they constantly make the two wrong assumptions we discussed earlier. Rather than making an effort to discover the answers, they concentrate on the problems...and in the end blame their hardships, their lack of abundance, and the imbalance in their lives on: 1) The world out there, or 2) God. We already know who is at fault when the tire is run with a "flat side." We already know where to place the responsibility when a life is run "out of balance." They have accepted the "failure" label because...they have chosen the wrong choices in life. Even the person that says, "Oh no...I just didn't make a choice!" has made the wrong choices...unknowingly. **NOT TO DECIDE...IS TO DECIDE.**

In the last chapter, you filled in your desired results in the six areas of your life. You have accepted responsibility for those areas. You have set in motion the six laws...and as you follow through with those six goals, you will create a more balanced life. **CONGRATULATIONS, WE** (you and I) already knew you could do it. You are already infinitely *more successful* this moment than you were before you filled in the charts. At that moment when your pen touched the charts, you proved yourself more successful than before; you have accomplished the more difficult step of the two essentials for success. You have set "desired goals". The "progressive attainment" portion of the two essentials for success is really the easier of the two steps. Once we have covered the six laws in a little more depth, I'll show you graphically... WHY YOU ARE ALREADY MUCH CLOSER TO YOUR GOALS IN THE SIX AREAS... much, much closer than you may have realized. You may have listed goals that you thought were only to be attained after 10, 15 or 20 years of constant striving, but I can show you that there is a good possibility that you can chop years off the deadlines in obtaining whatever it is that you want.

Let's look in more detail at the six laws... and discover a little more information about how they work in relationship to normal occurrences in this world.

10
In-Depth Study of the Six Laws

I find it amazing that the six laws that control and govern everything in this universe are not taught in the school system along with reading, writing and arithmetic. They (the six laws) are certainly as valuable as any essential social skills we might learn. And, they are certainly a thousand-fold more valuable than the thousands of different classes taught as fill-in material (on campus) across the nation. I think "Basket Weaving 101-A" is a terrific class...however, it could be an elective...after the individual had learned the six laws that would determine the outcome of every decision that could possibly be made by the individual. Maybe one of your children will be one of the lucky few that accidently reads this book before they have to make major decisions about "getting ahead" in the world. I doubt that this book will ever make the required reading lists of any school...that's a shame...but, an acknowledged reality. Let's look at the six laws in a little more depth.

THE LAW OF ORDER

There is ORDER to everything. You may not be able to see or understand the order, but it is always there. Sometimes the person that is involved in a situation cannot see the ORDER, but everyone else can see it. Sometimes no one can see the ORDER...that does not mean there is no ORDER, or that the ORDER does not exist. It only means that at this time, in these circumstances, with our resources, NO ONE HAS AS YET DISCOVERED THE ORDER. In the scientific field, this is a common situation and precedes most major break-throughs or discoveries. For years and years, everyone involved in a field may suspect (and search) for the missing link; the method for unlocking a particular baffling mystery. No one is able to discover the ORDER necessary to provide the answer. And then, in what seems to be an unusual manner, someone, perhaps accidently, discovers a fragment of the ORDER. Within a few short weeks, months, or years, a flood of scientific knowledge issues forth...the ORDER has become clear. You see, the ORDER was already there. The ORDER has always been there. Mankind in the role of scientist, merely becomes aware; discovers the ORDER. It is sometimes very easy to see and to understand the ORDER in highly complex function or situations. It is also very easy to not understand the ORDER in some very simple situations. For instance: Can you count to fifty? Can you add 25 plus 13 in your head, without pencil and paper? Can you repeat the alphabet from memory? Can you use a dictionary? Did you answer YES to each question? Highly complex functions...and yet you fully under-stand the ORDER. Now for some simple situations *requiring an understanding of ORDER:* What precedes happiness? Can you explain death? Why do "likes" attract? Which came first ...energy or matter? Why? You may be thinking, "What tough questions!" My point is only to emphasize that there is ORDER in everything...you will want to discover the ORDER in those areas that are important to you. The areas that will become very important to you...in terms of under-standing the ORDER...would naturally be; your family area, your financial area, your social area, the area of your physical being, the area of your mental being, and the area of your spiritual being. The more you can understand the ORDER surrounding you, and interacting in your life, THE MORE YOU WILL LIVE YOUR LIFE IN ALIGNMENT WITH YOUR "MAJOR PURPOSE."

I would like to share with you a fun thought...that is also a very serious thought. Think this through: 1) We live in a three dimensional world, 2) There is much (perhaps 99%) about this world that we still do not know HOW...WHEN ...WHERE...WHAT...or WHY it exists, 3) We have not discovered the ORDER that will unlock the door of understanding to these large areas of our not knowing. Now, imagine yourself living in a nine dimensional world! Oh, you find that difficult to imagine! Well, let's back up a bit. Wouldn't it be exciting to understand the ORDER in a four dimensional world (a few have)...or the ORDER in a six dimensional world? Wouldn't it be exciting to understand the ORDER of everything...beyond time...beyond and behind everything? Someone does know everything...you've probably already guessed who He is. Haven't you?

Once upon a time in my naivete, I thought that the six laws were (randomly) without order. I thought that way after spending the equivalence of two full years of study into the nature of the laws. This was a few years back, but I'll relate how the order came to me. When I decided that I would find the answers to how everything worked, I used my love for reading and an inquisitive mind to gather up the best that I could find in the way of known material. It took five years part time to read the works necessary for my research (10-14 books a week for five years does represent a fair amount of research). Fortunately I (like you) have a mind that never forgets anything I really want to remember. Once I had gathered all the materials I needed, I decided that the six laws were randomly existent throughout our universe. But that didn't make sense! The law of order negated that possibility. About four years later, the answer came to me one morning while I was taking a shower. How obvious it was...once I understood the order. I went over and over the order...and later that day shared the information with Mary Ellen. It was so easy. Order had to be the first law.

"In the beginning God created" (Gen. 1:1)

LAW OF VIBRATION

In this law, your science training classes may come in handy. Do you remember how it is that you hear and see and feel and smell and taste things of this world? That's right, you hear, see, feel, smell and taste things of this world based on sensory input (such as wavelengths transmitted to your sensing equipment). Do you remember how the physical appearance of matter can be changed by increasing the vibration rate? Do you remember all those facts you learned about; the speed of light, different wavelengths that produced different colors, plus the other wavelengths that produce heat, sound, feeling, and even brain patterns? People of the world are becoming so sophisticated in their learning that even little children know that the words we speak can be captured, and measured, and stored in the vibration state. It can then be transmitted by wires (or without) to another device that will recapture and reproduce the duplicate of the original voice. This duplicated voice can then be delivered to a series of nerves and organs that will perform another scrambling, transmitting, and reassembling process in a person's brain. I don't mean to bore you with a detailed explanation of the telephone. I just wanted to get you thinking about how much we take for granted the law of VIBRATION. Every great scientist understands parts and pieces of the law of VIBRATION. No scientist (living or dead) fully understands the law of VIBRATION. Every year we hear of research teams that make tremendous breakthroughs in the discovery of matter. The teams of research people are finally to the point of identifying some particles that are so small...they pass completely through the earth without running into a single atom during their journey. Other groups of scientists are constantly working on changing the vibration rates (and consequently the physical structure) of matter to create new forms...or to unlock the power source (or potential) locked within. Everything I have mentioned, and all that they are studying is *in comparison nothing*... when compared to the full understanding and usage of the law of VIBRATION. Mankind is only scratching the surface; we have only begun to understand. Here's the important point for you to think about in terms of understanding and using the law; anything you wish to change, everything you wish to have, whatever you want and need is already in some form of VIBRATION... **right now.** Everything is in the process of change right now... no thing (nothing) is without VIBRATION. There is absolutely nothing in this world that can keep you from your goals. Anything that is seemingly solid and immovable is (in reality) already dissolving, changing, and preparing for its change into another place or form or quality. Everything that seems solid is changing... while you read this book. As you begin to understand and use the law of VIBRATION more, you will probably accentuate and accelerate the changes you want and need. Remember, your thoughts are things; as solid and identifiable as anything of this physical world... and far more potent. Wouldn't it be great if you could control VIBRATION enough to create an uplifting, positive, highly receptive environment for change? Wouldn't it be wonderful if you could (understanding ORDER) set in motion the proper set of VIBRATIONS necessary to change the abundance you have *in each of the six areas of your life?* The "good news" is: **You can.** The "bad news" is: **You might not try.**

Of course, the ultimate use of the law of VIBRATION would be to merely voice the VIBRATIONS into existence, and have the physical world respond and change. You do realize what control you would have at that point... don't you? Physical matter and energy would be at your command. Do you realize *what power that would demonstrate?* To exercise dominion over every form of VIBRATION... is *more power* than you or I could handle. However, you do have some control over the law of VIBRATION, and as you exercise more and more control through understanding and using the law properly...you will always use it *properly*. An interesting thought about that total control over the law of VIBRATION: To have the total control at disposal, would make all things possible ...merely by asking...but, you already know someone that has demonstrated that kind of control. What He said had the power to move mountains, to create from the nothingness of air, to change lives instantly...the power of the Word is a full demonstration of the correct application of the law of VIBRATION.

"Let there be..." (Gen. 1:3-28)

LAW OF OPPOSITES

The law of OPPOSITES is a natural flowing of VIBRA-TIONS in an ORDERLY fashion...into complementary pairs. To see the oneness in everything is above and beyond our reach as human beings. What we see when we look out at our universe is: a perfectly balanced "package" of existence. Every-thing of this universe has an equal OPPOSITE. Sometimes you may not be able to see what the OPPOSITE *could be*...or where the OPPOSITE *could be found*...or how the OPPO-SITE *would appear* if it could exist. But, of this you can be certain, an OPPOSITE does exist; somewhere in some form!

The law of OPPOSITES is a very tricky law to understand. Sometimes the OPPOSITE is vastly different from its counter-part...and sometimes, they (the two opposites) appear to be almost identical in every way. The law of OPPOSITES is a very tricky law to fully utilize for your benefit. "Fence sitting" is virtually not possible in most cases...and in some instances may be "hazardous to your health!" Once you fully understand the essence of the law of OPPOSITES, you will constantly monitor your thought processes to ferret out the last vestiges of the five very negative words we covered in an earlier chapter. We spent many, many pages discussing the defini-tions of the five sets of words that easily cause over 90% of all the problems in our society. Each set of words discusses the OPPOSITE ends on different comparison charts. In an

ORDERLY fashion, all thoughts (causes) are channeled into VIBRATIONS. Different VIBRATIONS are set in OPPOSITION to form a perfectly balanced universe. Any thing (anything) that gets out of balance will cause *a very short-lived problem.* As soon as some thing (something) gets out of balance, it will seek a point of "rest". As soon as the balance is restored between the OPPOSITES, everything runs smoothly once again.

All mechanical devices have a flow pattern that takes into account the law of OPPOSITES. The pulse beat of your heart is an example of this law of OPPOSITES... as are the operations of all *other organs in your body.* The battery in your car is an excellent example of the utilization of OPPOSITES; as long as the positive and negative posts are separated... and, as long as the drain on one post is balanced perfectly with an influx of energy into and through the other post, the battery will remain charged. The reason the charged battery will start your car is because it is trying to seek "rest"... *it is not at rest*... it will willingly give up energy trying to seek the "rest". If you place a metal bar across both posts, in a snapping, crackling, energy explosion... the battery will seek its point of "rest". You'll have a different *life form* to deal with... a *dead* battery!

In the law of OPPOSITES can be found the answers for, "Why death?"... and "Is life worth living?" In the law of OPPOSITES, you can find the answers for every question you will ever have concerning attitude, behavior patterns, choice of lifestyles... and, where do you want your mind to dwell? Living a balanced life does not mean that you need to balance off the positive and negative thoughts you have! Your life will run smoothly when it is *run in balance* as we discussed in the chapter on the areas of life. Were you to try to contain both a fully negative nature and a fully positive nature within you, in a heart-rending, snapping, crackling, energy explosion, YOU WOULD SEEK A POINT OF REST! You would have an emotional or physical or mental breakdown. The tremendous emotional crises that many Christians face is when they try to live their lives with two OPPOSING philosophies. On the one hand, the newborn Christian has accepted a *new nature*, but on the other hand, there is an *old nature* that is everywhere in the physical world. A physical world that the new Christian *still inhabits, still enjoys, still must deal with on a daily basis.* This is not a new struggle that I am discussing, it is as old as recorded Biblical truths. It is very important that an individual search out their thoughts and come to an understanding of "WHAT DO I BELIEVE?" Ask yourself these questions...

WHAT DO I BELIEVE:

...IS THE PHILOSOPHY OF LIFE I WANT TO ACCEPT?
...IS THE TYPE OF LIFE I WANT TO LEAD?
...IS THE TYPE OF PERSON I WANT TO BE AND BECOME?
...IS THE QUALITY OF LIFE I WANT TO PURSUE?
...IS THE EXAMPLE OF A LIFE WELL LIVED?
...IS A MAJOR PURPOSE WORTH LIVING FOR?

Wisdom in the use of the law of OPPOSITES helps an individual remove confusion from daily living. Remember, as far in one direction as you can go, there is an equal OPPOSITE in the other direction. Every thought eventually finds its ways into physical existence. Therefore, you will find it advantageous... *extremely beneficial*... to make wise choices in the selection of which end of the OPPOSITES *you will become.* The world offers us every manner of choice to make. When we choose one end of the scale, we automatically remove ourselves from the OPPOSITE end of that scale. When you make choices concerning the five sets of words we discussed, **choose** the positive aspects (success, good, win, superior, and right) and throw yourself into the aspects fully. Remove yourself as far from the OPPOSITES (failure, bad, lose, inferior, and wrong) as is diligently possible. A proper structuring of your goals will accomplish this task, and we'll work on that in the next chapter. When you think of the law of OPPOSITES, it might help you to think of the extremes you can see in the available "models" we have. Once you've selected the attributes you deem "right" for you, try to find a perfect example (a model) that typifies the characteristics you wish to attain. As your thought patterns settle more and more into the pattern of the model, you will settle into your particular "niche" on the scale of OPPOSITES. There is a saying, in one of our businesses, by a man that has touched the lives of millions of people. Dr. Forrest C. Shaklee, Sr. said, **"What you think, you look. What you think, you do. What you think, you are."** Appropriately said, and certainly applicable to the model you wish to follow.

The law of OPPOSITES is everywhere. It is essential. It is primordial. It designates and differentiates all things.

"In the beginning God created the heavens and the earth."

(Gen. 1:1)

THE LAW OF CAUSE AND EFFECT

This is going to be an easy law for us to discuss. We have already covered the law in its entirety at least once in previous chapters. CAUSE (an energy form) sets into motion EFFECT (physical form). What you and I see in our daily world could be described as the EFFECTS, of EFFECTS, of EFFECTS, of EFFECTS, of EFFECTS, etc. and etc. and etc. We do not "see" CAUSE: we think CAUSE. CAUSE (the energy form) is everywhere in our world. Every CAUSE has a distinct, unique quality (rate of VIBRATION). Just as, every EFFECT has a distinct, unique quality (rate of VIBRATION) that sets it apart from all other objects. CAUSE, in its unique VIBRATION pattern, will manifest (bring into view) an EFFECT that will have a similarly unique VIBRATION pattern. Every CAUSE is subject to the law of OPPOSITES, and to the law of VIBRATION, and also the law of ORDER. The laws work **in everything!**

Because the law of OPPOSITES is always in existence, a CAUSE at one end of a scale (let's say: a positive, uplifting thought) will always produce an EFFECT at a similar end of a scale in the physical (such as: a positive, uplifting experience). The law of CAUSE & EFFECT is *a perfectly just law;* it always rewards degree for degree, measure for measure, reaping exactly what is planted.

I'd like to share an insight I have had hundreds of times in my work with over 40,000 sales and marketing people. I have shared this insight with the sales staffs of every company that has ever had me "in-house" in the capacity of "trainer." In every field of selling, the salespeople have a variety of terms (labels) that they assign to the "suspects" (potential prospects that might need their products). In many industries, sales-people call the prospects "turkeys" and "flakes" and in other industries they are called "mooches". And unfortunately, in some industries, the labels are unprintable. I always try to point out the irrationality in allowing this practice to continue. If the purpose for being in business is "to continue being in business", which includes *marketing* an adequate number of *units* (whatever), at an agreed-upon *price,* so as to provide a margin of *profit,* then derogatory labeling is counter-productive to the primary purpose of the company. Thinking a person is a "turkey" (CAUSE) will create a physical EFFECT at a similar end of the scale in question. However, the practice continues!

In our workshops, Mary Ellen and I stress the "Non-judgmental acceptance of everyone that views your business." To do otherwise is counter-productive to the goals of being in business to provide a service or products. The law of CAUSE and EFFECT gives you exactly what **you** have asked for **in your mind.**

Of the six laws, the law of CAUSE and EFFECT may be the *easiest to understand*…and the *hardest to consistently use positively* in your life. The Bible references the law of CAUSE and EFFECT thousands of times. There are complete books of the Bible devoted to the wisdom and understanding of this law. The 31 chapters of Proverbs are one constant lesson with almost one thousand examples of the law. Seeing the law of CAUSE and EFFECT *in print* is not the same as **living the law** of CAUSE and EFFECT knowledgeably day after day...as a way of life. *Everyone* lives the law daily...but *not everyone* lives the law in wisdom and understanding. The law of CAUSE and EFFECT is so easy to comprehend once ENERGY = PHYSICAL is explained. What you think...you create! Know your thoughts...and where they dwell. **Make the law work for you!**

Once an individual begins to see the pattern formed by the laws, he or she can appreciate more fully the workings of the law of CAUSE and EFFECT.

#1 In the proper ORDER

#2 With a certain intensity of VIBRATION

#3 At the desired point on the scale of OPPOSITES

#4 YOU WILL CAUSE THE EFFECTS YOU DESIRE IN YOUR LIFE

"For as he thinks within himself, so he is." (Prov. 23:7)

"By wisdom a house is built,
And by understanding it is established;
And by knowledge the rooms are filled
With all precious and pleasant riches."

(Prov. 24:3,4)

THE LAW OF ATTRACTION

The law of ATTRACTION is easy to understand...as soon as we can agree on *what* ATTRACTS, and, *what does not* ATTRACT. In the law of ATTRACTION, "like" ATTRACTS "like". Many times people will say, "Don't OPPOSITES attract?" No...opposites don't attract; they complement each other. Follow this through; opposites sit at either end of a scale...as far as you can go in one direction, you can go in the opposite direction to find an *equal balancing opposite*. If opposites attracted, all the pairs of opposites would end up in some sort of "mid-point" of mediocrity.

Opposites complement and by doing so, they form a

whole. Man and woman are two opposites that complement and *in their union create one unit.* A magnet has a positive end and a negative end. To think that opposites attract would mean you thought the positive field and the negative field would pull towards each other and meet in the middle of the magnet. It doesn't work that way! The positive end and the negative end stay in their respective places; *opposed* to each other... but *complementing to make a whole magnet* (a unit). If you have a long magnet (about 2 or 3 inches long), and you decide to break it in the middle... do you know what you will get? You won't get one piece of magnet that is *all* negative field... and one piece of magnet that is *all* positive field. **YOU WILL GET TWO PIECES OF MAGNET**... and each piece will be a complete unit with a positive and a negative end. Remember the law of OPPOSITES every time you start to think of what *cannot* ATTRACT.

Now let's cover the significance of "like" attracting "like". There is a great deal of truth in the cliches centering around this law. "Likes" are drawn to each other because they VIBRATE in tune with each other. They are in harmony. They align with one another. The greater the degree of "alikeness", the greater the tendency for the attraction process to take place. People seek out their companions according to this law. You select business partners according to this law. The tangible symbols of success and prosperity flow according to this law. Even *your choice of spouse* is subject to this law. You may have just balked at what I said. Did you inwardly say, "Wait a minute! You said opposites complement... and now you're saying spouses are attracted; 'like' attracts 'like'... how can that be?" Follow this through and you'll see why some couples fit together so nicely; OPPOSITES complement, and likes ATTRACT. Therefore, a man and a woman make a *perfect pair* because they balance each other as a complementing unit. Now, forget about the "man/woman" labels that have made one unit, and let's concentrate on the thousands of other labels (traits, character, personality, hobbies, abilities, talents, etc.) that are separate from gender or the essence of "man/

woman". The more "likes" that are in agreement, the greater will be the ATTRACTION. As a couple (man/woman) match up similar trait to similar trait...hobby to hobby...ability to ability...personality to personality...positive philosophy to positive philosophy, the "likes" will ATTRACT and create a firmer bond.

Can you see why some couples have so much trouble? They ignored the law of ATTRACTION when they first met...*or* during the first three or four months they were seeing each other. So many times young couples meet, experience a physical reaction that *they think* signals "a perfect attraction", and rush headlong into a lifetime of misery. The strong physical reaction is not the problem; the problem is *misreading or not understanding* the two laws (OPPOSITES & ATTRACTION). The strong physical reaction is the law of OPPOSITES signaling a completion of a unit; the law of OPPOSITES is "in balance" when opposites complement to form a whole. What if the two people have absolutely nothing in common? They have "no likes" that are even close. Imagine the *wildest mismatches* you have ever heard of amongst your friends and family, and you get an idea of what goes on in the world of "boy meets girl". By the time the mismatch is discovered (12 months of fights and a little baby that will be blamed for the break-up), a new statistic will be added to our soaring divorce rate in the United States.

I could take more time describing every match-up; friend to friend, associate to associate, man to woman, success to success, failures to failures, Christian to Christian, tangible to tangible, trait to trait, etc. What I think is more important (now that you know that like will ATTRACT like) is to realize "like" *doesn't always mean* two people. Any two objects, force fields, attitudes and so forth can be the "likes" that attract. And, the two things that attract can be very *dissimilar* in many, many ways. In fact, the two things might be similar in a very limited number of ways; but those few point of similar VIBRATION may be so strong...the ATTRACTION of "like forces" will draw the two together.

You ATTRACT to yourself according to your thought patterns. You ATTRACT to yourself people that are of "like" persuasion. You ATTRACT to yourself the fulfillment of your goal structures. And, you are ATTRACTED to thought patterns that parallel yours. You are also ATTRACTED towards people whose life-view philosophies are similar to your own. And, you are ATTRACTED into situations that will provide avenues and vehicles for the fulfillment of your goals.

What I have just described is a very important point. The law of ATTRACTION works in both directions; you bringing into your sphere of availability "likes" similar to your thought patterns, attitudes and characteristics...and, you moving into other spheres because of someone else's thought patterns, attitudes and characteristics.

The law of ATTRACTION is a perfectly just law. It rewards in exact proportion, without bias or prejudice, attracting to each person exactly what they "put out" or "seek" or "ask for" or "silently desire". Happy people ATTRACT happy people and happy situations and happy results. Unhappiness ATTRACTS unhappy people and situations and results. Successful people ATTRACT successful people and situations and results. Failures "put out" and ATTRACT failures in people, situations, and results. Good ATTRACTS good. Right ATTRACTS right. When an individual makes plans in the social area of life, I usually tell them, "Adequately describe the moral, ethical, good attributes of the kind of friends you would like to have in your environment." Once they've done that, I then request this, "Become that type of individual and you will ATTRACT *exactly what you seek.*"

Let me tell you of a perfect example of the law of ATTRACTION. Remember the inner core that we labeled *"me in the beginning"?* The whole complete you that existed *before all the labels of the world were attached*...remember? Have you ever wondered why people with their billions of different combinations of characteristics and faults are ALL pleasing to the Lord when they finally come to Him. The law of ORDER has been fulfilled...at that time. The law of

VIBRATION has been fulfilled...the Word never returns void. The law of OPPOSITES has been fulfilled...by choice a decision has been made. The law of CAUSE and EFFECT has been fulfilled...perfect cause is reaping perfect effect. And, the law of ATTRACTION has been fulfilled...the *essence of God's love* (acceptance) has sought and attracted the *"like"* that was buried deep inside beneath the labels of the world. There is a part of you that is in perfect tune with His essence. He seeks it *within you*...and you seek it *within Him*. It is the most beautiful example of the law of ATTRACTION you will find anywhere in the opposites; Heaven and earth.

"This I command you, that you love one another.

(John 15:17)

"Behold, I stand at the door and knock;
if anyone hears My voice and opens the door,
I will come in to him"

(Rev. 3:20)

THE LAW OF DUALITY

This is a simple one that states "As above, so below." In the law of DUALITY can be found the constant repetition process. This is not as difficult a world as most people would like you to believe. The six laws are really simple to understand. They are not always simple to put into *positive application.* The law of DUALITY is very important because it will take most of the work and "bloody noses" out of learning the "lessons" of this world. Any "lesson" you learn on the small scale can be applied to hundreds or thousands of situations ...larger or smaller. The people I shake my head at are those people that make the same mistake time after time after time. **Don't get me wrong! I've done it, too.** *But,* some people make "dumb" mistakes on little trivial inconsequential things ...time after time after time. Then, they spend all their waking hours moaning and crying the blues about "How they never have any time to accomplish anything 'big' in life." How they ever think they'll accomplish anything "big" is beyond me...they won't even try to learn the lessons on the small scale.

Can you see how the law of DUALITY works? Watch the workings of the five previously discussed laws...they all work on the large scale...they all work on the small scale...they all work if applied negatively...they all work if applied positively ...they all work *in your life and in my life.*

We are about to end this chapter...not for a lack of additional material but rather because, *it is not necessary* to try to prove the laws with thousands of examples. If you understand the law of DUALITY, you will automatically see within the examples of truth given, the essence of each law...and how each law could be expanded upon in countless separate stories and examples. If you understand the law of ORDER, then you have seen "how" and "why" the other examples would work if shown. If you understand *the beginning and the end*...you've **got it! Congratulations!** You've made it! I can take my reference book, and in it find thousand upon thousand upon thousands of examples of the laws. My Bible has some pages with over 40 examples of the laws *on each page.* On other pages, there will be only one example, but that example will be discussed in depth, it will be looked at from many viewpoints, and told in many ways...and finally it will be brought to a close. The six laws presented within this book are all there is to "understanding" and "wisdom". Anyone that understands the six laws and uses them properly will be thought of as a very wise person. Anyone that understands the six laws and then...*uses them improperly*...is stupid! That may sound very harsh, but it is the truth. It's one thing to be ignorant of the facts and make a mistake. It is an entirely different story to be aware and totally violate what you know to be true.

If I were to suddenly end this book with this page, there would be two different reactions exhibited by the large numbers of readers; one reaction would come from those who realized the importance of the six laws just discussed, and the other reaction would come from the group of people that did not understand the importance of the six laws. Therefore, if you would be disappointed by my ending the book with this page, you might want to rethink through the laws and how they "impact" your life.

We have a lot of chapters to follow which demonstrate how the laws can be used in daily living to better your life. I would like to bring this chapter to a close with a Bible passage that demonstrates the law of DUALITY.

> "You shall love the Lord your God
> with all your heart, and with all
> your soul, and with all your mind.
> This is the great and foremost commandment.
> The second is like it. You shall
> love your neighbor as yourself."
>
> (Matt. 22:37-39)

II

Understanding

11
Closer Than You Think

In this chapter we are going to view your preliminary goals in a manner that will show you exactly how far away they really are from being attained. I am certain that I can show you graphically that your goals are really closer than you think. In fact, most people are astounded when they discover that everything they want and need for a "balanced life" is only a few seconds, minutes, or possibly, days away.

It is very important that you spend time on the material in this chapter...enough time so you will really understand "why" the material works. It is important that you take the time to follow through with the basic concepts of the chapter. When I say, "follow through", I mean talk the material over with yourself...weigh it against what you now know about the six laws, and then consider what would happen "if" you used the material in your daily activities. If you read over any concept without "following through", you will have merely *read another book* or *skimmed another idea.* And as you will remember from earlier chapters, the negation of positive ideas by the mind is the great downfall of most PMA people throughout the world; they negate the laws of the universe *working positively* in their lives. This is not going to be a long chapter, but it will have "impact". This chapter will explain many inconsistencies you may have noticed about: 1) People that are always setting goals but never getting anywhere. 2) People that rise to great heights and then sink...only to rise and sink again. 3) People that attain their goals and become a totally different person in the process (*what kind of person...is the big question*).

As you look at the diagram on the following page, you will notice that it is divided into three sections: 1) An area in which an end result (goal) may be defined. In this area would be written one of the six areas of a balanced life, and a generalized or well-defined end-result that is desired. 2) An area in which may be written the generalized or well-defined feelings, emotions, and attitudes (labels) that you feel would be appropriate to wear upon reaching the particular end result (goal) that is in section #1. 3) In the third area should be written the actions you feel are appropriate for maintaining the end result (goal) on a continuing basis. In other words, what would a person do, or how would they act after reaching the goal...if they wanted to retain the goal. I will help you fill in the sample diagram so you will have some experience when it comes to filling in the diagrams relating to the six areas of your life.

This is an exercise in the use of the six laws of the universe. Please take your pen or pencil and work this example through with me. This example will answer a lot of questions you might have regarding wealth, the accumulation of wealth, the retention of wealth, and why some people deal with wealth so easily...and others are destroyed by it.

In the sample diagram, write a generalized wealth statement such as: MY GOAL IS TO BE INDEPENDENTLY WEALTHY AND TO BE HAPPY WITH MY WEALTH...or any other statement of wealth that appeals to you. Please do that now in section #1. In section #2 list all the labels you would take out of the CLOSET OF YOUR MIND and wear ...if you were INDEPENDENTLY WEALTHY AND HAPPY WITH THE WEALTH. List all the generalized feelings, emotions and attitudes you would expect an individual

RESULTS:

LABELS:

ACTIONS:

SAMPLE DIAGRAM
FINANCIAL AREA

(such as yourself) to wear upon attaining that goal. Perhaps you would list 15 or 20 predominant labels such as: Happy, Successful, Confident, Powerful, Superior, Winner, Prosperous, Enthusiastic, etc. Don't let me hold you back. You list *your feelings.* How you would feel if you were in total control of your wealth...and very happy with the wealth. DO IT NOW.

And now for the third section. List how you feel you would *act and react* in the world upon reaching the goal of INDEPENDENTLY WEALTHY AND HAPPY WITH THAT WEALTH. Start listing your conceptions of how people act that are very wealthy and want to retain and protect that wealth. Remembering the law of OPPOSITES, you will find that your list of actions can take one of two slants. You could list...people that have wealth are Generous, Kind, Helpful, Giving, Benefactors, Easy-to-be-around, Gracious, Courteous, Warm, and Loving towards the people in their environment. Or, you could list...people that have wealth are Careful of who they are around (lest others take advantage), Closed to others, Guarded, Suspicious, Difficult-to-be-around, Stand-offish, Jealous of others' wealth, Cold, Rude to "little" people, and Snobbish towards the people in their environment. Please list now your honest feelings about the actions of wealthy people. DO IT NOW.

If you filled out the diagram (which you should have), you will have *the key to wealth...and the key to being happy with the wealth...and the key to the retention of wealth.* Another interesting fact you may have noticed about the diagram, I did not ask you to list the "effects" of wealth. I didn't ask you to put down all the "things" people think of as wealth such as: Money, Cars, Travel, Real Estate, Bank Accounts, Stocks, Bonds, Art Collections, Jewelry, etc. These "things" are the physical "effects" of wealth. They are effects, of effects, of effects, of effects leading back to "cause" that started the process. Does this sound familiar to you? Certainly it does. Everything you are reading in this chapter, and what you will be reading in the chapters to follow, will always be direct applications of the six laws as they apply to your world, and to my world also. Because all those "things" are only effects of effects, we don't need to list them. If you use the diagram as a model upon which to base your selection of labels from the CLOSET OF YOUR MIND, you will set in motion the proper application of the laws to attain your end result (goal) which was INDEPENDENTLY WEALTHY AND HAPPY WITH THE WEALTH.

Now comes an important point of understanding. The goal is listed in section #1, the proper labels are listed in #2, but what is listed in #3? What you have listed in section #3 *is the key to the retention of the goal.* If section #3 is a natural continuation of the labels listed in section #2, then, the goal can be retained. But, if the actions of #3 are not a natural continuation of the labels listed in section #2, then, the end result (the goal) *will not be retained.* I'll cover this material again in just a moment. Some people understand it immediately while others, like myself, have to think about it for a little while before fully accepting the concept.

Section #1 is the end result you desire, and the more detailed and well-defined you can make the end result...the better. Section #2 lists the labels you feel are appropriate to wear to attain that goal. Do you realize that you listed a wonderful collection of labels for yourself? And do you realize that you could choose to wear that terrific collection of labels if you wanted to do so? And, if you feel they are the appropriate labels to wear **when** you are INDEPENDENTLY WEALTHY AND HAPPY WITH THE WEALTH, then it is absolutely essential that you wear those labels (CAUSES) to have any chance at all of attracting wealth! What you thought were the labels that you should wear "when"...are really the labels you should wear "before." Once you start working on the other diagrams, you'll see a general pattern of labels that are constantly repeated. As you fill in the diagrams for all six areas, the constants will make themselves quite apparent.

Now, we come back to section #3 and its importance in relation to your desired end result. If the characteristics and actions listed in the third section are a natural outgrowth, a natural progression, a natural continuation of the labels listed in section #2, then, the end result *can be retained*. For instance, the labels are positive…and the actions upon attaining the goal are positive methods of dealing with the environment …THEREFORE THE GOAL IN ITS ENTIRETY CAN BE RETAINED. But, what if the characteristics and actions listed in the third section are in opposition to the labels listed in the second section? Then, the end result (the goal) cannot continue *as it was originally stated*.

Let's say that an individual follows through with section #2 and by wearing the proper labels starts to see the "effects" of "effects" accumulating about them on the physical basis. They are wearing Happy, Successful, Prosperous, Good, Energetic, Outgoing labels (original thought forms…CAUSES) in their dealings with the environment and the people that make up that environment. But a change comes over that person. They begin to talk very negatively about their former friends, they become suspicious and guarded, they think that everyone (that has less than they have) is totally imcompetent. THEY CHANGE THEIR LABELS! You and I know what has to happen if the "cause" is changed. Right, the "effects" will change. It's scriptural. It will happen. There is no doubt that it will happen. It is only a matter of how fast. They will lose a portion, or all, of the original goal as it was conceived and defined. Perhaps they will lose the happiness associated with the wealth. Perhaps they will lose the wealth. Perhaps they will be thrown out of balance in trying to control the goal. Perhaps other areas will become "disaster areas" in order to accomplish the destruction of the original goal: INDEPENDENTLY WEALTHY AND HAPPY WITH THE WEALTH.

You may think I have painted a very gloomy, forbidding picture of wealth…but, I have not! I have described exactly what will happen once an individual starts to attain their goal. Once the goal is attained, the laws don't magically stop working! They continue. And if a person sets in motion a new thought pattern (opposite from the first) the new cause, with new effects, will attract different "likes", and *new results will come about.* It was necessary that we work through at least one example (one diagram) with some explanation so that you would see how the laws work when applied to all the goals we'll be setting. It sometimes takes a lot of words to describe a very simple process, but once the understanding is there, it seems so very simple. Doesn't it?

In each goal area we'll go through a similar process. First, we'll list *the end result in a well-defined manner.* Then, we'll list the identifications; the feeling, emotions, and attitudes **(labels)** you identify with the end result. And lastly, we'll list the supporting **actions,** the characteristics, the behaviors that will sustain and support the end result.

A few chapters back you wrote some preliminary goals; a written goal for each of the six areas; Chart "C". Flip back to those pages and rewrite the preliminary goals into the six diagrams on the following pages. **Please do that now**…you had six goals for six areas, and there are six diagrams that need to be filled in.

Now, go through the process of filling in sections two and three in each of the diagrams. Be descriptive when you list the feelings, emotions, and attitudes. Imagine yourself…see yourself…describe yourself. You should be able to list ten or more labels in each section. It is important that you fill in your diagrams before proceeding with the reading. PLEASE, complete the diagrams.

ARE YOUR DIAGRAMS COMPLETE?

Two important points to be made are these: 1) Have you found a preponderance of labels that are generated time and time again throughout the six diagrams? Excellent…if you have. Not so good…*if you have not.* 2) Have you found it easy to draw a continuation of the section two (labels) into the **actions** of section number three in each of the diagrams? You found it easy…good. Your section three was opposed to your section number two in most cases…*problems.*

FINANCIAL AREA:

RESULTS:

LABELS:

ACTIONS:

CHART D

FAMILY AREA:

RESULTS:

LABELS:

ACTIONS:

CHART D

SOCIAL AREA

RESULTS:

LABELS:

ACTIONS:

CHART D

PHYSICAL AREA:

RESULTS:
LABELS:
ACTIONS:

CHART D

MENTAL AREA:

RESULTS:

LABELS:

ACTIONS:

CHART D

SPIRITUAL AREA:

RESULTS:

LABELS:

ACTIONS:

CHART D

I am not saying that someone that would rate, "Not so good" or "problems", should just give up. If your labels don't match up, or your section three actions are opposed to the labels necessary to retain your goals, you have some changes to make. BUT, THAT'S NO PROBLEM. In the first chapters of the book, we already decided that "change" might be necessary. By the way, sometimes a person fills in their diagrams and comes out looking like a "champ". But what they put on paper in the diagrams... and the way *they really lead their life* leaves a lot of room for improvement.

I have seen people list their **end result** in the family area: A HAPPY FAMILY LIFE WITH GOOD INTER-PERSONAL COMMUNICATION THAT FOSTERS WARM, PERSONAL RELATIONSHIPS. Then they list **the labels (emotions and attitudes) as: HAPPY, WARM, LOVING, FRIENDLY, KIND, GENEROUS, PEACEFUL, PLEASANT, ETC.** Finally, **they list the actions** of a person that had the end result as: THEY WOULD BE RESPECTFUL OF OTHER FAMILY MEMBERS, THEY WOULD BE CHEERFUL AND PLEASANT TO BE AROUND, THEY WOULD BE INTERESTED IN THE HAPPINESS AND ACTIVITIES OF OTHER FAMILY MEMBERS, THEY WOULD USE KIND, LOVING, HELPFUL WORDS TO COMMUNICATE, ETC.

But, what are the "real" labels they wear around the house? What are the actions they demonstrate in dealing with family members? That's where "The rubber meets the road" ... are they wearing the labels and performing the actions that will earn them the desired "effects"? Probably not. That's why they are trying to change.

In both cases, change is necessary. Now, I don't want you to get the wrong idea and think that you should change because Michael Jaress says you are something that you should not be. You are exactly what you should be...based on all the labels you currently wear, and based on all the actions that you now portray, reveal and expose to your environment.

But, **IF...your desired end results** are different from the way things really are (right now)...then, you may want to try something a little different so your world will work out a little different. I think that IF you've been honest with yourself ...and, IF you've known what it's like to experience down-times and problems and negatives...and, IF you're not solidi-fied like stone, then it is possible and probable that you would be willing to strive for something new and exciting in your life. And that will require some changes be made.

In the beginning of this chapter, I told you "**your goals, your desires, and your end results**" were closer than you think. I even told you that your goals might be only "minutes away" from realization. It's true. It might take you seconds, or it might take you minutes, or even a few days...to change your labels and to start the laws of the universe working for you.

Sometimes people in workshops will say, "But, when do I get the money?", or "How fast can I expect my spouse to change?", or "Will it take very long for me to see improve-ments in my health?" These questions indicate that the per-son is still locked onto their "old" thoughts, and have missed an "Ah-hah" along the way. I am not saying the questions are "wrong" to ask. They are perfectly normal questions. But when a person gets the "Ah-hah" about the six laws of the universe and the process we just covered concerning goals ...they will understand that the material "effects" have been set in motion, and I don't have a time scale for "delivery"...no one does. And, *in reality,* the physical "effects" are the least important step in the process. I repeat, "The physical 'effects' are the least important step in the process."

Let's take our "WEALTHY AND HAPPY WITH WEALTH" goal and discover why the physical "effects" (the effects of effects of effects) become rather unimportant. Answer the questions: "Why was the goal "WEALTHY" set?" "What had you listed would be your label structure if the goal was already in hand?" In looking back at the diagram we find that the attainment of that goal would create labels of: Happy, Successful, Good, Superior, Prosperous, Confident, Powerful, Enthusiastic. In other words, the material "effects" were necessary only in so far as they were the "vehicles" for producing labels that you desired! What could be more simple; wear the labels before, during, after the "effects" are in your grasp.

I sometimes "go around and around" with people that are slow in admitting they can see what I'm saying. For instance, someone will say, "But, being those labels doesn't replace the cold, hard cash in the bank!" To which, I will reply, "Why do you want the cash?" "So I can buy things.", is the general reply. "What would you buy?", I ask. "Cars, a house, trips, jewelry, stocks.", they say. "Why would you want to spend the money?", I ask. Finally, they start to understand, "Well, the new car would sure make me feel good, and a bigger house would sure make the family happy, and I enjoy wearing expensive jewelry...it makes me feel successful and confident to know that I can afford the nice things in life." AH-HAH! The physical "effects" were only props in a stage play so the players would know where they were to stand, and how to act, and how to feel. Have you ever seen the "props" that are set up for a fake movie scene? They are there for the viewing. They are real, but unreal. They'll be torn down once their useful life is through. They provide the scenery and the color and the background, but it is the emotions, and feelings, and attitudes of the players that make for a great play or movie.

You are closer to your goals than you think. They are just around *the corner of your mind.* The labels are hanging in your closet. You have already completed your diagrams. Now it is the proper time to proceed with some tools that will help you implement goals. Until you knew where you wanted to go (goals, directions, end results, etc.) I couldn't help...and, all the tools in the world would have been useless. In our workshops, I repeat a certain phrase often that disturbs a lot of people. I say, "I hate seeing someone lose by default, and when you don't set goals and plan to attain those goals you have settled on being a failure by default. What a shame to play the game of life and lose by default." Remember the mortality rate? One per person! This is not a practice run ...this is your shot at life on this world...don't lose by default.

I am going to list some of the tools and concepts we will be working through in the rest of the book. It is my desire to offer you as many solutions as possible in rapid-fire order...because I want you to get excited. Excited enough about what you're reading that you'll want to carry this book around with you and read it even when you're supposed to be doing something else. Excited enough that you will get lost in thought and ignore the "cares of life" that constantly drag on you. Excited enough that you will get a little irritated when you have to put the book down or someone interrupts you. I know how excited I got when I realized the order for the six laws; I spent 17 hours over a two day period writing and collecting my thoughts. I still managed to handle all my responsibilities with companies and dealing with people, but it was frustrating...because I wanted to spend my time learning this new "concept" in my life. Here are the tools and concepts that will help you in getting **whatever it is that you want out of life.**

WE WILL COVER:

SUCCESS CYCLES...WHY THEY WORK AND HOW TO GENERATE THEM

FAILURE CYCLES...HOW THEY START AND HOW TO AVOID THEM

THE THREE STUMBLING BLOCKS IN ATTAINING GOALS

THE LABEL RIP OFF GAME AND HOW TO PLAY IT SUCCESSFULLY

USING SOME SIMPLE "RIGHTS" TO BUFFER NEGATIVE PEOPLE

DEVELOPING A MORE POWERFUL IMAGE THROUGH SIMPLE TECHNIQUES

HOW TO INCREASE YOUR PRODUCTIVITY 400% IN ALL AREAS OF LIFE

THE ONLY TRUE POSITIVE MENTAL ATTITUDE THAT WILL PERSIST

12
Thought Cycles

In the last chapter, you probably experienced an "Ah-hah" when you viewed the six diagrams in their completed states. **The main ingredients** for balancing a life **are a series of labels** that hang in THE CLOSET OF YOUR MIND. The physical "effects" of the world are the results that will be added on once life "comes into balance". In this chapter, we'll cover the thought processes that eventually end up as "SUCCESS CYCLES" or "FAILURE CYCLES" in a person's life. It is very important to understand the cycles. All of life is a series of cycles. If you were to chart your life, your highs and your lows, you would be able to see the cycles. Everyone has repeated patterns...but not everyone can see themselves. To fully understand your cycles, you will need to understand how a simple thought process looks on paper.

The chart on the next page resembles a clock with letters instead of the traditional numbers. Each time a person makes a minor or major decision, they go through the thought process or cycle.

At **point A: THINK.** This is the "cause" stage; a weighing back and forth of material from the past, present day knowledge, and the potentials or possibilities of the future. Rarely does an individual think without the use of all three time frames.

At **point B: DECIDE.** This is still the "cause" stage, but

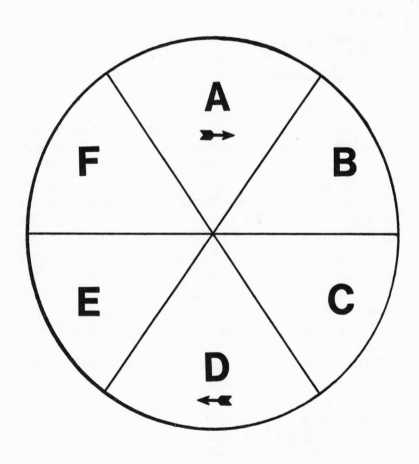

CHART E

once the decision is made, the thought vibrations have accepted one end of the spectrum of opposites. The law of cause and effect is about to bring into physical "beingness", the decision.

At **point C: ACT.** It is at this point that we see some physical "effects"; plans on paper, physically in motion, performance, activity. It is at this point that movement towards a goal, or a direction of thrust can be first seen.

Now you might think that is all there is to a thought cycle, but there's more to come. Up to this point, it has been a fairly uncomplicated process. If this was all there was, millions of problems would instantly cease to be...on this world. There are three additional points on the face of that clock. Let's take a look at them.

At **point D: RETHINK.** It is at this point the individual brings into play "the real person" that hides below the facade the world sees. This is where the big 10 words come into action; Success, Failure, Good, Bad, Winner, Loser, Superior, Inferior, Right, and Wrong. It is at this point a person's *understanding of the six laws*...and *their life-view philosophy*...everything combines into a **rethinking process.** What is amazing is...The measurements upon which to base the rethinking are exactly the same as before point C. Nothing has changed in the world regarding the physical dimension, or details, or extenuating circumstances...the only change is in the mind of the thinker.

At **point E: WORLDLY EFFECTS.** The physical universe is a mirror in which we see reflected our thought process. The world has positives and negatives. The world has good and bad situations. The world has successful ventures and failures. And, within the same situation will be success and failure...depending on *"who" is looking for "what".* A person that has "locked onto" the negative side of the Law of Opposites will be blinded to the opportunities and positive possibilities inherent in a particular situation. I have seen this thousands of times in business. Individuals start through the thought cycle, reach **point B,** and make a very wise business decision. They then proceed through **point C** by acting upon their decision. It is at the next stage of the thought process they experience problems. At **point D**, their rethinking is totally negative. The rethinking (**point D**) can sometimes occur within 15 minutes of **point C**. Nothing has changed, no new facts are known, all information remains the same...the only change is the life-view philosophy of the individual (coupled with their particular label structure) locking onto the "wrong end" of the spectrum in terms of opposites. What you look for...you will find. **Point E: WORLDLY EFFECTS**, is not reserved for business decisions. Every area of life has the law of opposites working within it. No area is without the laws...they are always at work; equally, fairly, justly for all.

At **point F: IDENTIFICATION FOR THE FUTURE.** Based on the outcome of the decision, what was seen in the physical world, the individual makes a vow, a pledge, a confirmation, a reinforcement, a modification of their thinking processes. Based on "the experience", the individual reconfirms their rethinking process (**point D**) for future use.

Of course, you can see the problem when the individual reconfirms **point D**. If the **point D** was different than **points A, B, and C** the individual has negated their ability to THINK WISELY...MAKE WISE DECISIONS...AND BE DECISIVE IN THEIR ACTIONS. They have placed their faith and their destiny in **point D**...which I often label the point of DOUBT. What so often happens is...people begin to let the **point D's** rule their lives. The destruction of the individual begins when they start to blame **points A, B, and C**; first they blame **point C** and start avoiding action...then, they blame **point B** and stop making decisions...and finally, they blame **point A**...and stop thinking. We joked earlier about "solid like stone", but it's not always a joke. Some people lead such negative, browbeaten, harassed lives...they have given up any attempt at original thought. **Point F** is the bail-out time for the negative thinker, and the super-charged happy point of confirmation for the positive thinker. The negative person "leaves the field" discouraged at **point F**. The positive person gets so excited and recharged at **point F** they almost bubble over with enthusiasm. Their joy and happiness and sense of fulfillment is so great, they can improve the environment by just walking into a room.

That's a rather quick explanation of the thought process; **quick but thorough.** Once a person completes the cycle, they are usually involved in another cycle immediately. Thinking, deciding, acting, rethinking, seeing the effects, and identifying and storing the results for future use. You and I and everyone else... *we've all learned* to go through the cycles. The big question to be answered is this; are your cycles predominantly **success cycles** or are they **failure cycles?** The difference is how you handle the rethinking at **point D.** If your rethinking is a support system (a reinforcement) of **points A, B, and C,** you will constantly see your thoughts and decisions turn out positive. If your rethinking runs contraproductive (in opposition) to **points A, B, and C,** you will constantly see yourself making wrong decisions, mistakes, and undertaking losing operations.

In the world of business, highly paid professional management people are highly paid because they have the ability to THINK, DECIDE, and ACT... and, because they believe in their thinking, and their decisions, and in their ability to act... they are successful more often than not. This does not mean that they are *always right*... it just means they are right most of the time... *when it counts.*

Very successful people expect the world to reward their efforts. The failures of the world expect everything to go wrong. There's nothing new about that statement. I have not found some magical formula hidden in a box somewhere. You realize the statement to be true. Can you also see the truth in the diagram demonstrating a thought cycle? I hope so, because the **point D's** of your life may need some changing if you are to realize the fulfillment of your goals.

I am going to use some double-talk on you for just a moment, but I'll explain it fully so it will be meaningful. A success cycle is a success cycle because **point F** is a reinforcement of **point D** which is a reinforcement of **points A, B, and C**. A failure cycle is a success cycle for a failure, because **point F** is a reinforcement of **point D** which is all a failure can see as real in their world. A person that is in a failure cycle gets very little reinforcement of **points A, B, and C** in their lives. Consequently, it becomes easier and easier for them to allow the rethinking process to over-ride their "original" thinking, their "original" decisions, and their "original" actions. They soon become proficient at being successful...unfortunately the process they become proficient at is the process of being successful at being a failure...constantly.

This chapter is designed to get you thinking about your rethinking process. What are your *predominant* thought patterns once you have started acting upon your decisions? What labels do you reach inside and put on to wear after you have passed the **point C's** in your life?

I am going to quickly discuss some failure cycles. As I do, listen for the voice inside that talks to you. Listen and hear what that voice is telling you about the way you have dealt with the **point D's** in your past.

The examples I will use are fairly commonplace, such as: Going back to school...Changing jobs...Learning to dance ...Building your own business...Buying a new car...Getting married...Selecting a new outfit...Becoming a Christian... Investing your money...Going to a new restaurant...Taking a new route across town...Picking an occupation...Selecting a movie...Deciding to follow through on the methods of this book.

We'll use the chart E for reference and mentally fill-in the points as we discuss the thought cycle appropriate for each situation. We'll cover enough of the examples to establish the pattern *for a failure type person...and the failure cycle* they will constantly create.

GOING BACK TO SCHOOL: A - I think I'll go back to school...**B -** Yes, that's what I really need to get ahead in this world. I'll do it...**C -** Fills out enrollment forms, selects classes, etc...**D - Rethinks.** This is going to be real difficult. It was hard years ago in schools, and I've gotten older (whatever that means), and I've got so many responsibilities that need my attention I won't be able to find study time. It was probably a dumb mistake to think I could do it. **NOW COMES POINT E** - The physical world reflects back exactly what the individual expected...**F - Bail-out time.** I knew I couldn't do it. I knew all my other problems and responsibilities would keep me from studying. I knew it was a dumb mistake. I told myself weeks ago...I should have listened and saved myself all this hassle.

CHANGING JOBS: A - I think I ought to change jobs. I'm not getting ahead in this job. I'm not happy at this company...**B - Yes**, I'm going to change jobs...**C** - Fills out job applications, starts interviews, accepts offers (maybe even makes the move)...**D - Rethinks.** This is going to be difficult. I'm not going to know any of the people (whatever that means) on the new job. What if they ask me to do things I'm not comfortable with doing? What if the management people aren't like the people at my old company? It was probably a dumb mistake to make a move. I wonder if I shouldn't just stay at my old company? **NOW COMES POINT E** - The world reflects back exactly what they had expected to see...**F -Bail-out time.** I knew I shouldn't have made a move. I just knew everyone would be different at that new company. I knew it was going to be a dumb mistake. I should have listened to myself when I first thought it was a mistake.

LEARNING TO DANCE: A - People really look like they're having fun dancing. I think I'd like to learn to dance and have fun too...**B - Yes**, that's what I'm going to do. I'm going to get involved right away....**C** - Joins a dance class, or goes to a location where people can dance. **D - Rethinks.** This is going to be awkward. I haven't danced in years. I won't know what to do. Everyone will probably think I'm "foolish looking". I never was very good at dancing. It will be hard for me to learn the new steps. This was a dumb idea. **NOW COMES POINT E** - The world will supply them exactly what was expected. In the beginning, the dance steps are different.

They are uncomfortable on the dance floor. They think every-one is looking at them...**F - Bail-out time.** I knew I couldn't do it. It was stupid to drag myself out on the dance floor and make an idiot of myself. How embarrassing! I'll never do something foolish like that again. That just proves how uncoordinated I am. Never again.

BUILDING A BUSINESS: A - I think I would like to build up my own business. I understand that almost 90% of all the wealthy people in the United States own their own busi-nesses. Sounds really good to me...**B - Yes,** that's exactly what I'm going to do. I am going to start a new business...**C -** Investigates business opportunities. Collects data. Invests time and effort and money into a business start-up...**D - Rethinks.** Here I am putting my time and effort and money on the line, and I don't even know if it will be a success. I've never operated a successful business before. What if the econ-omy is unstable (tell me a time when it wasn't) and my business fails? There's going to be a lot of problems in getting this business off the ground. I know things are going to go wrong. They always go wrong in everything I undertake. Maybe I'll be able to cut my losses short if the business starts to fail. **NOW COMES POINT E -** The world rewards them with exactly what they looked for; instability in every newspaper article, problems around every corner, the potential for loss in every wrong move...**F - Bail-out time.** I just knew it was a mistake to try to own my own business. I just don't have what it takes to be self-employed. I told myself I shouldn't have stuck with it. It's a good thing I was able to get out before I lost my shirt entirely. I should be able to recoup the $3,000 I lost as long as I don't do something "stupid" like owning a business again.

I think I'll...**BUY SOME STOCK: A -** I think getting involved in something safe like good, solid stocks would be a good idea...**B -** Yes, that's exactly what I'm going to do. I'm going to find myself a reliable stock broker that really knows what's up in the market, and put my money to work...**C -** Watches the stock market, talks to brokers, invests the money, receives stock certificates...**D - Rethinks.** I probably did a dumb thing. I put all my faith in one stock broker, and now my money is tied up in stocks. What if the economy is unstable (same old story) and my stocks lose value? What if the broker made a mistake. After all, it isn't his money that would be lost. If those stocks start to drop, I'm going to call and tell the broker to sell immediately. But, what if I sell, and then the stock picks back up. Oh, this was a foolish thing to do. Well, I'll keep an eye on the newspaper and call him if the stock drops. **NOW COMES POINT E -** Stocks rise and fall. The economy is always in the process of change. There is good, and also, bad. There are positive and negative situations. Sooner or later, the world will reward our failure cycle person with exactly what he or she wanted....**F - Bail-out time.** Sell the stock at a loss. A vow and a pledge and a condemnation all wrapped up together; I was so foolish to think that I could outsmart the "big boys"...I'll never get involved in something risky again. Maybe a savings account...oh no, the interest's too low.

Let's take a look at one more major decision. I won't waste your time with all the little decisions that will fit into this diagram. Little decisions that end up *contributing* to the failure cycle. Little decisions like "buying a new outfit", "taking the freeway as opposed to taking the surface streets", or "should I order the veal dish?" The **point D's** of life can infiltrate into every life situation and decision...souring the joy and happiness of *even* "the Sunday drive". A very important point to realize is this: I AM NOT SUGGESTING THAT ANY OF THE SITUATIONS ARE "BAD" DECISIONS OR "GOOD" DECISIONS. I am saying that people go through the thought process and at **point D,** they *create good or bad results* for their lives. Every one of the examples could turn out positive if the individual was in a success cycle. I mentioned in the very beginning of these examples that I was going to demonstrate "FAILURE CYCLES". We can just as easily go back through the examples and create success cycles.

I am going to demonstrate a failure cycle once again. As my example, I am going to use a very serious subject matter.

Subject matter that is of major importance to me...and hopefully to you. The subject for discussion is the decision of *a Christian to witness.*

SHOULD I WITNESS: A - I Think it would be a good idea to express my Christian feelings to the people in my life that are important to me. It always makes me feel so "uplifted" to share Christ, and I know that the joy of bringing someone to Christ is without words...**B -** Yes, I am going to start opening myself up to people. I have decided, I am going to spread the Word...**C -** Get a little more into the Bible. Talk with some people that I respect in the church; people at their place of work....**D - Rethink.** This is going to be difficult. Most people are set in their ways. It's easy to think of God, but the minute you bring up Christ you just don't know what your friends will think. I'll probably feel really uncomfortable, and who am I to interfere in another person's life. Most people will look at me as though I was one of those "weirdo characters" that float around with Bibles tucked under their arms. I'll probably lose the friendship of some people that resent my sharing. **NOW COMES THE WORLD...POINT E -** The world contains all situations, but the individual that expects the worse...*will reap exactly what they have planted* in their rethinking process. This individual will approach other people in their environment (maybe one or two) *looking for the rejection, the criticism and the "turn down"*...**Bail-out time** ...**POINT F -** I knew I couldn't do it. I just knew the guys at work would be shocked. I told myself that Bill and Sue would think me a little weird, and now they've started cancelling out on some of our invitations for social activities. I should have listened to myself; you just can't impose on people to listen. Well, that's one part of the Bible I just can't go along with in my life. I can go along with everything else except:

"Go therefore and make disciples of all the nations, baptizing them in the name of the Father and the Son and the Holy Spirit, teaching them to observe all that I commanded you; and lo, I am with you always, even to the end of the age." (Matt. 28:19, 20) and...

"Blessed are you when men cast insults at you, and
persecute you, and say all kinds of evil against you
falsely, on account of me." (Matt. 5:11)

and a few dozen other choice passages sprinkled throughout
the Word.

Every time you as an individual allow the **point D's** of life
to run, and to control your life, you give up the fantastic
potential the Lord has given you to be decisive in your thinking...to be decisive in your actions. When you let **point D's**
rule your life you have reached the point where thinking...
original thought...is being ruled by the labels of the world.
Remember the labels that the world hung on you for the
convenience of the world?

Success cycles go through the same six steps, but the
difference is the control the individual exercises at **point D.**
The control I'm talking about is the ability to overrule, to take
charge, to dwell on the more positive end of the spectrum of
Opposites. The control is the learned ability to "choose the
appropriate labels", to interject your goals, to identify yourself
with a long-term "major purpose" that will use each success
cycle to progressively attain long-term "major goals."

Everyone does not have that control. When I went
through the examples of failure cycles, you were probably
noticing similarities between some of the examples and people, or situations, in your world. In fact, you might have been
thinking, "Most of the people I know seem to be locked into a
variety of failure cycles." **That's right!** That's why so many
people are realizing so little joy and happiness and success and
prosperity in their lives. Let's talk about changing the cycles.
Let's talk about what can be implanted at **point D**...that will
change the cycles to success cycles.

In the next chapter, we will capture one major concept; the
understanding of "Major Purpose" as it relates to your goals.
When you wrote goals for the six areas of life, you were
beginning to design an all-encompassing "Major Purpose" for
your life. I don't want such *an imposing set of words* to shock

you. The only way I could express my idea of goals stacked upon goals...and all leading towards a common multi-layered huge goal...was to use a set of labels, "Major Purpose." Let's take a look at "Major Purpose", and how easy life becomes when we have one.

13
Major Purpose

The dictionary defines PURPOSE as "A result aimed at. The end to be attained. To propose as an aim to oneself." Whichever way we choose to view PURPOSE, it is quite apparent the subject matter will be linked with goals and directions. A "Major Purpose" could then be thought of as an all-encompassing "result" or "end to be attained" or "aim in life". That is the way I am going to use the thought "Major Purpose" in relationship to all that has gone before us in this book. You might have a feeling of being overwhelmed by such lofty terms, but don't let it scare you. Some people can state their "Major Purpose" in a handful of words. Mary Ellen uses only seven words to express hers...I'm a little more wordy, I take just over twenty words to cover mine.

Your "Major Purpose" is a compilation of your goals, and what you want to accomplish in your time on this world. It is an over-riding theme upon which your goals will flow towards completion. It is exciting...more than that, it is thrilling, to finally write down your "Major Purpose". You will find that an amazing *process* will start once you have identified, voiced, and committed to paper your "Major Purpose".

I am going to describe *the process* for you. If we've met in the past years, you know that I am a methodical person...even though I'm in marketing and management. Most marketing people rush ahead and then have to go back over their "tracks" to pick up all the loose ends. I like to cover every step in detail as I go. I save hundreds of hours of "pick up" time each year that way. I'll cover the four steps in the process so you'll know where the process leads...prior to writing your first draft of a "Major Purpose".

A well-defined PURPOSE is suggested by every great book in the field of personal development, but I propose instead that you have an all-encompassing, larger-than-life, huge, PURPOSE that will embrace *all of your goals*...for all the areas of your life. It is possible to have an over-all PURPOSE that will be that large...that inspiring...that all-encompassing. *But, it won't be possible* if you follow most of the textbooks that have you define your PURPOSE as it relates to one small segment of life, or to one tiny corner of your business world. The first step in the process is **PURPOSE.**

The result you will see in your life upon setting and defining your PURPOSE will be **DESIRE.** The larger your PURPOSE...the larger and greater will be your DESIRE for the fulfillment of that PURPOSE. DESIRE is often thought of as "the strength of feeling" and implies "very strong intentions". If PURPOSE is thought of as the target to be aimed for, then DESIRE is the driving force to reach that target. The greater the PURPOSE, the greater the DESIRE to reach it. The second step in the process is **DESIRE.**

If you have a tremendous DESIRE to accomplish *something...or anything,* you will find the means to bring about the end result. The means for accomplishment will come to you through **INSPIRATION.** The six laws of the universe are always working...always bringing thoughts and energy patterns into physical beingness. In every field of endeavor, great discoveries are made by individuals that set themselves a PURPOSE, work themselves into a high state of DESIRE to accomplish that PURPOSE, and then gather together whatever it takes to solve the situation. From where does the formula come? How is it that one man unlocks so many secrets? How does God know who needs to be lifted up with an idea? If I would bottle INSPIRATION and sell it...the price tag would be millions per bottle. There are that many people that want it. But, why even consider trying to bottle something that is free for the asking. Anyone that really wants INSPIRATION will have to go through the process to get it. They will have to come up with a PURPOSE they acknowledge as worthwhile. They will then get a measure of DESIRE...just enough to accomplish their PURPOSE. If they select a little PURPOSE, they will get a small measure of DESIRE. If they choose a large PURPOSE, they will have a larger measure of DESIRE. And the DESIRE will cause them to seek out the necessary means for the successful accomplishment of their PURPOSE. They will receive some INSPIRATION to help them along their way. The original PURPOSE will set in motion how much DESIRE, and also the amount and direction of the INSPIRATION. If their original PURPOSE was of a positive nature and in balance, then their DESIRE and the INSPIRATION they receive will also be of a positive nature and in the proper balance to bring about the right results.

INSPIRATION in the dictionary is defined as "guidance" or an act or force that "influences". I believe that without INSPIRATION all the DESIRE in the world would not find solutions; DESIRE does not discover new means, new methods, or new ideas. DESIRE provides the drive, the strong feelings and intentions, but INSPIRATION provides the means. The third step in the process is therefore **INSPIRATION.**

When the three steps in the process are combined in the proper balance, the PURPOSE (whether large or small) will be brought to a state of accomplishment and realization.

At the point of realization, a fourth step or state will come about. The fourth step can be labeled in a variety of ways; Happiness, Joy, Ecstasy, and Energetic Synergism are the most common ways of expressing "the charge" that goes through an individual when they complete the steps. The fourth step (let's call it **HAPPINESS** or **JOY**) is an essential part of the process...in fact, an absolutely essential step. If it (the fourth step) does not come about, an individual would be totally drained in the process of accomplishment; totally drained perhaps to the point of ceasing to exist. The fourth step of **HAPPINESS or JOY** recharges, revitalizes, and replaces all that was drained out of an individual in the creative process. The HAPPINESS and JOY comes because there is tangible proof that the PURPOSE has been fulfilled. This fourth step completes the cycle...it recharges and "feeds back" into step number one.

You have before you a four-step process that reads: **PURPOSE** creates **DESIRE** which calls forth **INSPIRATION** which upon fulfillment summons forth proportionate **JOY** which fuels and gives life to PURPOSE.

I can demonstrate this process on the small scale and the large. It can be demonstrated in every field of human endeavor. It explains why some people live their lives in apathy and mediocrity, and it also illustrates why others live lives of genius, high intensity, and great service to their fellow man.

Let me describe the mediocre: PURPOSE...just to make it through the day with as few hassles and as little energies expended as possible. DESIRE...just enough to barely get by, and as little interest as possible. INSPIRATION...virtually none. JOY...none.

Now, let me describe any one of **thousands of people that have benefited mankind** *with service, discoveries, dedication, knowledge,* or *benefits* beyond the normal range of performance. PURPOSE...well defined, large, identifiable. DESIRE...high intensity, driving, consuming, strong. INSPIRATION...creative, productive, imaginative, internally guided. JOY...extreme happiness upon fulfilling PURPOSE, self-actualized, self-fulfillment bordering on ecstasy.

It is now time for you to bring forward some of the information you worked on in previous chapters. The information we'll need brought forward can be found in Chart "D's". They contain "the labels" you will be wearing when working towards your goals. Please transfer that information to the chart on the following pages. You are going to have a

LIST BELOW THE MAJOR LABELS IDENTIFIED
IN THE "D" CHARTS...PREVIOUS CHAPTERS.

CHART F

chance to write your "Major Purpose" based on what you want out of life, and we'll need that information in order to do it...please complete it now.

You now have some choices to make in writing your "Major Purpose". The choice you have is whether to rearrange the labels, tie them together into comfortable sentences or paragraphs...or, write a PURPOSE that is all-encompassing and contains the essence of the labels that are listed. I will offer you some suggestions, but I cannot do the actual writing for you...nor can I tell you *which is right for you.* It will only take you a small amount of time once you have the idea of which direction you wish to take. The final words should be your choice...not just copies of the suggestions I will make. However, if it happens that your exact wording ends up similar to something in the text, don't think that you have to change it. Write your "Major Purpose" so it has meaning for you...that's all that counts. The suggestions are only that ...suggestions; appropriate for some people, and unsuitable for others.

SUGGESTIONS

A person whose major labels centered around:
Happy, Prosperous, Generous, Respectful, Kind, Successful, Friendly, Peaceful, At peace, Sociable, Outgoing, Influential, Enthusiastic, Healthy, Strong, and Respected...could develop a "Major Purpose" that would read (remember, this is only one suggestion):

"MY MAJOR PURPOSE is to lead a balanced life fulfilling my goals in each of the six areas of life. I am building a balanced life based on my ability to select and wear Happy, Propserous, Successful, Healthy labels. I am At peace, Respectful, Friendly and Kind with the many individuals that play their parts in my balanced life."

Another person might write with brevity:

"MY MAJOR PURPOSE is to develop harmony in the six areas of my life. Each day as I accomplish goals in the different areas, my life is filled with Happiness, Prosperity and Good Fortune. I am Happy with myself and At peace with all that fills my world."

Others write veritable short essays or stories which include all the labels written in the six diagrams, plus minute details of how the six laws will come into play in their MAJOR PURPOSE.

I have seen the very long...and the very short...such as:

"MY MAJOR PURPOSE is to be a centering point for Happiness." This would be an all-encompassing statement that contains the essence of all the labels listed.

The other type of MAJOR PURPOSE that would be said to be all-encompassing and a vehicle on which all goals (present and future) could be carried would be one such as Mary Ellen's:

MY MAJOR PURPOSE is "To glorify God in everything I do." This encompasses every action, every deed, every thought, and relationship. It serves to set the tone for all decisions and contains the essence of all positive labels.

Or my own:

MY MAJOR PURPOSE is "to lead a balanced life in all that I am. My life is balanced upon the pivotal point of Christ; my talents are His to use in all areas of life." Against this purpose I weigh my decisions.

Now, I would like to share with you one of the saddest examples of "Major Purpose" I have ever seen perpetrated upon any group of people. One morning as I sat typing, I could hear the television in the background. Suddenly, the voice on the TV started talking about real estate...a field in which I am qualified, and somewhat interested (I have trained over 6,000 real estate people in marketing techniques). I stopped typing, got up, and went into the other room to see what was going on. It was a program that trains real estate people in the techniques and skills relevant to their field.

As I entered the room, the discussion was on "losing" ...and how by being a "loser" enough times, you would gain the experience needed for the field. Then, came the major purpose part of the show: "You should repeat over and over and over to yourself. 'MY MAJOR PURPOSE in life is to become the greatest real estate person in the world.' You should eat it, sleep it, breathe it, live it every minute of your day. It should become the most important thing in your life."

That was about all I could take, I walked over and snapped off the TV...and thought to myself "How sick!" What a totally out of balance, small, self-destructive way to state a "Major Purpose". I thought about all the hundreds (or maybe thousands) of beginning real estate people that would be chanting those words day after day. I thought about the statistics for success in the field of real estate: 75% of the people that enter the field, leave it within the first year as failures, and the real estate field is one of the top occupations in the United States for divorces. The average real estate person in California makes approximately $4,000 per year. Sad facts ...but true.

You've come this far in the book, and we've shared a lot of thoughts between the lines, can you see the lack of wisdom in that TV show? I talked it over with Mary Ellen before including this example...neither of us like negativity...it is foreign to our nature...but, I thought the example would prove a point. Perhaps it shocked you also.

There is a really important point to be covered right now. It is a point of contention which is very confusing to many people, and if we don't cover it right now, you may end up with some confusion in your mind regarding "goals" and "Major Purpose". Many, many people fail to see **the distinction or the differences** between "goals" and a "Major Purpose". If you will think through the next paragraphs, you will understand ...fully understand...the vast differences. Once you fully understand the differences, you will never make the mistake of confusing the two and thinking they are one and the same thing.

A goal is an end result, an objective, or a performance level you wish to attain in *any one of the six areas of life.* I, for instance, can have a goal to be a very competent, highly paid, creative management consultant. At the same time, I can have a goal to be a warm, loving, attentive, supportive husband. In addition, I can have a goal to be a physically active, very healthy, nutritionally sound human being that will live in good health past one hundred years of age. Do you see what I have done? I have set **goals** *in different areas of my life.* When you set goals, you are doing the very same thing; describing end results, objectives, or performance levels...but always, the goal will be in relationship to **an area of life.**

A major purpose encompasses **all your goals.** It is larger than all the individual goals that funnel into, or act as vehicles in, your journey through life. Most of the books that describe "purpose" are teaching an inaccuracy. They talk about "purpose" when they should be using the term "goal". This is why I have had approximately two thousand people approach me in confusion over the last three years. They are confused over how to write a "Major Purpose". Their confusion is because they thought they had been writing their purpose...as they followed the instructions in PMA books...but, it turned out they had only been writing goals. Let me make this very clear: Writing goals for the different areas of life is very, very important, but writing a "Major Purpose" is **even more important.** In fact, writing goals without having a "Major Purpose" (that will act as a guideline) is almost always a waste of time. The "Major Purpose" is essential as a guideline for setting worthwhile goals. If a goal in an area brings you closer to attaining your "Major Purpose", it will tend to create a positive experience. If a goal is set (in any area) that runs contraproductive to your "Major Purpose", you can imagine the chaos, the confused and unorganized state that will be created...can't you?

You have written an all-encompassing "Major Purpose" if...you can *systematically and progressively attain your purpose* regardless of the area of life in which your are involved. This means that you should be able to feel accomplishment of your "Major Purpose" *any time* you are working on *any goal.* Can you see the joy in life that results when every goal has as its end result the promotion of YOUR MAJOR PURPOSE.

Now it's time for you to put some of your thoughts on paper. Combine the words...develop a thought...write... change...do something. There are no"A's" for excellence of grammar. Just the satisfaction that comes from finally doing it. Years from now, you'll read back over your notes, and thank yourself for putting down your thoughts. Mark my words, the day will come *when you'll look back.* If you have continued reading without writing, please stop...and write ...please stop reading and finish the diagram marked "My Major Purpose". Later in the book you will need to come back to this diagram and recopy your statement, and it will be more meaningful if you have completed "Major Purpose" at the time it was fresh in your mind.

MY MAJOR PURPOSE

FIRST WRITING

SECOND WRITING

FINAL WRITING

CHART G

In the next chapter, I will share with you the three stumbling blocks to success in every human endeavor. Remember the definition of success? "The progressive attainment of desired goals." The three blocks (of which I speak) are the three conflicts that an individual faces in the "progressive attainment" portion of the definition. We have a saying in our business world. Mary Ellen and I say it thousands of times each year to tens of thousands of people. It goes like this:

"Will your daily activity support
the end result you desire?"

Let's get on with a short, but thorough, explanation of the three "stumbling blocks" that get in the way of everyone that has ever sought to "progressively attain" any daily activities.

14
Stumbling Blocks

There are only three "Stumbling Blocks" that will get in your way once you have done the work to identify your goals, your labels, and your "Major Purpose" in life. This book is an action, doing, performance book, and I want to make certain that you know about the three problem areas before you have to deal with them. It's important that you think through the handling of the three "Stumbling Blocks", so you will have a plan of action when they arise. I am not saying that you should consume hours and days in thought on these negative items; just be aware that they exist and know how you'll deal with them when you come upon them.

If you were walking down a pathway that was twenty feet wide, and suddenly came upon a cactus plant that was about six feet tall and two feet wide...you'd have some choices to make. Now, one choice would be to pretend that the cactus plant (with it's sharp spines) didn't exist. And, using your best "PMA attitude", just walk right through it. A second method would be to imagine the six foot cactus as being much smaller than it really is; to rationalize it away as insignificant compared to your abilities. Get a good run at it, make a super human effort, and try to clear it "in a single bound". Another choice you could make is to boldly approach, assess the situation, get your shovel and support timbers...and spend the next two years digging and churning in sand. You'd be

involved in building the most glorious, magnificent tunnel the world has ever seen... *under that cactus plant*. There is a fourth way that many people use when presented obstacles. They cautiously approach, focus on those long, sharp spines, and they decide that *they really didn't want to go any further on the path*. At that point, they either sit down and wail life away, or they go back on the path; grumbling and griping all the way.

You're probably way ahead of my writing. You've probably already decided that **the smart thing** to do would be: Sidestep, walk around, avoid that block in your path. That's why this chapter exists; to identify the "blocks" so you can *sidestep them...avoid them...walk around,* and get on with your goals in life.

The three "stumbling blocks" are: 1) Habits 2) Stress, and 3) Procrastination. "Habits", "stress", and "procrastination" are the names (labels) given to the three types of conflicts a person experiences when any change in "the order" is initiated. If you have a goal, you will encounter one, two, or possibly all three "stumbling blocks!" And, just like the cactus sitting in the middle of a very wide path, you can choose any one of the methods I outlined: 1) Pretend it does not exist and suffer. 2) Misjudge it, and your ability to hurdle the block. 3) Spend years in overcoming the block... instead of proceeding towards your goal. 4) Quit. 5) Understand the situation. Sidestep it, avoid falling, and continue on towards your goal.

In order to understand why the "stumbling blocks" exist, we need to use the six laws of the universe, and apply them to the situations. I want you to imagine a large platter of freshly cooked liver and onions. Imagine the aroma, all hot and steaming, rising from this dish. You've had a reaction, and the reaction was either positive or negative. The law of OPPO-SITES works that way...even with the few people that say, "Well, I don't feel too strongly one way or the other." **Not to decide, is to decide!** If you did not align yourself with those that "like", you have taken a position. You must be one of those people that *don't like* liver and onions...and that's okay. It's perfectly fine to like or dislike liver and onions. I'm just using liver and onions as an example.

Everything of this world is judged positive by some people and negative by others...this is called *a conditioned response.* Some of the readers of this book almost got sick when I mentioned liver, and others have very positive reactions (if you're on a diet, I hope I haven't made you hungry). Let's take a look at a very incomplete list of words that will be judged *very positive by some people and very negative by others:* Liver and Onions, Tuna Fish, Steak, Spinach, Strawberries, Snails, Family Outings, Work, Freedom, Cadillacs, Free Enterprise, Love, Marriage, Happiness, Boating, Tidiness, Handicaps, Loafing, Rock Music, Company Loyalty, War, Reading Books, Goal Planning, Children, and the list goes on forever ...until we list everything. The items you feel positive towards, you will want in your life. Those you feel negative towards, you exclude as much as possible.

Positive and negative feelings (conditionings) are easy to understand. Now, let's put our understanding to use in looking at the three "stumbling blocks". On the next page, you will see the three "stumbling blocks" as they appear once the conditionings (the positive and negative reactions) are placed properly. The three boxes on the right side of the page indicate how you feel and react at this time in your life. The three boxes on the left side of the page are going to indicate something new you are bringing into your life.

HABITS

We'll talk about habits first. On the diagram, you will see that the right hand box contains a "positive" sign. That means you in some way *like, approve, need, want* or *desire* "something". And now, you have decided to bring something new into your life...something that you feel is positive also. The conflict comes about when the two positive "somethings" are both competing for the same time frame, and/or have end results that are diametrically opposed.

OH BOY!   **OH YEECH!**

HABITS
STRESS
PROCRASTINATION

SOMETHING NEW: FEELINGS NOW:

CHART H

I'll give you some examples that demonstrate both. Let's say your right side positive "something" is...you like to watch TV. It's an accepted way of life in the United States. The average TV is on for approximately 8 hours daily...so, someone feels it is positive. And, you like and desire and want to watch TV...and that's okay. Until you find out that you could use some of those 56 hours each week to make yourself a fortune in extra money. Now, you really want what the extra income would provide...that's positive. But, something else is competing for the same time frame. You would now have a "positive-positive" conflict. The end result in both cases might be "the enjoyment of my leisure time". Two different methods or pathways...but, the same goal.

An example of diametrically opposed end results would be if your right side positive "something" was *something like;* eating to obesity, drinking to excess, drugs that destroy, smoking like a chimney, or any others of the things we often call habits. Don't get me wrong, I'm not passing judgment on any of these habits. I choose to view them as negatives, and other people choose to view them as positives. That's why they do them. I have my own particular way of spending my 168 hours each week...**and so do you.** Some people would view my habit of reading 10 to 14 books each week as a total waste of precious time...and that does "smack" as being a little negative in response...doesn't it?

Let's get back to our individual that has a habit they would like to change. Let's pick on the eating habit...after all, approximately 60 million people in the United States want to lose weight. Which tells me "SOMEBODY'S EATING THE FOOD", and liking it (positive). The habit is on the right side of the page, and the new behavior (and subsequent end result) would be listed on the left side of the page. Diametrically opposed goals, and the problem is compounded by the inability to totally eliminate the right hand side positive. We would therefore have a "positive-positive" conflict that might rage within the individual for the entirety of their life.

Enough talk about the different kind of habits. Let's look

at the process for side-stepping the conflict. I'm going to describe a simple process that describes how and why you do your habit so very proficiently...and what needs to be done **if you want to change!**

1. You do something now. You do it with perfection. You do it without conscious thought. You can repeat the pattern of doing it...almost unconsciously.
2. You change. In the beginning, you perform, imperfectly. You must consciously think through every effort. You cannot repeat the pattern...unless you consciously think it through.
3. You continue the new pattern. You do it with perfection. You can only perform it perfectly with conscious thought. You can repeat the pattern perfectly as long as you think it through each time.
4. The new pattern becomes your habit. You do it with perfection. You do it without conscious thought. You can repeat the pattern...almost unconsciously.

It is amazing how proficient an individual can become at: Watching TV or eating or sleeping in late every morning...or any of the ten thousand other things you do by habit. William James, a philosopher and early writer on psychology, wrote "Ninety-nine hundredths or possibly nine hundred and ninety-nine thousandths of our activity is purely automatic and habitual, from our rising in the morning to our lying down each night." Anything you perform consistently can become a "habit".

You will be able to side-step old habits if you will use the materials in this book. Think of it this way, "Your habits have you doing exactly what you do...for exactly the results you have...right now." If your diagrams (on goals) contain anything new, or different, you must attempt something new. I'll share with you another sobering thought, "Every habit, every repeated action, everything you do is part of the CLOSET OF YOUR MIND". Each morning you clothe yourself in the labels that you choose, and some of those labels are directly opposed to **your goals and your "Major Purpose" in life.**

STRESS

Stress is an interesting situation that many people feel is too far beyond their ability to read and understand...but, that's not true! On the page with the six boxes, you will see a negative sign in the right hand box labeled stress. In the box on the left side of the page, is a positive sign. What we have here is a conflict that is caused when you bring something new into your life that you feel will be a positive...and *part* of your label structure reacts negatively. You would then have a "positive-negative" conflict that might immobilize you temporarily. This is what usually happens when someone stands up to give a speech. It doesn't matter what their label is, or how important they are, or the gravity of the message...they may be unable to voice the words due to the stress. The right side box contains a negative sign, and usually signifies "fear" to the individual. The fear may be extreme. Extreme to the point of causing a short-circuit in the person's body, or extreme to the point of causing long-term illness. "Why would anyone risk their life to stay in a situation that causes that much stress?" you might ask. Imagine a person that has dedicated their entire work career to rising within a certain corporation. The income they are paid has risen with the responsibilities. Their entire socio-economic lifestyle is now dependent on that income and position. Suddenly, they are transferred to a new division in the corporation or the corporation makes changes that change the "climate" of the environment...and, they are told to turn the division profitable within six months or "heads will roll". They want to perform, they must have the money, their prestige is on the line (all positive desires), but they are now experiencing fear. When the desire, and the fear, are wrapped up in the same task ...watch out...there's trouble brewing...in this, an extremely stressful situation.

I am going to share with you the three most terrible things that could occur in our day-to-day worlds.

1. **You might be rejected.** Someone at work, or home, or

"out there", might reject your thoughts, your ideas, or you.

2. **You might be severely criticized.** Someone might criticize your ideas, your work, your abilities, or you.

3. **You might make mistakes and people will think you are dumb.** Someone may laugh at you, or your ideas, OR WHAT YOU DID.

We can stand almost anything, except...criticism and rejection by our fellow man. But, I'm going to share with you an astounding truth:

> *They* may reject, and *they* may criticize, and *they* may scoff when you try something new...but it's all an attempt on their part to elevate their own importance or to keep you "in the mold" where *they* feel you belong.

They don't have to live in your body. *They* have no right to determine happiness for you. *They* really don't know where you want to go with your life, and *they really don't care* (for the most part) if you get there or reach your goals. Most of the stress that you will ever experience in implementing your goals and your "Major Purpose" will be caused by other people trying to get you **to give up...to quit...to revert.** You will be able to handle the small twinges of negative feelings caused by other people once you know how to play "THE LABEL RIP OFF GAME". That's a great game you'll learn to play a little later in the book...look for it to be a real "eye-opener".

PROCRASTINATION

This is the last of the three "stumbling blocks", and for most people that take one of our workshops, the least troublesome to handle. On the right side of the page, is a negative sign...and on the left side of the page is...*a negative also.* Procrastination comes about when the action at hand is negative, and the alternatives are also negative. What a state to be in...nothing positive...no desire to perform...no interest. The tendency will be to put off the task. Maybe tomorrow things will be more positive...more interesting...more exciting.

Does that sound like the problem of procrastination that strikes most people? It certainly does! The problem of course is: Most people do not bring into their lives exciting, positive, stimulating tasks. Why? They have ill-defined goals. They have no idea what their "Major Purpose" would be if they wrote it. And, they have no ideas about setting priorities for accomplishing "whatever it is" that would make their lives make more sense.

I can promise you this: If you have been filling in the charts and diagrams throughout this book, you will find within those charts positive ideas...positive goals...and excitement. There is something exciting and electrifying about seeing your future in print...spread out in front of you. In the back part of this book, I will share with you some time management techniques that will give you hundreds of extra, unencumbered hours each month. You can use those hours to accomplish whatever is important in your life. Effective time management is exciting!

Many times, business people ask us to conduct seminars on time management techniques. Mary Ellen and I enjoy the workshops...and it is always a great experience to see people become more productive in their businesses, and I enjoy sharing the most important techniques with you. You are going to have an advantage over the people we see in a seminar within a corporation, because...you will be able to take the time to apply the techniques **to all six areas of your life.** You will be able to go over the material time after time...and systematically adjust your plan of action. In this way, you will get a finely tuned program *that will be personalized...just for you.*

In the next chapter, we are going to collect together all the notes we've been making throughout the book. We'll collect our thoughts, crystalize the label patterns, and get set-up for the final chapters on techniques and tools. It would be advisable to set aside at least 45 minutes of uninterrupted time for the exercises. You'll also need your pen or pencil, some scratch paper, and you might want to refill your favorite beverage before we start.

15
What's It Going To Be?

What's it going to be like in your world from now on? This chapter is a series of exercises that will help you collect your thoughts, your diagrams, your goals, your labels, and your "Major Purpose"...and condense them into a workable arrangement. Remember when we covered the chapter on the six laws? I mentioned that not one out of perhaps ten thousand people know what the laws are...or what they control ...or how to use them. *We will use what we have been studying* in the series of exercises within this chapter. There is a saying in the business world that goes "IF YOU DON'T USE IT...YOU LOSE IT!" Many good ideas are dropped because someone temporarily sets the idea aside...they didn't use it...and consequently, they lost it. Each time we run through the material, a greater portion is used and retained by your mind. Let's quickly check the order of the laws: 1) ORDER... 2) VIBRATION... 3) OPPOSITES... 4) CAUSE and EFFECT... 5) ATTRACTION... 6) DUALITY. Remember?

This book was written in reverse order. I started with DUALITY and worked backwards to ORDER. I started with HAPPINESS and JOY (of the four steps PURPOSE, DESIRE, INSPIRATION, and JOY) and worked backwards through tools and goals to PURPOSE. The book was written from an EFFECT position backwards to CAUSE. In doing this, I knew you would be able to see results immediately. Also, you would be able to see the laws at work in every event in your life. When I say "every event", I mean seeing the laws at work from your very first thought in the morning upon rising...to the final, last act you will complete on this world; daily...and ultimately!

Sobering thought isn't it? It certainly is, and it is also a very exciting thought. Perhaps some of the most exciting news we can share is this: fortunately...you are accountable.

You are accountable for what you do in this world.

You are accountable for your success...or failure.

You are accountable for the good you do.

You are accountable for all you do that is good for nothing.

You are accountable for the balance in your world.

You are accountable for the example you demonstrate.

You are accountable for the uplifting of mankind.

You are accountable for the lives you help or destroy.

You are accountable for the knowledge you are given ...and give.

You are accountable for that which you believe.

You are accountable for what you give in return for your gifts.

You are accountable for the talents entrusted to you.

You are accountable for the kind of person you can become. I see within the six laws a gigantic plan of growth, potential, order and inspiration spread before the human race. **You and I** are a part of this universe, this whole, *and as such, we have options to exercise.*

Let's exercise our options to the fullest. Let's become all that we can in the short stay we have upon this planet. Let's at least accomplish the goals we say we want, and live our lives with intensity.

One of my children said to me "Dad, I hope this next school year goes real fast so summer will get here quickly." My discussion with her went like this "Honey, I hope it seems to take forever for next summer to get here..." And, I went on to explain why including the good, happy things that would happen during the year. Perhaps, you feel that way also. I hope so. I like to fill each day with so much living, so many exciting tasks and accomplishments, and so much learning that sometimes weeks seem like they are years long. Remember, life is worth living. If you've fallen into the trap of wishing away the weeks to get to the weekends, or promising yourself, "Oh, I'll be happy when...", perhaps this chapter will be a pivotal point in your life. Remember the definition of a pivotal point? "A point in time, place and circumstances when the decision that is made affects the quality of life from that point forward."

We are at the point of collecting all the good thoughts and decisions you've made on charts throughout the chapters we've already completed. Let's collect that information onto the charts on the pages that follow. The double page of charts contain spaces for your decisions made in charts "A", "B", "C", "F", and "G". Use the following instructions to properly collect the information:

MY MAJOR LABELS

You have a collection of MAJOR LABELS of identification that you wear. These labels of identification encompass the major relationships in which you are involved at this time in your life. You will find them in CHART A. Please transfer them from CHART A to the proper place in the double page charts that follow.

You also have a collection of MAJOR LABELS that identify feelings, emotions, and attitudes of a positive nature. Take a piece of scratch paper and go to CHART "B". Collect only the positive labels that are conducive to the accomplishment of your goals. Once you have collected the labels from CHART "B", proceed to CHART "F", and collect the labels that you have identified as absolutely essential for you to wear...if, you are to acquire your desired goals. Once you have collected all the labels having to do with emotions, feelings, and attitudes,

MY MAJOR LABELS
FROM CHART "A"

IDENTIFICATIONS:

FROM CHART "F"

FROM CHART "B"

FEELINGS, EMOTIONS AND ATTITUDES
THAT WILL HELP ATTAIN MY GOALS:

MY MAJOR GOALS
FROM CHARTS
LABELED "C"

SPIRITUAL:

FAMILY:

FINANCIAL:

SOCIAL:

PHYSICAL

MENTAL:

MY MAJOR PURPOSE IN LIFE
FROM CHART "G"

transfer them to the proper places in the double page charts. Do not, I repeat, DO NOT LIST ANY LABEL THAT IN ANY WAY RUNS CONTRAPRODUCTIVE TO YOUR GOALS. Some labels that seem very "worthy" when standing by themselves, are in reality, detrimental to the attainment of your goals. When you start actively wearing the labels you have selected, you will want to make sure you don't get "in a bind" by wearing inappropriate labels for what you want.

MY MAJOR GOALS IN LIFE

Bring forward the statements of your goals from the six areas of your life. You will find the six goal statements in the charts labeled "C" in the first section of the book. You should collect those statements now...and place them in their proper places in the double page charts.

MY MAJOR PURPOSE IN LIFE

In the chapter on "MAJOR PURPOSE", you wrote out a description of your "Major Purpose". You should bring that statement forward to its proper place in the double page charts. You will find that statement in the chart labeled CHART "G".

Once you have collected all that information onto the double page, you will have in front of you:

INFORMATION REGARDING YOUR GOALS, YOUR ASPIRATIONS, YOUR NEEDS, AND YOUR DESIRES. IN FACT, YOU'LL HAVE MORE INFORMATION ABOUT WHAT NEEDS TO BE DONE FOR YOUR LIFE TO PROSPER...**MORE THAN YOU WOULD HAVE KNOWN** BY SPENDING $5000 TO $10,000 FOR CAREER COUNSELING.

PEOPLE THAT FILL YOUR WORLD

There are people in this world that will be affected in the

implementation of your goals. Some of these people will whole-heartedly support your goals...others will react negatively to any change you desire to make. That's the facts ...some people will be shocked that you want to change, and they will react negatively. By understanding "your support people" and "the potential destructive forces", you can learn some tools that will help you through any rough spots.

List below the people that will be rewarded by your goals; those people that will find the new labels pleasant and attractive and positive.

_____ relationship to you _____

_____ relationship to you _____

_____ relationship to you _____

_____ relationship to you _____

_____ relationship to you _____

_____ relationship to you _____

_____ relationship to you _____

If you need more spaces in the beginning, cut a piece of note paper that you can use as a bookmark. Put their names on it, and place it between these pages.

Now, let's take a look at the negative side of the picture. You should have a fairly good idea of the people in your environment that will react in a negative manner to any changes you undertake. You usually know who is "a label ripper" by their past performance. First, we'll identify the potential problem areas, then we'll discuss how you can play "THE LABEL RIP OFF GAME." Who's a potential negative force:

_____ relationship to you _____

_____ relationship to you _____

_____ relationship to you _____

_____ relationship to you _____

_____ relationship to you _____

_____ relationship to you _____

_____ relationship to you _____

_____ relationship to you _____

_____ relationship to you _____

_____ relationship to you _____

If you need more spaces, use your note paper. It is convenient to have this listing for this reason also...as you turn a negative person to your side, you can scratch them off the negative list and add them to your list of supporters.

You will probably have a large group of people that you feel are neither highly POSITIVE nor terribly NEGATIVE. As you follow through with your new labels, you will treat this large group as though they are in the POSITIVE group; highly supportive of your actions...they soon will be.

HABITS

Now, let us take a look at how you spend your time (HABITS) each week. How do you spend your time? How much of your time is already "spoken for" in terms of necessities? What is necessary...and what is not? Fill in the following blanks with what you use of your 168 hours weekly:

_____ hours sleeping (a necessity)

_____ hours eating (a necessity)

_____ hours working (got to pay the bills)

_____ hours in personal care (grooming, etc.)

_____ hours in personal time (devotions)

_____   WHAT'S THE TOTAL

You have just added together a number of hours that will total somewhere between 95 and 135. Which leaves you 30 to 70 hours a week of discretionary time to be accounted for. Are you in the habit of getting very little out of those discretionary hours? Would you like to get more done in less time? Would you like to accomplish perhaps twice as much in the 100 (or so) hours that are necessity hours? In the tools section that follows this chapter, there is an answer for that problem. We'll get into that section as soon as we outline the other potential problem areas.

STRESS

If you were to list the six areas of your life in order of the most stressful first, and then the second most stressful, and then the third, etc., etc...how would you list them?

Most stressful area _____

Second _____

Third _____

Fourth _____

Fifth _____

Sixth _____

Next to each area, could you write the name of the person that causes you the most stress in that area. If there isn't a person that accounts for the stress in the area, that's good. That will mean you are only dealing with an effect of an effect, etc. But, if there is a person responsible for the stress, you will need to learn techniques that will "neutralize" the effects of that person. And eventually, bring that person to a more positive position in your life...or, walk around them if necessary...just like the cactus plant. The first decision to be made regarding a negative person that causes you stress is this: Are they essential for your being successful...or can you accomplish your goal without them or their help?

Secondly, you will want to answer this question for yourself: Is it...or would it be in their best interests to support your goals and "Major Purpose?" Sometimes a person will cause you stress and openly oppose you because they cannot see the connection between their success and your being involved.

Some other questions that you should think about concerning someone that causes you stress: Do you know what labels they normally attack? Do you know what they do that makes you react? Do they trigger-off labels from the "CLOSET OF YOUR MIND" that you normally don't wear with anyone else? In other words, do they have an "inside track" on making you reactive? In the tools section that follows this chapter, we'll cover some "rights" you have that will neutralize the negative effects of others.

PROCRASTINATION

I don't care how great a procrastinator you used to be. If you have listed all the information in the proper charts, and you will start implementing some of the desires into your

daily living, YOU WILL CEASE TO BE A PROCRASTINA-
TOR...in the areas that count in your life!

I have a saying that I like to use in my business world. It
goes like this:

ONCE YOU KNOW ALL THERE IS FOR YOU TO DO
ALL THAT'S LEFT...IS FOR YOU TO DO IT!

POINT D's IN YOUR LIFE

Let's check out your rethinking processes at POINT D in
the cycle of thought. Remember the SUCCESS and FAILURE
cycles of thought? When you start working on all the goals
you've selected, do you know which way you will think at the
POINT D's? Think about your "Major Purpose" right now.
Can you remember the essence of what you wrote? Your
"Major Purpose" is the "key" to overcoming the POINT D's as
you will see in the diagram on the following page. You will
notice how each goal meshes and integrates with all the
others. Each goal becomes a support unit for the "Major
Purpose", and the "Major Purpose" becomes the measuring
stick against which every goal is measured. It is very difficult
to try to accomplish disconnected goals that are running in
many different directions. It would make it nearly impossible
if two or more of the goals were running in direct opposition
to each other. You would be "pulled apart at the seams" trying
to fly in every direction at once. That would be like two people
sitting in opposite ends of a rowboat; one rowing up the river
with all their might...and the other person rowing down the
river. The rowboat would go nowhere (except perhaps into
the rocks), all the energies of both people would be wasted.

You should realize by now that all new ideas and events in
your life have to meet the criteria of your "Major Purpose".
Any new idea...any new person...any new goal...everything
that tries to engage your time, must "stack up" as supportive
of your "Major Purpose". Everything you decide to do can be
weighed against your "Major Purpose" to see if it is worthwhile to you. If something cannot pass the test of measurment

EACH OF THE SIX AREAS OF LIFE, ACTS AS A
SUPPORT UNIT FOR YOUR **MAJOR PURPOSE.**

against your "Major Purpose", you certainly won't want to add it to your life. To add it to your life would violate the laws. Remember the law of ATTRACTION? Remember the law of OPPOSITES? Remember the law of CAUSE and EFFECT? Remember what will happen if you waste time on the small scale? Ultimately, you would be wasting time on the large scale... that's the way the law of DUALITY works... remember?

You hold the "key" to overcoming every negative POINT D you will ever reach in your life. That "key" is your "Major Purpose". If your "Major Purpose" is in line with the positive applications of the six laws (and it should be if you have been filling in the charts) your success is guaranteed.

Let's get on with the "tools" section of the book. "LIFE" has been called a "GAME", and as such, we have been covering some of the "GROUND RULES". "Rules", that control the outcome of everyone's attempt at being a participant in the playing. In the next section, we'll cover some of the tools you can use in dealing with the other participants and the other variables in the daily activities of being here on this world.

III

Application

16
Tools for Daily Living

As we enter the last section of this book, I hope that you will understand some changes I would like to make in my writing style and the manner in which I present material. In the beginning of the book (up through the chapter we just finished), I have tried to be as explicit as I possibly could... without being boring and redundant. Now I would like to let you know that there will be "gaps" in the material I will present. You will have to exercise your understanding of the concepts discussed... and by doing that, you will fill-in the "gaps" perfectly. My intentions are to give you a "limited number" of tools for dealing with four very large areas of life.

I say a "limited number" because, once you know the four areas, you will realize that it would take a medium size library to completely cover all the tools that could be discussed. Almost every non-fiction book that is listed on the most popular lists in book stores is (in some manner or form) offering tools for handling small segments of at least one of the four areas.

The tools that I will discuss will help you in dealing with these four areas of daily living:

1. PEOPLE
2. MONEY
3. TIME
4. YOURSELF

Now that you know the four areas, I'm sure you can see why I said there would be "gaps" in the material. There is absolutely no way to be really thorough and completely cover everything ...and every possible situation.

As you use the six laws in your daily thinking, you will find the tools helpful in creating the proper atmosphere for the attainment of your goals and major purpose. The tools are simple. They do not violate the six laws. They will prevent some difficult situations from becoming obstacles in your path of progress. However, having knowledge and wisdom does not guarantee you "no problems". There is no immunity to problems...once you understand that a problem comes about when "WHAT YOU WANT...IS DIFFERENT FROM WHAT EXISTS". As you become more adept at using the six laws and following through on your goals and purpose, you will become more aware of "problems" that you would like to see solved. Fortunately, with the proper tools, you can also see the "solutions".

As I am sure you realize, most people are into the comparison games we discussed in the chapter "What Labels Do You Wear". A long time ago, I learned it is next to impossible to change "anyone"...let alone to try to change "everyone". You can be responsible for your set of labels. You can control which ones you take "off the hangers", and by doing that, you can ultimately control the rewards, the results, you will receive in this world. Knowing that most people are into the comparison games of criticizing and judging, it will become very, very important to learn and practice the tools offered here.

Let's get on with the tools I would like to offer you as additions to the many concepts shared earlier.

17
What "Right" Have You Got?

The information I will share with you now is in preparation for the the LABEL RIP OFF GAME that follows. What I'm going to list are a series of "rights" that you have...if you are willing to exercise them. If you are *unwilling to exercise a "right"*, you lose it. The "rights" are a lot like talents and abilities where you must "USE IT...OR LOSE IT".

There are a couple of things you need to know about the "rights" I'm going to list. You should: 1) Understand the different "rights". 2) Understand the consequences of exercising your "rights". 3) Be willing to grant identical "rights" to other people.

I did not state that you should use your "rights"...*always, constantly, in certain instances, never...or any other qualification.* I did state that you should *understand* the "rights". Whether you ever want to use them, that would be up to you...once you know what they are.

The best way to demonstrate items one, two, and three above is to take one "right" and run a practice session. My question to you is this "Do you still make mistakes?" Was that a "yes" I heard inside you? Good! You have a "right" to make mistakes as long as you are willing to accept the consequences for your mistakes. And, of course, as long as *you are free to make mistakes,* **you would and should be willing** to grant a similar "right" to other people.

When you hop in your car and take off down the street, you are exercising your "right" to possibly make mistakes. If you make an error, you will have to accept the *consequences* (a ticket or an accident) after all, those *were possibilities* when you undertook the venture, especially if you make mistakes. Now, comes the third, and very important, point...you should understand that other people "out there" might make the same mistakes you could. Grant them the "right" to be human also...and don't get your insides so churned-up when someone accidently waits two seconds after the green light comes on...before they move through the intersection.

Isn't this fun? Knowing that it's okay to "mess up" occasionally? Just accept the consequences (as a responsible adult surely you are accountable for your actions) and get on with life. Now, don't forget to let other people "botch it"...okay? By the way, that includes kids.

Well...here's the list...have fun reading them:

YOUR RIGHTS

1. YOU HAVE A RIGHT TO...be the only judge for your own feelings, thoughts, and behavior. (good old CLOSET OF YOUR MIND)
2. YOU HAVE A RIGHT TO...offer your desire as the only reason for what you do in life. (you won't have to justify goals)
3. YOU HAVE A RIGHT TO...make mistakes and errors. (that's how you learned everything you know up to this point)
4. YOU HAVE A RIGHT TO...change your mind. (fortunately...or I'd be an anesthesiologist who abhors blood)
5. YOU HAVE A RIGHT TO...be illogical. (being logical is not always being right)
6. YOU HAVE A RIGHT TO...refuse to solve other peoples' problems (thank goodness)
7. YOU HAVE A RIGHT TO...say, "I don't understand."
8. YOU HAVE A RIGHT TO...say, "I don't know."

9. YOU HAVE A RIGHT TO... say, "I don't care."
And last, but not least,
10. YOU HAVE A RIGHT TO... let other people be dis-
     appointed or angry. (they will... no matter what you
     do... so why worry?)

Those are your "rights"... if you want to use them... and
accept the consequences (mild to harsh)... and grant the same
"rights" to others. Once you become secure in the understanding of the "rights", you no longer need get all upset inside in
dealing with people. You will know that you have the option
as to whether you should... or shouldn't exercise a particular
"right".

Sometimes you will use a "right", and at other times
(almost the same circumstance) you'll choose not to use the
same "right". Some of the "rights" are more harsh sounding
than others... for instance: If someone criticized you for taking five minutes (instead of four) to explain your position at a
town meeting... YOU COULD 1) Choose not to use a "right",
and beg forgiveness or offer to punch them in the mouth. 2)
Choose "right #1", and say "I thought the subject matter was
important, so I took the time I needed to explain my position."
3) Choose "right #3", and say "Oh well, mistakes happen." 4)
Or even choose "right #9" by saying "I don't really care. I took
the time I needed."

Each of the replies would be appropriate in certain instances, and each of the consequences would be different depending on the person that criticized you... the importance of the
material... what was at stake... your intensity of involvement
in the subject matter.

You will probably come to a point of liking one or two of
the "rights" over all the rest. Even though you grow to like a
certain few, remember the rest.

You may have some extremely negative people that float
through your life occasionally (or is it constantly), and the
"rights" allow you to deal with very negative people that
trample over the feelings of everyone that gets in their
pathway.

The "rights" give you *the option* of being assertive in dealing with people. In the every day activities of the business world, having the "rights" gives you an alternative to acting passively or becoming reactive and acting aggressively. In the long run, you will lose respect if you grovel at the feet of people who are aggressive. You will also lose respect if you are constantly aggressive and demanding of the mild-mannered that are everywhere in our society.

The "rights" are not an excuse to be a rude, crude, obnoxious person. They are a method for dealing with the people that will give you "flak" when you decide to change. It is my belief that most people have one or more areas of their lives in which...they would like to see some changes. I honestly think more people would make the beneficial changes..."IF" the negative people of this world would just keep their noses out of everyone elses' business.

Remember the examples I used about the "flak" people will send your way when you start to change? Remember the lawyer that wanted to own a business? And the housewife that wanted to add new interests to her life? And the teenager that decided to get better marks in school? It was back when we were first talking about how you are what you are, by the general agreement of the people in your environment. You are a   (your occupational label) , because your school, your teachers, your company, your friends, and the society *agrees; that's what you are.* Let's look at the LABEL RIP OFF GAME as it is played...and how you can use the "rights" in the "game".

18
The
Label Rip Off
Game

Properly learning the way this game is played will help you in hundreds of situations...in all areas of life. The game is especially important when you decide to make changes in your goals and life directions. When you decide to implement your goals, your new labels, and your "Major Purpose", you may notice an increase in the frequency of games played as people try to change your mind.

Look at the couple in the illustration on the next page. Don't they look prim and proper and nicely clothed? You'll remember that the clothes they wear are labels of identifications, feelings, emotions, and attitudes. We covered that in the chapters on labels as extensions of ourselves. The labels all hang in the CLOSET OF YOUR MIND, and each day we select the proper labels to wear...as has this couple.

Along comes the world of people; friends, relatives, associates, acquaintances, strangers, and a group known as "I know what's best for you!" Let's give our couple more labels. We'll call them Fred and Betty. Let's also assume they represent the lawyer and the housewife...and at home is their "poor" student teenager, David.

Conversation begins...

Friend: Why, Fred and Betty, hello. How are you doing?

Fred/Betty: Just great. How are you?

Friend: Oh, so-so. Money is getting tight with the inflation problems.

Fred: Don't I know it! That's one of the reasons I'm getting out of XYZ company. I'm in the process of setting up my own firm. I figure we'll turn it profitable by the end of the year or the first of next year.

Friend: Fred, I just cannot believe you'd be that foolish.
(rip off) You've got all those years invested at XYZ. You've never had the management training to own your own business...and you know about 80% of all new businesses fail.

Fred: I've thought it out and know I'm doing what's best for me.

Friend: Betty, I hope you've got more influence with
(rip off) him than I do. Maybe you can talk some sense into him before he bankrupts the family. By the way, how is the family?

Betty: Oh, everyone is just great. Our son David has really taken a liking to his classes this year. It looks like he's finally going to pick up his grades.

Friend: What's wrong with him...is he ill or some-
(rip off) thing? He's always had problems according to my son, Jimmy. I'd keep an eye on him. Usually when the kids do something unusual like this, they're sneaking around behind your back. Maybe he'll get back to normal as the school year progresses.

Betty: I'm sure David is doing what's right for him. In fact, now that he can drive, he's being much more considerate of how he spends his time... and what he does. I've got more free time since he doesn't need to be driven everywhere, and I've been considering exhibiting some of my art...and maybe studying under a professional.

I think if I improve my design studies, I might be able to get some contracts as a consultant in my spare time.

Friend: Oh Betty, not you, too! You've always been the
(rip off) center of your family...it just doesn't sound like you talking. I cannot imagine you going out into the business world...and, as far as the "art field", what a mistake that would be. I thought you were a better person than that...the art field is so full of those "weirdos" you know.

Betty: I'm really looking forward to doing what I want to do.

Fred/Betty: Well... friend (?) , we really must be going, BYE!

Well, did you see the "LABEL RIP OFF GAME" in action? You were probably thinking that when you learned to play the game, *YOU* would learn to rip labels...DEFINITELY NOT. The labels that are ripped and torn in "THE LABEL RIP OFF GAME" are yours; **your labels.**

Here's the most important lesson to be learned in preparing yourself for the game: *Everytime* someone rips at your labels, it will be for **one of the following two reasons.** People rip at labels to: 1) Elevate themselves by "putting you down", or 2) Manipulate your behavior in some way. Your part in the "LABEL RIP OFF GAME" is to decide *which reason is their motive.* That's the only role you take in the game...your role is NOT TO SEE IF YOU CAN RIP THEM ONE BETTER! Let me run the reasons why back and forth a couple of times. If you rip back, you will rip for one of two reasons: 1) To show them they can't put you down (which means, you put them down **to elevate yourself**). 2) To make them feel guilty or ashamed or ruin their day (which means, you ripped, in some way, **to manipulate their behavior**). Just remember, your role in the "LABEL RIP OFF GAME" is to decide *which reason is their motive.* In our example of Fred and Betty, they could have started ripping back at their "friend" with the sly, witty-...biting...cutting remarks we've all learned to use since grade school. There were many chances in the exchange where they could have been real nasty: Money is tight (what is their friend doing about the situation...failing?)...our Jimmy (Jimmy is one of the most undisciplined children the school has ever seen)...art (some low-class, low-brow people never have understood "art".)

What could possibly be the reason if Fred and Betty had "ripped" back? Certainly it would not have been to create an uplifting, positive conversation about what was going on in their world. They would have been "ripping back" to put their friend down. To rip back negates the positive aspects of the laws of the universe...it would have created nothing constructive for Fred and Betty...nor will it create good in your life...or in mine.

Because Fred and Betty chose to play the game from a position of strength, THEIR LABELS ARE INTACT... THEY FEEL SUCCESSFUL, GOOD, SECURE AND VERY POSITIVE. They are winners in the game of life. They played using the laws...instead of playing the game according to their friend's "rules".

It will take practice on your part to perfect skill in your role in the "LABEL RIP OFF GAME". Your part is to evaluate and decide on the motives behind "The Ripper". It will take some time for you to totally perfect your skill...and here's why.

YOU WILL BE RIPPING BACK IF YOU:

1. Verbally attack back with a spiteful statement.
2. Verbally attack with the sly innuendo.
3. Non-verbally attack by punching them in the nose.
4. Non-verbally attack with body language.

Numbers one and three are very easy to understand. I'll explain a little more thoroughly numbers two and four.

When a person uses number two, they will sometimes use a double-edged phrase statement. What is more probable is they will use a single word or sigh that is designed to register as "disgust". Have you ever heard yourself or someone else say, *"Well, surely* you've heard about _____!" The special emphasis on "surely" was designed to be a "LABEL RIP OFF" and put the person in *their place*. Parents do it often with their children "I *would think* you would know how to do this *by now…we've shown you* how three times!" Husbands and wives do it in public everywhere… *"Must you always* _____ _____!"* It's not a question, it's a statement of disgust…a "put-down"…a slice with the razor. Let's fill in the extra words that were insinuated in each statement. "Well (you stupid, ill-informed, dummy) *surely* you've heard about _____ _____!"* "I would think* (any stupid moron would understand) that you would know how to do this *by now* (unless you are totally dumb, perhaps incompetent)…we've *shown you* (even an idiot could understand something this simple) three times!" *"Must you always* (you are such an embarrassment, and disgust me…how distasteful) _____!" In each case, the statement was issued to damage another person's self worth…and as such was **a label rip-off.** When you decide to eliminate label rip-offs from your communication tools, you will automatically elevate yourself **in the eyes of all viewers.** You will be wearing a new label and the world will reward you for that new label. Remember, the world (universe) rewards you for every label you wear. Let's follow through with number two a little further…remember the single word…the sigh? People that have become masters at the art of the "put down" shorten their long sentences into single words or vocal expressions. It is not to their credit that they have done this. It is far easier to restrain yourself from uttering a ten word sentence, than it is to stop yourself before the sigh is issued …or the single word escapes. For instance, a mother might say, "Jimmy (heavy sigh)!" Which means, "Jimmy (you are exasperating, such a chore, a true brat, how disgusting to have to put up with you, I wish you would dry up and blow away)!" In business, one associate will say to another, "Sure, John, you can have the floor, we're interested in your report…(heavy sigh)." "The heavy sigh meant (I hope we don't sleep through it…you are so boring.) Husbands and wives perfect the single word "rip-off" with a single sound…"tsk". The "tsk" is probably the ultimate in put-downs between family members. In many families the "tsk" takes the place of most talk.

Imagine a family sitting in a nice comfortable restaurant. A mother, a father, a twelve year old son, and a nine year old daughter; a perfect picture of Americana out for dinner. Husband clinks water glass against coffee cup as he prepares to drink. Wife utters "tsk"...which means (can't you ever be careful, you are never careful). Son forgets to change fork to "right" hand as he takes too large a bite. Father utters "tsk"...which means (you uncouth, stupid idiot, have you no manners, maybe we should have let you eat with the local pigs, disgusting.) Sister notices, so she sits up straighter and very carefully eats her next bite. Brother looks at sister, and utters "tsk"...which means (you "worm", you are doing that on purpose, it won't be long and you'll spill your milk like always, then we'll see.) Daughter hears brother's "tsk" and chokes on a piece of bread. Mother says "tsk" which means (how distasteful, if you wouldn't jam food in like that, you wouldn't choke, dummy.) Husband hears wife's "tsk" and utters "tsk" at wife...which means (who are you to talk, always trying to be seen in just the "right" restaurants, this whole idea of coming here is nothing but a pain, and now you're picking on the kids, why don't you shut up.) Son notices the unkind remark to Mom and looks at sister and says, "tsk" (well, here go Mom and Dad again, it sure will be great when we're grown and can get out of here, they want us to be perfect...why don't they try it!) AMAZING...no words spoken.

Become a watcher of people, and you will sooner bite off your tongue rather than continue to play "THE LABEL RIP OFF GAME" as the "ripper". *Become a watcher of the people that watch.* It will only take one or two restaurant experiences, and you'll understand fully how the "LABEL RIP OFF GAME" works...as you view..."the rippers". Watch the reactions of the watchers (people at other tables that have empathy) as they "read" the subtle messages. **They will be shocked.** Possibly, shocked to the point of losing their appetites. Someday, you too will lose your appetite *for even watching the game*. There is not a lack of communications in the

American family. What does exist is not "a lack", but rather an increasing dependence on negative "game-playing" where NO ONE IS A WINNER! NO ONE ENDS UP FEELING GOOD! NO ONE COMES AWAY LOOKING OR FEELING SUCCESSFUL!

Once you make some basic philosophical decisions relating to the concepts, tools and methods contained in this book...you and the members of your environment may notice some changes. With the changes will come *new results.* With the change in labels, there will come a change in the results...the rewards aligned by the world. One reward is a new respect from all viewers for your calmness, your stature, your unruffled manner in dealing with people that are playing the part of the "ripper" in the "LABEL RIP OFF GAME".

The final test of *your skill* in learning to play the "LABEL RIP OFF GAME", is your ability to control your usage of method number four; Non-verbal attack with body language. It has often been estimated that up to 90% of all communication is non-verbal in form. If so, then possibly 90% of all the label rip-offs in our society are... non-verbal. The hand on the hip that means (I'm irritated with how you are doing that), the drumming of fingers while your spouse is talking which means (why don't you just SHUT UP, how boring you are), the pursing of the lips accompanied by a negative wave of the head which means (stupid, if you do that one more time, I'll break your arm!), the "I told you so look", that is for the benefit of onlookers, when you look at a child which means (how did I ever foster such an idiot for a child, you insignificant, dumb, worthless piece of humanity.)

You can start right now. You can start today to practice your role in the "LABEL RIP OFF GAME" and perfect your skill. By the time you have selected the changes you will want to make in your labels, you will be skilled at playing the game. Your role is always the same, to evaluate "the why" (the motive) behind the ripper's attack. When you correctly evaluate the motive behind the attack, YOU NEUTRALIZE THE EFFECTS OF THE ATTACK.

The dictionary definition for neutralize is: *"to destroy the effectiveness of: to nullify."* NOTHING could be more effective. You will have *nullified* the criticism, *nullified* the sting, *nullified* the control that person sought to use over you.

YOU WILL RECEIVE ONE EXTRA BENEFIT BY PERFECTING YOUR SKILL...YOU WILL AUTOMATICALLY *ELEVATE IN STATURE*...IN THE EYES OF EVERY VIEWER. The husband that rips at his wife in public...is scorned by the viewers. The parent that verbally destroys his child...is scorned by the viewers. The female that cattily attacks others...is scorned by the viewers. The businessman that attacks subordinates...is scorned by the viewers. The businessman that rips his competition...is scorned by the viewers. The couple that belittles their elderly parent, the old that despise the young, the whites that put down the blacks, the poor that malign the rich, the healthy that loath the sick...each group lessens their own stature in the eyes of viewers...and the immutable laws of this universe will not work positively for the individual that "rips" another. I am not saying, *"The laws will not work."* I am saying the laws will not work *positively* in the life of that individual. With each "rip", something is lost. With each "rip", there is a backsliding process. With each "rip", the laws will reward...but, the reward will be of a negative nature. Certainly you've at some time heard the passage, "Judge not lest ye be judged; and by your standard of measure, it shall be measured to you." Or perhaps it was written, "Do not judge, and you will not be judged; because the judgments you give are the judgments you will get, and the amount you measure out is the amount you will be given." (Two versions of Matt. 7:1,2) Or in the same chapter, "Therefore whatever you want others to do for you, do so for them, for this is the *Law* and the prophets." (Matt. 7:12) There are hundreds of passages dealing with the six laws of success. I bring them into this book as illustrations that we (you and I) have at hand; they are the instructions needed to fulfill ourselves. If anyone chooses to ignore or violate the laws, the laws shall go right on working...the laws work for everyone... they never fail to provide the proper measure based on the "cause". There is a special passage in Galatians that would speak directly to every "ripper" that has ever existed. "For if anyone thinks he is something when he is nothing, he deceives himself. But let each one examine his own work, and then he will have reason for boasting in regard to himself alone, and not in regard to another. For each one shall bear his own load." (Gal. 6:3-5) and "for whatever a man sows, this he will also **reap**." (Gal. 6:7)

Right about now, **you are** in the process of thinking and making decisions regarding the "LABEL RIP OFF GAME", and your role in it. I want to describe one more situation. Actually, it will be a more fully described situation... we've already touched on the husband and wife relationship... but, we have not covered the full extent of the damage caused by the game.

I think that by using an example that is very close to home, you will more fully understand why you should never "Rip Back" in the "LABEL RIP OFF GAME". There is one person in your environment with whom you should not play the "LABEL RIP OFF GAME"... you should never have to if *you both* understand *the motives* for ripping. I'm sure right now, you're saying to yourself, "You're kidding! Husbands and wives are always ripping each others labels. I see it everywhere; in stores, at restaurants with friends, at conventions, even on vacations." I didn't say it doesn't happen... I am saying they shouldn't! And, here's why. We'll use a new couple, Jim and Nancy for illustrative purposes. Jim and Nancy have one set of labels that are unique. This unique set of labels works like this: Jim wears a "husband" and Nancy wears a "wife" label... and those labels are unique... totally unique. "NOT SO", you say. "Lots of people wear *husband* and *wife* labels." Maybe I should state it thusly: Jim wears a "husband" label with an asterisk that leads to a subtitle Nancy's husband... Nancy wears a "wife" label with an asterisk that leads to a subtitle Jim's wife. The "husband" and "wife" labels that are unique in this case are *shared* by Jim and Nancy. It's almost as though

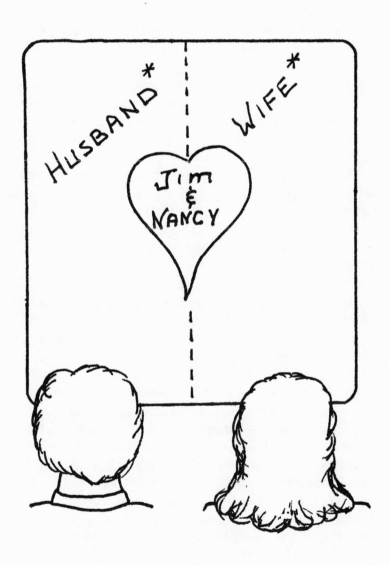

they wear one gigantic label that stretches when they are apart. On one end of the label is written JIM, HUSBAND OF NANCY..., and on the other end of the label is written NANCY, WIFE OF JIM. The labels are interrelated and dependent on each other. Now let's look at some hypothetical situations to show why husbands and wives would do better to "bite off their tongues" rather than attack the labels of their partners.

If you know there are only two reasons why people attack other people's labels, then...what motive could it be when one spouse attacks the other spouse's labels. Is it to "put the partner down — so they can feel superior", or is it "to manipulate...by making the partner feel guilty or rotten or sad."

Consider this also, the more precious a label, the more it will hurt if ripped. If there is only one totally unique label between husband and wife, what label would you attack if you *really wanted to hurt?* That's right, attack the most precious label...the most personal label...the one that is connected to the most emotions.

Now consider this, Jim cannot attack Nancy's "wife" label without indirectly attacking himself. Nancy cannot attack Jim's "husband" label without indirectly attacking herself. A cutting slash of razor sharp sarcasm...the caustic remark that shocks everyone within ear range...slices through both labels. It doesn't stop at the dotted line that divides the side that becomes Jim's half of the label. When Jim uses his words to hurt, the cutting edge eventually ends up...in him.

While I do not profess to have the only solution for stopping this label ripping process that goes on between partners, I do know this, husbands and wives that will follow through on the reading and using of this book will have a new respect for each other. In addition, using this book will rid your family of one of the greatest destructive situations that can ever exist in the family life. A destructive situation that exists in almost all families; the lack of a well-defined set of workable goals. A family that has defined its goals, and knows what and where and how *and why* they are doing what they are doing... that will be a happy family with everyone working for the good of each individual. It'll be a family where everyone pulls together and enjoys life, and living, and loving. It's amazing how much of the harshness can disappear, once "Purpose" enters into a household. A household that has neither goals nor direction, has no reason or direction for being.

If the "Major Purpose" (defined by the participants in the household) is centered in all six areas... the household will be truly blessed. It doesn't take much "reading between the lines" in my writings, for you to get the idea that I feel that a family that builds its life around a solid, mature, growing spiritual life will benefit in every area.

The LABEL RIP OFF GAME has no place... is without benefit... and, should be removed from your arsenal of communications. Playing the game as a "ripper" is not using a tool... *it is playing with a weapon that will eventually be turned on the user.*

Using your "rights" without malice is one of the easiest ways you will ever find for fending-off the attacks of the "rippers". Certainly, the "rippers" are going to be sprinkled throughout our society, but you will have *nullified* their "effects"... and **affect,** on your life. Isn't it wonderful that you can protect the integrity of what you believe... you can protect the labels you have chosen... and, that you can proceed with your "Major Purpose" regardless of what others choose to do with their lives?

19
Is There Life in Those Eyes?

I have a favorite topic I would like to share with you; a tool we share at all our workshops. I share the tool with thousands of people each year. It's one of the most remembered tools we teach...we call it "twinkling" when we talk about it. I like to "twinkle" at everyone in the audiences. I like to "twinkle" at everyone I meet in the business world. I like sharing a "twinkle" with people at church and at local community meetings. Sharing a "twinkle" with members of various civic groups is always enjoyable. You're probably wondering "What in the world is a 'twinkle'?" A "twinkle" is a smile with your eyes ...from your eyes...and through your eyes. It's not even necessary for your mouth to get involved in the "twinkle". All that is necessary for you to "twinkle" is for you to learn to let the life and happiness inside you...shine through your eyes.

You have probably seen thousands of people that look like they are "dead" inside. If you haven't, you haven't been looking at the people that fill this world. They walk along the streets on their way towards "whatever". They work and put in their 40 hours. They take up space, but they are totally uninterested in existence. When you glance at people that have that "dead inside" look, their eyes lack luster. Their eyes lack life. If you were to sit down with them and talk about goals in life, you would find that they have given up hope. They are really just putting in their time waiting for the end. It's a typical case of the old joke line "Dead at 30, buried at age 65!"

If you want to draw out the best responses in other people, and if you want to show that you are someone that has purpose in life, then let it show through your eyes with a "twinkle". Here are the rules for "twinkling":

1. A "twinkle" is a smile with your eyes, so be sure you look into the eyes of other people when you do it. Many people can accept only limited eye contact...so keep it brief: a couple of seconds at a time is long enough.

2. Your "twinkle" should be given to everyone; young and old, male and female, friend and stranger. Your "twinkle" should be turned on in group meetings and when you are one-on-one with individuals.

3. Your "twinkle" should become a learned response. In the very beginning, you might have to remember to do it, but in a short period of time, you will find it becomes a permanent part of your personality.

4. When someone returns your "twinkle" with a "twinkle" of their own, you have found a kindred heart; someone that is alive and happy inside. When someone "twinkles" back, be sure to say *something positive* to them. This reinforces them and you; it is a direct extension of the law of CAUSE and EFFECT.

As a public speaker, I have found that audiences can feel, and will respond to a "twinkle", from as far away as 200 feet; pretty powerful tool...wouldn't you agree?

20
Who Gets To Keep The Money?

This is going to be a short chapter about a very delicate matter; **money.** How do you act around money? What does money mean to you? How do you think about money? Can you handle money. Does money control you...or you it? Does money turn you off?

Interesting questions, aren't they? Knowing the answers to these questions...*is very important because, most people cannot handle money comfortably.* I can make this statement based on my personal observations of both myself...and thousands of other people...many of whom had plenty of money.

On the surface, money seems to be a rather simple matter. It has been described as: "a medium of exchange" or "a measure of service designated by wealth". But, underneath, there are many uncomfortable feelings connected with money and wealth. I will not try to cover all aspects of the subject ...just some personal observations that may be of some help to you. I have not included this section to try to preach to anyone; these are just some observations that you may find interesting.

1. Money is an "effect" of an "effect" of an "effect", etc.
2. Money is a quasi-necessity...that is worthless to keep.

3. Money controls unless you own it.
4. Chasing after money is a hopeless race.
5. It takes very little money to be rich.

I'll spend a little bit of time on each of the five items.

First, as we've already covered in the six laws, money (the physical stuff) occurs somewhere down the line of laws as an effect of effects of effects. Nowhere in this universe can you find anything that starts out in the physical form. Everything must pass through the ORDER before it will eventually turn up in the physical form. This is a very abundant universe, and when it comes to money, there is an ever increasing supply. It is everywhere... *in very large amounts.* You don't have to create it... it already exists... someone has it. You probably have a goodly supply right now. In fact, if you are going to live another 20 years, you are probably in line to reap the effects of effects of effects that will amount to $500,000 or $1,000,000... or perhaps even five or ten million depending on your ability to use the six laws positively.

Second, money is a quasi-necessity that is worthless to keep. Money is necessary, but not really. Many people never even see their money. They receive a check that is deposited automatically... and their bills are automatically paid from the same account. No money actually changes hands. Trying to keep money for money's sake is worthless. The only use of money is the manner in which you exchange it. I am not saying that you should become a spendthrift. When you invest or save money in an account, you are exchanging your money for future money plus interest; nothing wrong with that if your goal is to have increased money in the future. When you fully accept the idea that all abundance (including money) is temporal, you will probably enjoy all abundance much more (including money.)

Third, money can control you... if you don't own and control it. Let me offer you a few stories to explain what I mean. I have seen very strong business people destroy their otherwise ' strong position" while quibbling over a 25¢ mistake in a $25 lunch tab. Hopefully, you are not controlled by a quarter, but what if we raise the stakes a little. I've heard of people being killed while quibbling over a $2 bill...haven't you? Would you give up your life over two dollars? Probably not. But, what would you do if you dropped a five dollar bill that blew into rush hour traffic? Would you risk your life trying to dash out into speeding cars to try to retrieve it? How about a twenty...or a hundred dollar bill? If you own the money, you can freely give up the loss. If the money owns you, you will gripe about the loss forever. That five dollar bill could become the most talked about, grieved over bill in your life.

I would like to share with you something you might want to consider doing. Decide on an amount of money that you can freely give up...an amount of money that you will not quibble about. Decide on an amount of money that you would freely give to a friend...not as a loan, but as a freely given gift.

I will share a personal experience that may be a little extreme, but will illustrate the value in giving up the grieving over an amount of money. Once upon a time, I lost almost $80,000 in a business transaction because some friends made some very poor business decisions, and I chose to believe their miscalculations rather than to be cautious. The more I thought about the money, the more destructive I became. Over a period of years, that loss controlled me and cost me additional money in lost revenues; time that could have been put to use earning money. It took giving up that money to free me from it. When I gave up the angry, hurt feelings, I was then free to go about my business...and make more money. Understand this, I was not free to make more money to replace the money I gave up. I was now free to think "good causes"...to continue my business career...which had as an effect, of an effect, of an effect...money.

I hope you own your money. I hope you can use it freely. I hope that the six laws have given you some new thoughts about acquiring your share of the abundant stuff we've been talking about.

Fourth, chasing after money is a hopeless race. Have you ever heard the quote about happiness being like a butterfly? If you chase it, happiness will fly away...but, if you remain quiet and still, it will land softly upon your shoulders. So it is with money! When you prepared goals for the six areas of life, and wrote your "Major Purpose", you set in motion the most powerful method...the only method...that will assure you having exactly what you need in terms of money.

And **fifth,** It takes very little money to be rich. Of course, what is rich but a state of mind! Once upon a time, when I was eight years old, I exchanged two dollars I had saved for a roll of nickels. Imagine my surprise when I counted the nickels and found 41 in the roll! I was rich, and happy, and excited. I must admit that in my naive young mind I figured that if I traded enough dollars for enough rolls of nickels, I would soon have a huge bank account. But, is that any more naive than adults that think they can somehow give shoddy service and become rich? Or is it any more naive than people that think they can become rich in a flim-flam "get rich quick" deal that has a hundred losers for every supposed winner? Think of how many people you know that think they can continue being "poor in mind", but "rich" someday in material abundance.

It takes nothing more than a plan of action to be rich. Success is the progressive attainment of desired goals...**sound familiar?** Sure it does. If your well-defined, well-thought-out goals include riches, you are rich every step of the way. If your goals include abundance, and that abundance includes a measure of money, you are rich long before the goal is reached. Remember to take heed of the person you become in the pursuit of your desires. If you wear the proper "set of labels", you will attract the proper results...and become, in the process, the kind of person *you deserve to be.*

21
Time:
The Non-Negotiable Variable

You and I and everyone else...we are all locked into a non-negotiable 168 hours per week. Every week you have ever lived has been 168 hours in length. You spread out your activities and filled those hours with whatever you did. Now, you have a new set of goals spanning the six broad areas of your life. You have almost certainly expanded the scope of desired results in your life. But, the non-negotiable variable still exists; there are only *168 hours in each week*. How will you handle these new time demands?

I will offer you a time management technique that will assure you a way to get more done in less time. And, what is more important, the technique will assure that you get the really important priority items accomplished. The technique is called the 80/20 rule in the business world. It's called common sense when we apply it to life and career planning.

When you plan goals in all six areas based on an overriding, all-encompassing "Major Purpose", you are setting in motion a synergistic plan of action. That means...the total effect will be much more than the sum of the parts. In synergism, one plus one equals much more than two. One plus one plus one plus one plus one plus one equals a truly remarkable sum...*far, far greater than six*. It is very important that you accomplish the most important goals in each of the six areas...so you will get this multiplier effect. When you get the multiplier effect, your results come more quickly and you will gain the support of the people in your environment more easily. Everyone likes to back a winner, and there are many people in your world that need a "success" model to identify themselves with...and you may be the right model for them.

The 80/20 rule works in every area of life *on this earth*. It is not a universal law, but rather an immutable law of business. When I say immutable, I mean...*unchanging, a constant.* The rule states that 80% of the positive potential in any venture comes from 20% of the activity or effort expended. In other words, 20% of your activities will result in 80% of your happiness, your profits, your accomplishments, your progress, etc. The remaining 80% of your activities will result in only a 20% measure of accomplishment.

Let me give you a few examples to demonstrate:

80% of the profits in a business come from 20% of the activities.

80% of the sales are made by 20% of the salespeople.

80% of a company's progress can be attributed to 20% of employees.

Now, let's apply the 80/20 rule outside the business world. Let's apply it to the social world, the family area, mental and physical development, and finally to the spiritual realm. The 80/20 rule can be applied to the spiritual area of life in terms of your activities on this world in the support of your individual beliefs. By this, I mean: 1) Your church activities 2) Your study in the Word 3) Your fellowship activities, and 4) Your witness. Your salvation does not fall in the realm of the 80/20 rule. You either have it 100%, or you don't; it is outside the realm of this world.

The 80/20 rule works under the six laws in each area of your life. Here are some examples of its working in the six areas of a person's life. As you read through the examples, you can make some decisions regarding your use of time in the future. This is not an efficiency study, but rather, *it is a study in* effectiveness. In the business world, I rarely get involved in efficiency studies because, efficiency studies usually mean everyone on the job becomes more and more efficient at doing even *the useless tasks*. Effectiveness studies, on the other hand, are designed to discover the most important, the most essential, and the most profitable activities...and then accentuating the activity in those areas. Every executive in the world that makes $100,000 a year or more...is paid that money for being "effective" in specific areas of importance. Let's look at your important areas.

FINANCIAL AREA: If you make an arbitrary $35,000 salary, and put in a sixty hour work week, the 80/20 rule would indicate your income and effectiveness thusly:

20% of hours worked (60 hrs. x 20%) = 12 hours weekly
The 12 effective hours had as their yearly result...
80% of money earned ($35,000 x 80%) = $28,000

Twelve effective, very productive hours each week earn you $28,000 a year. The remaining 48 hours are far less productive each week; they earn you a total of only $7,000 a year. Ask any manager, any salesperson, any operations person, any professional person, the following questions: "How many hours of each day are wasted by needless problems? How many hours are chewed up each day in non-productive activities?" If they cannot give you an answer, it's probably because they have never done an effectiveness study on their work flow. If they are honest about their answers, you'll hear the 80/20 rule repeated back to you.

If we then apply the 80/20 rule to the 48 hours weekly, and the $7,000 yearly figures, we discover this:

20% of hours worked (48 hrs. x 20%) = 9.6 or approximately 9½ hours each week that result in yearly income of...80% of money earned ($7,000 x 80%) = $5,600

When we add all the figures together we find that a total of 21½ hours weekly (12 + 9½) result in the earning of 96% of the income ($28,000 + $5,600 = $33,600) earned. Remarkable! One third of all the time spent results in all but a few hundred dollars of the money earned. This is why I maintain that there are plenty of hours in even the most busy person's schedule to include...time for the family...time for friends...time for the church...time for health...time for mental development ...and time to be alone with your Lord. I don't believe in the "workaholics" syndrome. I believe that people that call themselves "workaholics" are avoiding their responsibility to take control over...and balance, their own lives.

I'm sure you will agree that work can be productive, profitable, and pleasurable...but, most people feel that they are in jobs or professions where none of these wonderful feelings are enjoyed. Why? They are violating the 80/20 rule and confusing "time on the job" with "productivity", and doing that, they perform the whole job half-heartedly. When you apply the 80/20 rule to the financial area of your life, you will probably not work harder...but you will certainly work smarter.

FAMILY AREA: How much time do you spend in the company of your family each week? An hour in the morning...90 minutes around dinner...a couple of hours watching TV each night. What does that add up to on a daily basis? Perhaps five hours daily including a little extra time on the weekends. A grand total of 35 hours each week. Now let's apply the 80/20 rule to the time that is spent, and you will find about seven "quality" hours each week. Seven good solid productive hours where meaningful communications come about. Let's face it, how much meaningful communications go on during two hours of TV programming? You are saying to yourself, "We don't spend 35 hours together as a family. Everybody's running around getting ready for work in the morning. Everybody 'wolfs' their dinner down in 13 minutes flat...if they're even home for dinner. And, nobody's interested in discussing the quality of the TV programming because there is no quality." Perhaps, this is why studies have shown that the average father in America spends less than 7 minutes a week in meaningful communications with his children. Shocking statistics, but true! The top of the list in reasons for divorce is constantly...a breakdown or lack of communications. There will be plenty of time in your goal planning for the "quality" time...if you have made the family area goal in alignment with your "Major Purpose".

SOCIAL AREA: Apply the 80/20 rule to your social life also. Perhaps you spend 8 to 12 hours weekly in social activities. Do you enjoy each and every one of those hours, or are you like many people that attend functions because "you should" and then resent every minute of your being there. Of course, I might be assuming too many hours in this area of your life. Perhaps, your social activities have been cut to almost zero time in this hectic "rat-race" world that has engulfed so many people. In which case, you will probably really enjoy opening up some leisure hours for friends and family members. Just remember...concentrate on making them "quality" hours that fit in with your purpose.

PHYSICAL ACTIVITY AREA: The human body requires approximately 36 minutes of sustained activity each week to maintain physical health. If you want to improve physical health, it takes about 72 minutes of vigorous sustained activity each week to do so. Twelve minutes a day, three times a week to maintain...twelve minutes a day, six times a week to improve physical health. But what do most people do in terms of the exercise they give their body each week? Sporadic exercise, haphazardly applied...with little thought and little usefulness. When you set aside time for your physical body and its development, make sure you set aside "quality" time...spaced properly. This is a once in a lifetime chance to go around in this body; SURELY IT DESERVES 12 MINUTES every other day at least. Twelve minutes out of the 1440 minutes a day seems like such a small contribution when compared with the alternatives. If you enjoy physical activities that use up more than 12 minutes, just be certain that you give your body the 20% "quality" time necessary of sustained exercise...it will give your body the 80% or more of activity necessary for the maintenance of health.

One of the activities we participate in as a family is our exercise program in the mornings. We incorporate a little family time into our aerobic exercises and laugh and have fun while we're enjoying "quality" time exercises. We put on a fast-paced record album that lasts about 12½ minutes, kick up our heels, and enjoy ourselves. Our girls enjoy it, we enjoy it, our bodies enjoy it...and need it also. Try it if it fits "your style" of exercise program...you'll love it.

MENTAL AREA: Think about the reading you do and the development of your mental abilities. If you are like most people, approximately 20% of the material you read gives you 80% of your growth. When it comes to most books, 80% of the material is only filler...put in to "plump up" the size of the book. The "meat" of the book or material is in that small fraction; the 20% factor. Consider also the thoughts you think; 20% of them give you 80% of the good you reap. A few good thoughts can often be the determining factor between being a key executive...and an "also ran". One of the best spin-offs you will enjoy from this book is...during the time you have been reading, you have concentrated on mental activity designed to focus on the 20% of thoughts that will give you everything **you have ever wanted!** Not what Michael Jaress wanted, BUT WHAT YOU HAVE WANTED. You may have already given up years of your mental capabilities thinking about what other people wanted. You may have unknowingly been a victim of the negative thoughts of other people. "Quality" time is what I hope you read into every line in this section of the book. The "quality" 20% of the time that gives to you...over 80% of all the rewards you desire in life.

SPIRITUAL AREA: It is difficult to apply the 80/20 rule to the "true" spiritual area of your life. We can apply it to the physical aspects of your spiritual, religious activity. So much of the religious activity in churches throughout the world is spent in activities other than the Spirit feeding the spirit of the individual. You may know of people that are caught in the situation of attending many hours of programs weekly...and wishing they were somewhere else. At least 80% of those hours are therefore wasted, non-productive. It's the few precious hours or minutes, the 20%, that are truly meaningful and inspirational.

Now, if we discuss the spiritual area in terms of conviction, there is no 80/20 rule at work. Once we move out of the physical realm of this world, the spiritual area becomes a 168 hour each week activity. It is then, the oneness of the Lord abiding in you... and you in Him... 100% of the time. There is no middle ground, you are either at one with God or you are not. Christ is either your Lord and Master or He is not. And, a person that does not know where they stand in relationship to Jesus... that person has already answered their own question; they are separated... and would certainly profit from the time that they could set aside for the spiritual area each week.

Let's bring it all together into a 168 hour week. The reason I have not separated out the hours you sleep is: 1) Sleep is an essential activity in everyone's life. 2) Approximately 20% of your sleep time supplies your body with the "quality" time necessary for the healthy maintenance of the body. The rest of the time spent sleeping is "filler" of one type or another. Here's how it looks when the percentages are applied:

> 20% of 168 hours = 33.6 or approximately 33½ hours that are your truly effective, high performance hours... plus 20% of 134 hours (168 – 33.6 hours from above) = 26.8 hours

When we add the figures together... 33.6 hours plus 26.8 hours... we get approximately **60½ hours that give you 96% of everything you have going for you right now.** You may scoff at the figures, but I will issue a challenge to you; chart your time... account for what you do that is "quality" time during a one month period. After you have kept track for a one month period, then register your opinions. Keep track of all the time... pin it down... and be exact. Don't count as "quality" time the activities where you are wishing you were somewhere else. Don't count as "quality" time the two or three hours each work day you spend "hurrying up to get somewhere so you can wait." Don't count as "quality" time the angry times that are non-productive, the moaning and groaning time that eats up your stomach and accomplishes nothing.

Don't count as "quality" time the hours you spend tossing and turning in bed because you are worrying or ill-at-ease...or whatever. Don't count the time you spend watching a TV program for 90 minutes *after* you realize that it is totally dumb in content...or you realize you've already seen it once before. Do you get the idea? Just count the "quality" time that is spent in **productive systematic attainment of your desired goals** ...all based on accomplishing your MAJOR PURPOSE. In the Bible there is a passage that translates, we are accountable for all that we do that is "good" and "good for nothing." "Good for nothing" is... "putting-in-the-time accomplishing nothing of lasting worth" time.

You have the most fantastic, terrific opportunity facing you each and every day of your life. The opportunity to turn that which has been given to you...another day...into a miracle of accomplishment.

Mary Ellen and I learned of a tragic accident that happened recently to a family we know. This couple were members of our community and personal friends. They had everything going for them; they had finally raised their children...he was retiring from the service as a Navy Captain...they were looking forward to moving into their new home...they were healthy, happy, and still young in heart and years. He rounded a bend in the road leading to their home and struck a tree on the side of the curve. He was killed instantly. Dead at the scene.

Do you think he might have spent his last week on this earth differently had he known the 168 hours were to be his final ones? Might he have held his wife more tenderly each day before leaving for his work activities? Would he have been more intense in his handling the really important aspects of his life...to bring them to completion? Don't take what I'm saying in a wrong way, he was a good man...he loved his kids and wife...he did a good job...he was concerned about his church...he just didn't know THAT THIS WAS HIS LAST WEEK!

And, you don't know either. Nor do I know when will be

my last week or day. All we can do is to make certain that we make the time we have **productive and meaningful.** We can so structure our lives that we balance the six areas into a meaningful something. We can know our "Major Purpose" and seek to accomplish it in everything we do. In that way, you and I will have covered the most important issues...for us.

Remember the part of the book where I set before you the question of standing at the end of your days, and looking back over what had been? Every day we do that! It is by faith that we lay our bodies down to sleep. The probabilities are certainly in your favor that you will wake the next day...but, it is by faith that we allow ourselves the end of another day and the sleep that is to come...there is no guarantee. When you leave the house each day, the same situation exists. We live each moment by faith in the expectation of the next moment to come.

This is not a point of pessimism, and I don't intend to create an aura of gloom and tragedy. This is the mystery of life. We are part of something so large...something so magnificent...something so beyond the scope of the finite mind as to be beyond the knowing of the ORDER.

There is an ORDER to all of this, and the final chapter will give you a great deal of material for thought about the ORDER of things to be. This final chapter will probably give you subject for thought that will engage your mind for many years to come. Thank you for walking so far with me.

22
Can You
Live With
Yourself?

An interesting question...and of definite major importance; CAN YOU LIVE WITH YOURSELF? Happily? Comfortably? In peace? Confident of the future? Assured that you are accomplishing your purpose for being?

For you will see, now that you have completed the reading of this book, I will pose questions for you that will require you to reread the book. This chapter is really the introduction to the book. I had to put it out of place. This is the introduction ...and now the rest of the book follows...to be reread again. In this chapter, I will challenge you with questions concerning the "daily activities" that compose your daily life. All the long range plans in the world ultimately are laid waste if on a daily basis life is wasted...or left wanting.

The only "true" introduction for this book would have been the reading of the book. You've done that. And now, the book will have extra meaning for you the second time around. As you read this chapter, talk to yourself...have an inner dialogue with yourself...and be accountable to yourself for what you will look forward to each day.

This is the way the introduction to this book should have been presented:

INTRODUCTION

As a reader of this book, I would like you to sit back, for just a moment and contemplate. Isn't it wonderful that there is a way of life that improves every aspect of living! There is a philosophy of life that immediately removes the problems of the past, and the worries of the future! There is a simple way of understanding how every day can be the best day of your life! There are six laws that govern everything in this huge, glorious universe we live within! The absolute best reference book you will ever read concerning these six laws is the Bible; the Word of God! If you understand the Word, you will seek out the laws...and live life in *the positive applications of the laws!* If you decide to remain separate from the Word, you will ignore the laws...and suffer *the negative applications of the laws within your life!*

This book can do nothing to add to the six laws. This book cannot make you accept the six laws. This book cannot change, nor add to, the laws. It can only identify the laws, and by so doing, cause you to think and reflect on them.

If you fully understand the six laws, you will thoroughly enjoy this book...although, you will probably wonder why the book is written in a completely backwards manner.

If you are starting this book with a partial, fragmented understanding of the six laws, you will find this book very easy to read. In presenting the information, I wrote the book in reverse order...starting with the simple philosophies and working towards the complex.

If you have never been exposed to the six laws, you will be at a temporary disadvantage in reading this book. The only proper preparation for understanding the six laws is...the understanding of the six laws. Which seems like "double-talk", but is not. Just realize this, you will probably want to reread the book at least two or three times to solidify your understanding of the six laws and their importance to your success and happiness in life. You will find the six laws of utmost importance in the explanation of "why" everything in this universe works like it does.

The six laws work positively or negatively in the life of every person that lives...based on their proper or improper applications of the laws. No one is exempt from the workings of the laws, and to "not know" the laws, virtually guarantees some improper applications. I am going to list the laws in their proper order, and then, give a few examples that may "please" you or "shock" you...depending on your particular state of mind. After each example, I will pose one or more questions that will "search" the innermost convictions that you hold dear; your meaning for being.

The six laws can be listed and labeled this way:

THE LAW OF...ORDER
THE LAW OF...VIBRATION
THE LAW OF...OPPOSITES
THE LAW OF...CAUSE/EFFECT
THE LAW OF...ATTRACTION
THE LAW OF...DUALITY

THE LAW OF...ORDER: There is ORDER in everything. Neither you, nor I, will ever know the fullest extent of that ORDER. The fullest extent of that ORDER is known only to God, who in total wisdom, shares parts and pieces of that ORDER with us. You may choose to follow the ORDER based on your own decisions...or indecisions. In His Word, you can read the results that will accrue to you based on your choices. *You have absolutely no choice labeled...*"Chooses not to follow ORDER!"

My questions to you: Have you chosen a path in the ORDER that leads to life? Or death? Have you set your priorities in proper ORDER? Who is Lord and Master ...number one in your ORDER of allegiance and obedience? Do you understand the ORDER well enough...to fully understand why Jesus is an absolute essential in the ORDER that leads to life? Is your life today running smoothly, successfully, happily...in the ORDER you have chosen? Or, are you experiencing tensions, stresses, unhappiness...in the ORDER you have chosen? What is the path of ORDER you've chosen?

THE LAW OF... VIBRATION: There is VIBRATION in everything. Every thought, every word, every action, every physical body...everything VIBRATES in the ORDER. Just as "You are known by the company you keep.", you are known by the thoughts you think...the words you speak...the actions you demonstrate. The most powerful set of VIBRATIONS in the entire ORDER is the love of God flowing throughout this universe. You are accountable for every VIBRATION that emanates from you. You make your choice of VIBRATIONS based on your selection of ORDER.

My questions to you: Are you a force for good thoughts, words, and actions? Or, are your thoughts, words, and actions good for nothing? Since prayer is the expression of your innermost feeling VIBRATING your wants and needs, what do you inwardly think, feel, and express on a daily basis? Are you happy to be alive? Would you want your thoughts public record? Do you talk to yourself in positive, uplifting inner words? Or do you think, feel, and express the opposite? Do you understand how it was that Jesus, the Son of God, could "ask" and "receive" based on his understanding of the ORDER? Do you realize that "According to your faith" your thoughts, words, and actions have been rewarded? Your VIBRATION is in synchronization with the ORDER...but, in which direction?

THE LAW OF... OPPOSITES: Everything in the ORDER is subject to the law of OPPOSITES. The ORDER lists the OPPOSITES from which you may choose. In the Word of God, may be found alternate choices enough to fill anyone's quest for knowledge. With the choices are also listed the results that will accrue based on decisions to follow the different choices. As far as you can go in one direction, there will be an equal OPPOSITE in the other direction. Your choices are always to first pick which side of the OPPOSITES ...and then secondly, *to decide how committed you will become to your choice.* The more committed you are to your selection, the farther you will move from its OPPOSITE. The more successful a person becomes, the further they are removed from the arena of failure. The healthier a person becomes, the further they are removed from illness. As you become a happier and happier person, you are progressively more distant from the unhappy state that surrounds so many people in our society. Each person accepts their own particular end of the OPPOSITES. Each person makes their own choice ...and then becomes the kind of person that fits that particular end of the OPPOSITES. When you fully understand the laws of ORDER, VIBRATION, and OPPOSITES, you will then "know" why Jesus Christ is, was, and will always be, an absolute essential in bringing individuals from the end of the OPPOSITES that causes separation from God...to the end of the OPPOSITES that represents oneness with the Lord.

My questions to you: How does your life look to your fellow-man? Which side of the OPPOSITES do you demonstrate in your daily living? How does your life look to you? Which side of all the OPPOSITES do you live with in your thoughts and inner talk? How does your life look to God? Which side of the OPPOSITES have you really chosen? Have you been kidding yourself by thinking you could "kinda' live your life with two masters?" Would you think that you will be found "pleasing" in the eyes of the Lord?

THE LAW OF...CAUSE/EFFECT: Every physical EFFECT has as its origin an energy form CAUSE...which we call thought. Every thought eventually finds its way into physical manifestation. Every CAUSE eventually finds its way into physical manifestation. Every CAUSE eventually finds its way into becoming an EFFECT. An EFFECT cannot magically appear without a corresponding CAUSE. Also, a CAUSE cannot just disappear...there will always be a corresponding EFFECT produced somewhere, somehow.

My questions to you: Do you have a "well-thought-out" plan of where you want to go with your life? Do you like the EFFECTS that surround you in your life today? If your THOUGHTS last year were tape recorded, and all the positive THOUGHTS were placed in one pile...and all the negative THOUGHTS were place in another, which pile would be the larger? Is your life being run by "crisis management" techniques? Is your financial world rewarding you nicely? Is your family life filled with happiness and warmth? Do you have large numbers of highly supportive friends that wish you well and applaud your successes? Is your physical body in excellent health and full of energy? Does your spiritual life fulfill and fill you with the Holy Spirit? In other words, are you receiving EFFECTS that are pleasing? Or, are you desirous of some changes in the EFFECTS in your life? Do you understand how Jesus changed EFFECTS by his use of CAUSE?

THE LAW OF...ATTRACTION: "Like" ATTRACTS "Like" throughout the universe. OPPOSITES complement to make a whole, but "Likes" ATTRACT each other. Every thought ATTRACTS like kind. Every word ATTRACTS its equal. Every action begets its "like" through the law of ATTRACTION. Each end of the law of OPPOSITES will ATTRACT to itself "like" natures. Successful THOUGHT *will create* successful EFFECTS. Successful EFFECTS *always* ATTRACT similar successful EFFECTS. I would like you to temporarily erase "money" from your vocabulary...as I use the words "rich" and "poor" to describe the law of ATTRACTION. "Poor" people ATTRACT "poor" people. "Rich" people ATTRACT "rich" people. The book of Proverbs list over one thousand examples of this law...and only the most blind of the blind would think that this law only applies to making money. This law governs the ATTRACTIONS that exist between thoughts, feelings, emotions, attitudes, physical and non-physical entities, actions, reactions, and states of beingness. ORDER, VIBRATION, OPPOSITES, CAUSE/EFFECT, and ATTRACTION *exist in everything, permeate everything, control everything*...there are no exceptions.

My questions to you: What have you done to put yourself in the circumstances that now *exist in your world? Permeate your world? And control the daily activities of that world?* Are you where you are, by your "rich" choice in the ORDER? Or, are you where you are, because of a "poor" choice concerning the ORDER? As "rich" as you are, *could it possibly be,* that you have but "scratched the surface"? Can you accept the potential criticism of your way of thought? Not from others- ...but, from yourself? Of all the abundance this world can offer, what would you like to ATTRACT to yourself? What do you want? What do you need? What would help? Have you ATTRACTED the greatest positive force into your life? Or, have you ATTRACTED equal forces that are negative into your life? Look at the EFFECTS, and you will be able to gauge the quality of the CAUSE, and the scope of the CAUSE, and the direction of the CAUSE...what do you see? Can you see why the Word of God never returns "void"? Do you understand how ORDER, VIBRATION, OPPOSITES, and the EFFECTS create ATTRACTIONS in your life, and in mine?

The sixth law in just a moment, but before we cover it, some passages that should have more meaning for you...now that you have the five laws we just covered:

"And I say to you, ask and it shall be given to you"
(Luke 11:9)

"Again I say to you, that if two of you agree on earth about anything that they may ask, it shall be done for them by My Father who is in heaven."   (Matt. 18:19)

"Therefore I say to you, all things for which you pray and ask, believe that you have received them, and they shall be granted you."
"I am the true vine, and My Father is the vine dresser."
(John 15:1)

"I am the vine, you are the branches; he who abides in Me, and I in him, he bears much fruit; for apart from Me you can do nothing."   (John 15:5)

"If you abide in Me, and My words abide in you, ask whatever you wish, and it shall be done for you."
(John 15:7)

The laws are repeated...and repeated...and repeated. Thousands upon thousands of times they are repeated covering every conceivable worldly situation. It is in the sixth law that we finally learn the greatest lesson; the laws always work...in every situation...large or small. The sixth law covers all possible situations.

THE LAW OF...DUALITY: "As above, so below." What exists on the large scale, exists on the small. The laws work in the smallest corner of your own personal world...and throughout the far-flung heavens of all creation. When you learn to use one of the laws on the small scale, you can be assured of this, you have learned a law that will always work on every scale, In God's ORDER, there is no large and small scale; everything is of course...small. What works in one small case...will of course, work in another small case of similar nature. When you or I look at a problem, we have a tendency to gauge the problem compared to our own size. In God's ORDER, the problem that appeared so large to us...is immeasurably and incalculably small. Use the six laws to put your life in perspective. Use the six laws to put your problems in proper perspective. Use the six laws to positively influence your life...or you may use the six laws to their negative conclusion. It's your choice.

We are about ready to begin this book. In the pages that follow, you will find the concepts and tools, the laws and their applications that will help in the answering of all the questions posed in this introduction. There are approximately 55 questions positioned and presented along with the six laws. Questions whose answers will directly affect the quality of your life from this day forward. When you follow through with the directions and exercises within this book, YOU WILL FIND THE ANSWERS YOU SEEK. The answers are always available...it is up to you to implement them in your life.

There is one additional question to be asked. Your answer to the question is very important because, your answer will determine your acceptance or rejection of a "life-view" philosophy offered in the very first chapter of the book. Your answer to the question will indicate your position relative to the philosophy...plus, it will indicate where you stand in relationship to the laws of ORDER, VIBRATION, OPPO-SITES, CAUSE/EFFECT, and ATTRACTION. In addition, your response also determines whether on a daily basis you can live a life that will ultimately (on the large scale) be worthwhile...*in your own eyes.*

The question is this: IS LIFE WORTH LIVING?

If your answer is a "yes" that you truly mean, with all your heart and soul, then...tomorrow morning when you wake up...at that moment, *you are already more successful* than all the people that died in their sleep this night. You are already "richer" than the wealthiest negative person in the world. At that point of awakening, you have the fulfillment of the six laws *working positively* in your life.

What will you do with the rest of your "life" that stretches out into your future eternal? That will be determined by your answers to the 55 questions presented in this introduction to the book. The important lesson to be learned at that moment you awaken is this...

CONGRATULATIONS...You Made It Again!

Your "Major Purpose" in life awaits you. Read the next few pages, and let's get on with the book.

An Ending...
and a Beginning

It is time to end, and begin. These pages will be my last for awhile. I have written all that I knew to be important... *really important,* in the chapters you've finished reading. In the gathering of the material for this book, my life has been touched by many different people, and I have benefited greatly. I hope a similar occurrence has happened often in your life... and, perhaps happened again... through our relationship of writer and reader, and perhaps more... friend to friend.

A saying often quoted by speakers on the lecture circuit goes: "Don't walk behind me, I may not lead. Don't walk in front of me, I may not follow. Just walk beside me, and be my friend." This relationship is an example of perfect interchange; a perfect balance in the laws.

Therefore... as my friend, I have an exchange to make with you. I will share some beautiful lines of other writers with you. These lines have touched me deeply, and may become meaningful to you also. As you contemplate upon these lines, I hope you are filled with an intense desire to share with friends and loved ones... all that I have shared with you. Someone needs what you can give to them. Will you extend to them and *make the "exchange" complete?*

My bounty is as boundless as the sea,
My love as deep; the more I give to thee,
The more I have, for both are infinite.

William Shakespeare

The Savior is waiting to enter your heart,
Why don't you let Him come in?
There's nothing in this world to keep you apart,
What is your answer to Him?

(a passage in a hymm that
opened my heart to Jesus)

"Take My yoke upon you, and learn from Me,
for I am gentle and humble in heart; and
YOU SHALL FIND REST FOR YOUR SOULS.
For My yoke is easy, and My load is light."

(Matt. 11:29,30)